The prehistory an
of Southwark and

MoLAS Monograph Series

1 Excavations at the Priory and Hospital of St Mary Spital, London, Christopher Thomas, Barney Sloane and Christopher Phillpotts
ISBN 1 901992 00 4

2 The National Roman Fabric Reference Collection: a handbook, Roberta Tomber and John Dore
ISBN 1 901992 01 2

3 The Cross Bones burial ground, Redcross Way, Southwark, London: archaeological excavations (1991–8) for the London Underground Limited Jubilee Line Extension Project, Megan Brickley and Adrian Miles with Hilary Stainer
ISBN 1 901992 06 3

4 The eastern cemetery of Roman London: excavations 1983–90, Bruno Barber and David Bowsher
ISBN 1 901992 09 8

5 The Holocene evolution of the London Thames: archaeological excavations (1991–8) for the London Underground Limited, Jubilee Line Extension Project, Jane Sidell, Keith Wilkinson, Robert Scaife and Nigel Cameron
ISBN 1 901992 10 1

6 The Limehouse porcelain manufactory: excavations at 108–116 Narrow Street, London, 1990, Kieron Tyler and Roy Stephenson, with J Victor Owen and Christopher Phillpotts
ISBN 1 901992 16 0

7 Roman defences and medieval industry: excavations at Baltic House, City of London, Elizabeth Howe
ISBN 1 901992 17 9

8 London bridge: 2000 years of a river crossing, Bruce Watson, Trevor Brigham and Tony Dyson
ISBN 1 901992 18 7

9 Roman and medieval townhouses on the London waterfront: excavations at Governor's House, City of London, Trevor Brigham with Aidan Woodger
ISBN 1 901992 21 7

10 The London Charterhouse, Bruno Barber and Christopher Thomas
ISBN 1 901992 23 3

11 Medieval 'Westminster' floor tiles, Ian M Betts
ISBN 1 901992 24 1

12 Settlement in Roman Southwark: archaeological excavations (1991–8) for the London Underground Limited Jubilee Line Extension Project, James Drummond-Murray and Peter Thompson with Carrie Cowan
ISBN 1 901992 28 4

13 Aspects of medieval and later Southwark: archaeological excavations (1991–8) for the London Underground Limited Jubilee Line Extension Project, Heather Knight
ISBN 1 901992 30 6

14 The prehistory and topography of Southwark and Lambeth, Jane Sidell, Jonathan Cotton, Louise Rayner and Lucy Wheeler
ISBN 1 901992 31 4

The prehistory and topography of Southwark and Lambeth

Jane Sidell, Jonathan Cotton, Louise Rayner

and Lucy Wheeler

MoLAS Monograph 14

Museum of London Archaeology Service

Published by the Museum of London Archaeology Service
Copyright © Museum of London 2002

A CIP catalogue record for this book is available from the British Library

Production and series design by Tracy Wellman
Typesetting and design by Jeannette van der Post
Reprographics by Andy Chopping
Copy editing by Val Kinsler
Series editing by Sue Hirst/Susan M Wright

Printed by the Lavenham Press

Front cover: excavation at the B&Q Mesolithic site; lithics (scrapers, an awl/borer
and a knife) from the ploughsoils; reconstruction of the route of the Mesolithic
Thames in Southwark and Lambeth

Back cover: reconstruction of the B&Q Mesolithic site; conservators working on a
Bronze Age timber from the Vauxhall piled structure; Bronze Age side-looped
spearheads from the Vauxhall piled structure

CONTRIBUTORS

Principal authors   Jane Sidell, Jonathan Cotton, Louise Rayner, Lucy Wheeler

Fennings Wharf stratigraphic narrative   Trevor Brigham and Bruce Watson

Fennings Wharf cremations   Bill White

Fennings Wharf radiocarbon dating   Alex Bayliss

Phoenix Wharf stratigraphic narrative   Julian Bowsher

Vauxhall piled timber structure   Gustav Milne

B&Q lithic microwear   Randolph Donahue

Graphics   Faith Pewtress, Kate Pollard, Kikar Singh

Photography   Andy Chopping

Project managers   Richard Malt, Gordon Malcolm, Barney Sloane

Academic adviser   Nick Merriman

Editors   Pippa Bradley, Sue Hirst, Richard Malt

CONTENTS

FIGURES

TABLES

FOREWORD

by Dr Nick Merriman
Institute of Archaeology
University College London

Southwark and Lambeth are today associated with the cultural and economic revival of the South Bank, of which the most visible symbols are the Tate Modern and the London Eye. Past associations in the popular mind range from 'the Clink' and Charlie Chaplin to the Vauxhall Pleasure Gardens, and the Bankside theatres of Shakespeare's day. This important volume traces a much earlier history of the area, which lay beneath the feet of even the earliest Roman inhabitants. In its intensive concentration on a particular area, this is very much a work of local history and one which serves as the first academic synthesis of the prehistoric evidence for this familiar part of London, extending its history as it does to some eight thousand years before the arrival of the Romans.

Study of the prehistoric archaeology of such a densely settled urban area is fraught with problems. The evidence is often deeply buried, fragmentary and revealed only by accident. It is noteworthy that the principal sites discussed here were found in the course of pre-PPG16 developer-funded investigations aimed at answering completely different questions (the presence of a Roman road; the early foundations of London Bridge; the nature of an inlet into the Thames). It is a credit to their excavators that their importance was recognised and recorded at the time.

The informed publication of such fragmentary material is difficult. The current PPG16 regime (and indeed the period before its instigation) does not have a mechanism to fund the synthetic publication of evidence from a range of sites, which is clearly what is needed to make sense of disparate prehistoric material from this part of the Thames valley. English Heritage are, therefore, to be applauded for taking on this role themselves, and for sensibly allowing the authors to draw on material from a range of sources beyond those of the sites immediately in question.

The serendipitous nature of archaeological discovery, the strategies of the excavators, the support of English Heritage and the excellent analytical work of the authors have combined to produce this regional synthesis. It includes a complete sequence of vegetational development for the area from the Late Devensian to the Iron Age and analyses of key sites of regional or even national significance: the Early Mesolithic B&Q site, the intriguing Fennings Wharf ring ditch and the Phoenix Wharf boiling pit, and the subsequent evidence of ard cultivation. What makes the volume particularly satisfying is that the archaeological, palaeoecological and topographical evidence is presented as an interlinked whole, which allows the interplay between river level, environment and human exploitation to be appreciated. Most importantly, the evidence is discussed within its wider regional context and related, for example, to recent prehistoric evidence from east London and on the gravel terraces around Heathrow. The result is a work of genuine synthesis which shows that archaeologists are beginning to move beyond local description of evidence to the analysis of regional research questions.

Through its integrated approach and its accessible style, this volume provides a model for how the disparate prehistoric and palaeoecological evidence from a range of small sites can be studied together to provide a result which is much greater than the sum of the parts. All involved are very much to be congratulated on seeing such a long project come to such a useful fruition.

SUMMARY

This volume provides an account of the cultural evidence for human presence in the area of north Southwark and Lambeth, London, in the period c 9500 cal BC to c AD 50. It also documents environmental and riverine change throughout the period and examines the way in which the human communities caused and are likely to have reacted to such changes. An introductory chapter outlines the background to the study, which arose as part of the English Heritage Greater London publication programme. The study is the first concerted attempt to synthesise the available prehistoric and topographic information, using the data generated by the Museum of London Archaeology Service and its precursor bodies, much of it unpublished fieldwork from the 1980s, enhanced by the inclusion of as much new information from recent sites as possible.

The volume does not follow a strict chronological structure, as it became apparent during analysis that the conventional divisions of the three-age system, which define hunter-gatherers, sedentary farmers producing ceramics and then metalwork within a rigid dating framework, did not apply in this case. Instead, the evidence is considered within broad themes, starting with 'mobile communities', then looking at what has been defined as a 'ritual riverscape' and finally examining the evidence for 'settled communities'. These sections are effectively discursive, outlining the evidence, including a Mesolithic camp adjacent to a Late Glacial lake in Bermondsey in the first section, a burnt mound and ring ditch with an assemblage of cremations in section two, and a series of preserved ard marks in the final section. Evidence relating to the changing environment and river regime is woven into the text in discussions of the landscape and the interactions which took place in the context of the human population.

Following the outline of the available evidence, several short essays examine, firstly, the ecological succession and the human involvement and, secondly, the prehistory of Southwark and Lambeth in a wider regional context in order to gauge accurately what this new information means in the broader context of the Thames valley. Unsurprisingly, both similarities to and differences from some of the better known prehistoric centres such as Heathrow and east London are identified, such as the field systems of both Southwark and Heathrow, and the contrast between the lack of Iron Age settlement evidence in central London against the hillforts/settlements found further east.

A gazetteer of all identified findspots of prehistoric material has been produced, listing addresses, a brief description of the finds and published references and Greater London Sites and Monuments Record (GLSMR) records where available. The gazetteer numbers (GAZ #) are cross-referenced into the body of the text where a particular site is mentioned, and at chapter heading level where a site is discussed in more detail. Several technical papers have been included for the specialist reader. One presents details of the worked flint recovered from the study area together with the results of the microwear analysis carried out on the important Early Mesolithic assemblage from the B&Q site (GAZ 208). A second paper provides full details of pottery quantification, forms and fabrics for all the material described from the study area, and a final report lists all available radiocarbon determinations.

ACKNOWLEDGEMENTS

This publication is the product of a joint venture between English Heritage and the Museum of London Archaeology Service (MoLAS) to publish backlog projects identified in the London post-excavation review (Hinton and Thomas 1997). Particular thanks should go to Brian Kerr and Ellen Barnes who have worked closely with MoLAS throughout the archaeological project and have positively encouraged the approach taken.

The authors would like to express their thanks for the assistance rendered during the project by many individuals: firstly Richard Malt and Gordon Malcolm with Barney Sloane, Peter Rowsome, Andrew Westman and Hedley Swain for assisting in the management. Thanks should also go to the senior archaeologists for their original work excavating the sites, notably Dave Beard, Julian Bowsher, George Dennis, Wendy Rogers and Bruce Watson. We also extend our gratitude to the clients who funded the excavations, in particular the Greater London Council, the Highways Department of the London Borough of Southwark, Inner City Enterprises Plc, List Developments, the St Martins Property Corporation and Willmott Dixon Housing (Southern).

Much of the lithic analysis has built on foundations originally laid by Nick Merriman and John Lewis, while the environmental work has greatly benefited from the work of Rob Scaife, Ian Tyers and Keith Wilkinson, all of whom are gratefully acknowledged. Thanks are also due to Gary Brown, Frank Meddens and Vicki Ridgeway for providing pre-publication information and access to reports on the important assemblages of struck flint and pottery recovered from their excavations at Hopton Street (GAZ 54) and Three Oaks Lane (GAZ 180). Sharon Gerber-Parfitt is thanked for her help with the onerous task of inputting the B&Q lithic data; likewise Peter Rauxloh of MoLAS for his ready grasp of the potential of the data captured and for its expert manipulation. It is fair to say that no attempt could even have begun to be made on elucidating the importance of the B&Q site assemblages without the help of these two individuals. Alistair Barclay is thanked for his assistance with the ceramics from the Fennings Wharf (GAZ 130) central feature.

Thanks are also due to John Shepherd and his colleagues Alan Thompson and Steve Tucker for facilitating various searches in the London Archaeological Archive and Research Centre at 46 Eagle Wharf Road, London N1 7ED. The task of tracking down groups of struck flint and pottery would have been made immeasurably more difficult without their collective efficiency. Roz Sherris of the Museum's Early Department provided much needed secretarial assistance, not least with the tabulation of the gazetteer and other data. Paul Charlton and Barry Taylor of the Greater London Sites and Monuments Record also assisted with the compilation of the gazetteer. The summary was translated into French by Dominique de Moulins and into German by Friederike Hammer. The index was compiled by Susanne Atkin.

The project has benefited greatly from the guidance of Nick Merriman, who acted as academic referee, and the authors would like to express their collective thanks for his invaluable assistance. Pippa Bradley, Richard Malt and Alex Gibson are also thanked for providing additional peer review. Nevertheless, the theories and models proposed within this volume are the responsibility of the authors and any errors or misinterpretations rest solely with them.

1

Introduction

1.1 A brief history of prehistory in Southwark and Lambeth

Following the pioneering work of F C J Spurrell (1885; 1889) around Erith, further downstream, A D Lacaille (1966) was the first of the post-war fieldworkers to appreciate the prehistoric potential of the Southwark locality, based on a close study of its topography. His observations principally concerned the Mesolithic period, and followed a century and more of finds made casually during river dredging (Smith 1854; Franks 1864–7, 342–4), building work (Kennard and Warren 1903; Anon 1937) and small-scale archaeological excavation (Kenyon 1959).

A full-time archaeological team was established in the area in the early 1970s (Sheldon 1978, 13) and focused immediately on determining the extent of the topographic 'highs' suitable for Roman settlement, and on the Roman river regime (eg Willcox 1975; Milne et al 1983). Fuelled by the regular recovery of small pieces of flint and pottery, often from deposits sealed by the earliest Roman layers, members of the team soon sought to take account of, and seek explanations for, the prehistoric evidence uncovered during the course of their work (eg Graham 1978; Tyers 1988; Yule 1988). At the same time, it was quickly recognised that the peat deposits formed against the newly defined sand islands had the potential to provide a series of prehistoric and palaeoenvironmental markers, although attempts to correlate these with the 'Tilbury IV' horizon identified in the mid estuary by Devoy (1979) were ultimately to prove less successful (eg Rackham 1994).

Increasing developer activity during the 1980s allowed the examination of larger sites, both on and beyond the main Southwark islands, and direct and sometimes extensive traces of prehistoric activity began to be recognised. These ranged from hunter-gatherer flint scatters along the Old Kent Road (Rogers 1990) and in the shadow of Waterloo Station, to 2nd millennium cal BC ard marks etched into the sands of Horselydown (Heard et al 1990, 610). Merriman's influential contributions (1987; 1992) and the promulgation of Planning Policy Guidance Note 16 (Department of the Environment 1990) have since combined to prompt new and still more unexpected discoveries, such as the log trackway and palaeoenvironmental sequence at Bramcote Grove, Bermondsey (GAZ 215) (Thomas and Rackham 1996). Reports of other finds from local stretches of the Thames foreshore have also multiplied as a direct result of a recent survey of the inter-tidal zone (Webber 1999; Haughey 1999), and these include in situ deposits, artefacts and wooden structures, including a pile-driven structure at Nine Elms, Vauxhall (GAZ 6). Further discoveries may be confidently anticipated.

What follows is the first concerted attempt to synthesise the available prehistoric and topographic information from the area of north Southwark and Lambeth, using the data generated by the Museum of London Archaeology Service (MoLAS) and its predecessor bodies. The work of other organisations is also included within the Gazetteer, and is incorporated in the discussions where appropriate.

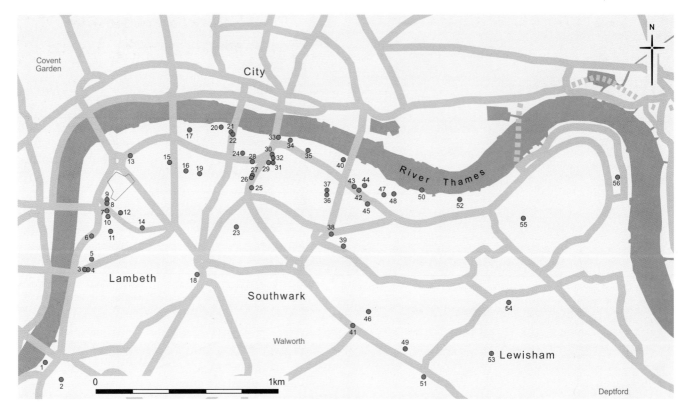

Fig 1 Sites in the study area (see Table 1 for key to site numbers) (scale 1:20,000)

1.2 Research aims

When this project was originally conceived, a series of research aims were proposed which would be applied to a study area reaching from Lambeth Palace on the southern bank of the Thames in Lambeth across north Southwark as far as the B&Q site in south Bermondsey (see Fig 1 and Table 1 for the full extent). A period of assessment (after MAP2, English Heritage 1991) was undertaken to consider the available material and establish its potential to address these research aims. These were consequently revised and submitted as follows (Westman 1997):

1) What were the topography and environment of the study area (Southwark and Lambeth north of Ordnance Survey (OS) national grid northing TQ 778) during the Holocene, and how did they change, especially as climate and sea level changed?

2) How would the changes in topography and environment have affected the suitability of the study area for human exploitation and occupation?

3) What human exploitation and occupation of the area were there during:
   the Mesolithic?
   the Neolithic and Early Bronze Age?
   the Late Bronze Age and Iron Age?

These chronological objectives gave a framework for the analysis, the results of which are published in this volume. However, a combination of factors has led to the further revision of these aims during the analytical stage of the project. This in part reflects the long duration of the project, and

indeed the time-span in question, the recent developments in prehistoric archaeology and a much more detailed scrutiny of the data. It was decided to dispense with the traditional age system used in the construction of the updated project design and to replace this with broader, more descriptive, categories observed in the archaeological record. This was done in an attempt to be true to the archaeology of the study area, and to reflect what is described and interpreted more accurately.

Therefore, the terms Mesolithic, Neolithic, Bronze Age and Iron Age will not be found as headings within this volume. They are occasionally used for convenience and clarity within the body of the text, but have been replaced as subdivisions by 'Mobile communities', 'A ritual riverscape' and 'Settled communities'. Time bands and human activity ascribed to these phases overlap with each other (see Fig 2), but better reflect the lifestyles adopted by human groups in the dynamic, often marginal, physiographic zone of the Thames floodplain.

1.3 Circumstances of excavation

The interventions described in this volume were all undertaken within the sphere of developer-funded archaeology, the majority of which were carried out before the promulgation of Planning Policy Guidance 16 (PPG16). Certainly all the sites had been identified and were being negotiated prior to its publication in 1990, while the first site, Copperfield Street (GAZ 58), was excavated in 1975. However, the majority took place during the late 1980s and 1990–1. The individual

Table 1 Sites in Fig 1 with gazetteer number and National Grid reference

Fig 1 no.	Address	GAZ no.	Easting	Northing
1	Thames foreshore, Vauxhall	6	530200	178000
2	Coronation Buildings & 30–60 South Lambeth Rd	9	530400	177770
3	129 Lambeth Rd	23	530660	178950
4	Norfolk House, 113–127 Lambeth Rd	25	530700	178950
5	Lambeth Palace Kitchen Gardens, Lambeth Rd	27	530740	179060
6	Lambeth Palace North Garden, Lambeth Palace Rd	28	530740	179310
7	Waterloo Station, Upper Marsh St	32	530910	179580
8	Addington Street, Waterloo	33	530910	179660
9	29 Addington Street, Waterloo	34	530910	179700
10	Upper Marsh, Waterloo site E	35	530920	179520
11	Carlisle Lane, Waterloo site F	36	530950	179360
12	Lower Marsh	39	531060	179560
13	127 Stamford St	43	531170	180170
14	4–10 Lower Marsh, 126–156 Westminster Bridge Rd	48	531300	179400
15	Joan St	51	531600	180100
16	206 Union St	53	531780	180010
17	47–67 Hopton St	54	531820	180450
18	Southwark Leisure Centre, Elephant and Castle	55	531900	178900
19	Copperfield St	58	531930	179980
20	Skinmarket Place, Bankside	65	532170	180480
21	2–10 Southwark Bridge Rd, Southbridge House	69	532280	180430
22	Park St	70	532300	180400
23	Brockham St	72	532340	179410
24	Courage's Brewery bottling plant, Park St	81	532410	180200
25	201–211 Borough High St	88	532510	179830
26	120–124 Borough High St	89	532510	179940
27	106–114 Borough High St	90	532520	179960
28	15–23 Southwark St	91	532520	180110
29	21–27 St Thomas St	113	532700	180100
30	1–7 St Thomas St	117	532740	180190
31	Guy's Hospital, St Thomas St	121	532750	180100
32	4–26 St Thomas St	122	532750	180150
33	Fennings Wharf, Tooley St	130	532810	180370
34	Chamberlains Wharf, Tooley St	137	532940	180340
35	Wilson's Wharf	148	533140	180230
36	12–16 Whites Grounds/4–42 Brunswick Court	154	533350	179750
37	Whites Grounds	155	533350	179800
38	Bermondsey Abbey, Long Walk/Abbey St	159	533400	179330
39	170–176 Grange Rd, 41–45 Grange Walk, Southwark St	not in GAZ but in main text	533530	179200
40	Mark Browns Wharf, Tooley St, Tower Bridge Rd	169	533530	180130
41	281–345 Old Kent Rd, Humphrey St	174	533630	178350
42	10–16 Lafone St	179	533650	179860
43	Three Oaks Lane	176	533700	179800
44	Queen Elizabeth St South	188	533760	179850
45	Phoenix Wharf, 4 Jamaica Rd	189	533790	179650
46	Bricklayers Arms Railway Yard, Rolls Rd	191	533800	178500
47	Wolseley St	199	533970	179750
48	Jacob's Island, Bermondsey	201	534080	179760
49	283 Marlborough Grove	204	534200	178100
50	Thames Foreshore, Chambers Wharf, Bermondsey	207	534380	179800
51	Old Kent Rd/Bowles Rd	208	534400	177800
52	Platform Wharf, Paradise St	212	534800	179700
53	Bramcote Grove, Bermondsey	215	535150	178050
54	Silverlock, Rotherhithe	220	535340	178600
55	Canada Water, Surrey Quays Rd	221	535500	179500
56	Bryan Rd/Salter Rd/Rotherhithe St	230	536530	179940

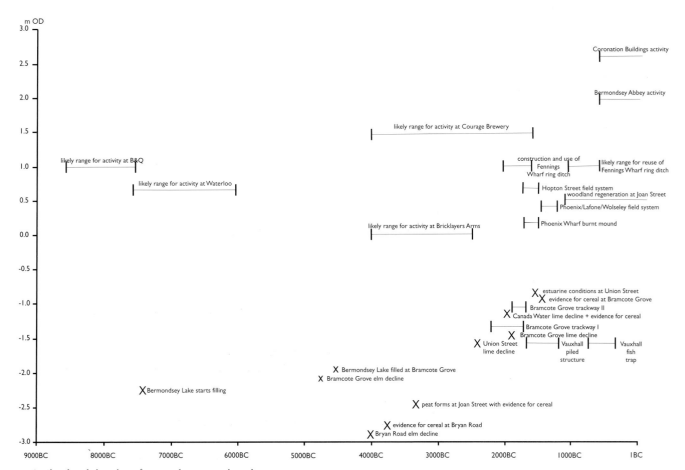

Fig 2 Altitude and chronology of events and activity in the study area

Fig 3 Excavation at the B&Q depot, Old Kent Road

projects ranged from large open excavations (see Fig 3) meticulously carried out over several months, such as the B&Q depot (GAZ 208) on the Old Kent Road, to small watching briefs lasting only a few days from which samples were collected, for instance the Joan Street (GAZ 51) intervention. Individual sites often yielded important information, such as the burnt mound and ard marks at Phoenix Wharf (GAZ 189) and the ring ditch at Fennings Wharf (GAZ 130).

1.4 The nature of the project

This project is an English Heritage funded backlog study; a synthetic publication of a group of sites dug in the main during the 1980s. Data recovery, rather than analysis and publication, was the priority during this period. In the 1990s, the problems caused by this approach were recognised and, in London, a programme was drawn up to publish many of these sites, using a thematic rather than single-site approach (Hinton and Thomas 1997). This volume, therefore, concentrates on a series of sites in Southwark and Lambeth that have produced data on the development of the area throughout prehistory. Several sites that contribute to the story but have been published elsewhere have also been referred to and comprehensively referenced, but the bulk of analytical text concentrates on the group of sites within the backlog project.

The recovery of cultural evidence was usually a result of simple serendipity during the examination of sites of later date, or of discoveries made in the context of topographic investigations designed to elucidate the extent of sand islands and associated channels. It is only recently that prehistoric data have been explicitly sought in their own right for what they might tell us about the exploitation of the floodplains of the Lower Thames. As a result the prehistoric database is much less well focused than that relating to the Roman period, although it is not without interest and regional significance, particularly with regard to the phases conventionally labelled Mesolithic and Bronze Age.

The character of the prehistoric evidence recovered from the study area is typical of the context types now regularly recorded from floodplains and estuarine inter-tidal zones (eg Allen et al 1997; Bell and Neumann 1997; Wilkinson and Murphy 1995). It encompasses a series of lithic and lithic/ceramic scatters, several of which are demonstrably in situ; a restricted range of usually truncated negative features including tree-holes, pits, ditches, post and stakeholes, as well as several groups of ard marks, and a small number of timber features/structures preserved in channel and lake sediments.

Aside from the fills of individual features, the most common generic context type from which prehistoric artefacts have been recovered comprises the horizontal deposits that mantle the surface of the terrace gravels and natural sand islands. These apparently similar deposits of dirty grey and sometimes charcoal-flecked sand have often been referred to by their excavators as 'weathered', 'disturbed' or waterlain flood silts. Although the absence of targeted micromorphological data renders interpretation hazardous and the adoption of a single causal explanation decidedly unwise, it is possible to suggest that some of these deposits represent the remains of former land surfaces and developed soil profiles disturbed by natural and human agencies (eg the B&Q site), while others overlying ard marks are likely to be genuinely ancient agricultural soils (eg Phoenix Wharf, Lafone Street (GAZ 179) and Wolseley Street (GAZ 199)).

The environmental and topographic evidence has been made available in several ways. Generally the data discussed in this volume have been collected from archaeological sites excavated by the Museum of London over the last 20 years or so. Some of the data referred to have been published elsewhere and are used here to make a more complete interpretation. Other data appear in press for the first time. Most of the environmental samples were collected as monoliths from undisturbed sedimentary sequences preserved by waterlogged conditions close to the modern Thames. Although every effort was made to ensure that these samples were of the highest quality, it is not always possible to be sure that they are entirely representative of the surrounding area. Owing to the nature of the sediments generally found in the study area, palaeoenvironmental reconstruction has tended to rely on pollen, diatom and sedimentary techniques in combination with radiocarbon determinations. The topographic data used to produce the base maps and model the changing courses of the Thames were collected from geotechnical sources as well as archaeological records. The constraints on such information are discussed below.

1.5 Organisation of this report

This book is laid out in six main chapters. Chapter 1 forms the introduction to the study area and the project. Chapter 2 examines the archaeological evidence for the floodplain environment and human activity within it using three broad headings outlined above, ie Mobile communities (9500–1500 cal BC), A ritual riverscape (2500–1500 cal BC) and Settled communities (2000 cal BC– cal AD 50). Chapter 3 pursues the twin themes of the changing environment and its effect upon the human communities set within the wider regional context. Chapter 4 briefly assesses the success of the project and identifies priorities for future research. Chapter 5 comprises a gazetteer of sites within the study area based on information from the GLSMR and the London Archaeological Archive and Research Centre. Chapter 6 contains detailed appendices on the lithics, ceramics and radiocarbon determinations. A full bibliography completes the volume. Within the text, context numbers (where used) are shown in square brackets and finds accession numbers are within angle brackets.

1.6 Topographic modelling

One of the major objectives of this project was to try and understand the nature of the changing topography of Lambeth and north Southwark from the end of the Devensian Glaciation. It was necessary to use extant data to achieve this and therefore geotechnical data that have been collected over the last 20 years were modelled. These range from isolated boreholes drilled prior to archaeological intervention to the database of boreholes drilled for the Jubilee Line Extension, which cuts a swathe across the study area. In addition to this, trench data from archaeological interventions formed a major component of the datasets. Three-dimensional co-ordinates of all differentiated strata were entered into a database, and then run through a modelling programme (Surfer TM [Win 32], 6.04). The data were then used to construct models of the surface of Pleistocene gravels and the overlying Holocene sands and peat horizons.

There are a number of problems with this type of modelling and this should be taken into account when examining the resulting maps. These are only proposed as tentative plots that will be modified in the light of future study. The difficulties include limitations of the data, ie boreholes are rarely drilled consistently across a geographical zone; neither are archaeological sites investigated in a consistent spatial pattern in the rescue context. In addition the quality of geotechnical descriptions and detail tends to vary between drillers, ie one driller could record a single facies as 'alluvium', while another could record the same as 'fine silt clay, fining up with occasional sand laminae and local organic flecks'. The same problem can also apply to archaeologists: the level of detail recorded will vary as will the differentiation of archaeologically sterile, but nonetheless important, sediments such as river silts. A further problem exists within the study area: terrace gravels are often overlain by sand, which is generally a distinct horizon formed under different conditions from the gravel, and often thought to be Holocene rather than Pleistocene. Unfortunately, the tendency for field archaeologists to define sand or gravel as 'natural' leads to problems in distinguishing these when using archive records. There are also limitations with the software when working with small datasets, most notably the problems of satisfactorily extrapolating between points in areas of restricted data. All these issues have been encountered with this project; however, if the results are treated as generalisations about actual sub-surface topography that can inform archaeological interpretation, then they may be seen as useful graphic tools.

1.7 Changing river regimes

Since the Anglian Cold Stage, roughly 450,000 years ago, the Thames has dominated the landscape of south-east England, flowing in constantly changing channels, without the restrictions of embankments and revetments that are such a feature of the historic period. However, the Thames is also an estuary and, over the last ten thousand years, there have been major changes to all estuaries in southern England as a result of glacial decay further north and the consequent rise in relative sea levels (RSL). This has affected the Thames no less than other estuaries such as the Severn and Southampton Water (Long et al 2000), although possibly the changes have been rather less well studied here. Alterations to the estuary geometry have affected the floodplain and therefore will have impinged upon the societies inhabiting it. This study is concerned with tracking the development of the River Thames in the stretch bordering Lambeth and Southwark and how this is likely to have influenced local prehistoric communities.

1.8 A note on the dating

The results, given in Chapter 6.3, are conventional radiocarbon ages (Stuiver and Polach 1977) and are quoted in accordance with the international standard known as the Trondheim convention (Stuiver and Kra 1986). They have been calibrated with data from Stuiver et al (1998) using OxCal (version 3.5) (Bronk Ramsey 1995; 2000). The date ranges have been calculated according to the maximum intercept method (Stuiver and Reimer 1986) and are cited in the text at two sigma (95% confidence). They are quoted in the form recommended by Mook (1986) with the end points rounded out to 10 years. Throughout the text, dates are given as calibrated BC dates with actual radiocarbon measurements given in parentheses. A chronological chart is also given (Fig 4) for ease of cross-referencing.

1.9 The archive

This volume has been compiled using a range of raw data. The individual site archives (context sheets, plans, section drawings, photographs, sample sheets etc) are held at the London Archaeological Archive and Research Centre (LAARC), Mortimer Wheeler House, 46 Eagle Wharf Road, London N1 7ED, and may be consulted upon application. Summary data are also held at the Greater London Sites and Monuments Record, English Heritage, 23 Savile Row, London W1X 2HE, and again may be consulted upon application.

OI STAGE	EPOCH	STAGE	PERIOD	FLANDRIAN CHRONOZONES	GODWIN ZONES	CULTURAL PERIODS	CALENDAR YEARS BC/AD	CALENDAR YEARS BP	¹⁴C YEARS BP
One	Holocene	Flandrian	sub-Atlantic	Fl III	VIIc	Post-medieval			
						medieval			
						Saxon & Danish	AD 1000 —	1000 —	1000 —
						Roman			
						Iron Age	0 —	2000 —	2000 —
			sub-Boreal		VIIb	Bronze Age	1000 BC —	3000 —	3000 —
							2000 —	4000 —	4000 —
						Neolithic	3000 —	5000 —	
							4000 —	6000 —	5000 —
			Atlantic	Fl II	VIIa		5000 —	7000 —	6000 —
							6000 —	8000 —	7000 —
			Boreal	Fl Ic	VIc	Mesolithic			
					VIb		7000 —	9000 —	8000 —
				?	VIa		8000 —	10,000 —	9000 —
				Fl Ib	V				
			pre-Boreal	Fl Ia	IV		9000 —	11,000 —	10,000 —
Two	Pleistocene	Devensian	Loch Lomond stadial (Younger Dryas)		III		10,000 —	12,000 —	11,000 —
			Windermere interstadial (Allerød)		II	Upper Palaeolithic	11,000 —	13,000 —	
			Dimlington stadial (Older Dryas)		I		12,000 —	14,000 —	12,000 —

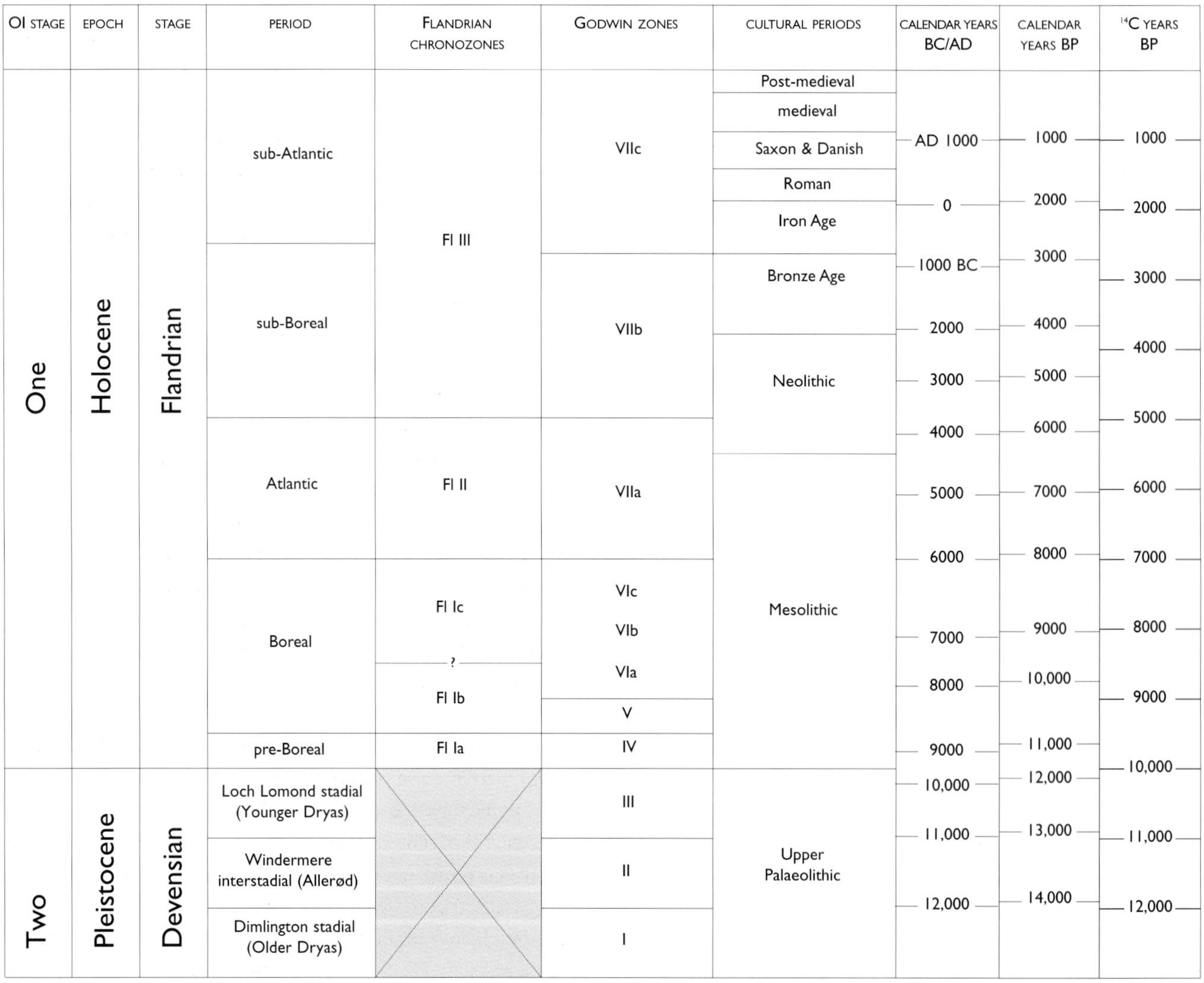

Fig 4 Chronological chart

2

The Late Devensian to the Roman Conquest: the prehistory of Southwark and Lambeth (*c* 9500 cal BC–*c* cal AD 50)

2.1 Introduction

Although this study takes the beginning of the Holocene as its starting point, a brief discussion of the Devensian/Holocene transition is useful to place the changes that occurred in the Holocene into a wider context. During the Devensian Late Glacial (Oxygen Isotope Stage 2 (OIS2)) climatic amelioration of the Windermere Interstadial (*c* 13,500–11,000 cal BC) (see Fig 4), the Thames followed a braided bed form. However, it would appear that many of the channels cut in the Shepperton Gravel were abandoned at the end of this period (see Wilkinson et al 2000) and the Thames was in transition between a meandering and anastomosing form. This may well have been because of the decreasing flow competence as a result of declining spring ice melts. Organic sediments accumulated in several of these abandoned channels during the Windermere Interstadial, the Loch Lomond Stadial (*c* 11,000–9000 cal BC) and finally into the Early Holocene. The site at Silvertown Urban Village, Newham (Wilkinson et al 2000), is a good example of this with organic sedimentation dating from the Loch Lomond Stadial. Some of these abandoned channels seem to have been relatively large, and at Bramcote Grove distinctive lacustrine sediments accumulated from before 10,000 cal BC until the Early Holocene, prior to the final silting of the extensive feature identified as the Bermondsey Lake (GAZ 215; Thomas and Rackham 1996). Other than these channel fills, little sedimentation seems to have taken place in the Thames floodplain during OIS2.

The sand eyots or dunes which have left relict features such as Thorney Island and the Bermondsey and Horselydown eyots are likely to have started forming in the Early Holocene. This would be consistent with the move from an anastomosing form to a single channel river depositing sand. None of these eyots has been convincingly dated, because of the inaccessibility of the basal levels and the relative difficulties of dating sand facies. A 4th millennium cal BC date has been obtained from a small piece of wood found in the laminated sands of Thorney Island, Westminster (Sidell et al 2000), but this is the only measurement that has been obtained thus far. Where the contact with the Shepperton Gravel has been observed, a hiatus is suggested, again adding to the difficulties of ascribing a formation date to the sequences. The eyots form topographic highs upon which significant amounts of prehistoric activity are known, such as the field systems on the Southwark islands discussed below. Therefore, the importance of establishing at what date they formed and would first have been available for occupation cannot be stressed enough.

Evidence relating to Late Devensian environments in the London region is relatively limited (see Rackham and Sidell 2000), though a typical cold periglacial environment should be envisaged, with limited tundra-like vegetation. The environment at the end of this period probably consisted of an open landscape dominated by herbaceous plants, particularly Poaceae (grasses) and *Artemisia* (mugwort). This is suggested by evidence from a range of sites including Bramcote Grove, the best example excavated so far in central London (Thomas and Rackham 1996). The Late Devensian levels show an environment dominated by herbs, including

Poaceae, Cyperaceae (sedges), *Artemisia* and *Thalictrum* (meadow rue). Few tree species are present; *Salix* (dwarf willow) and, to a lesser extent, *Juniperus* (juniper) and *Sparganium* (bur reed) are the dominant taxa and present a picture of a cold, open Older Dryas landscape with dwarf shrubs. The succeeding phase, equated with the Lake Windermere Interstadial shows a development to open *Betula* (birch) woodland with local *Salix* and *Juniperus*.

Evidence of London's early Postglacial landscapes is gradually increasing, beginning with a transition from a treeless open steppe-like landscape in the Late Devensian, to *Betula* and *Pinus* (pine) woods. This was later replaced by drier *Betula* forest and the development of *Pinus* woods, with heaths and waterside areas of herb and scrub vegetation including *Carex* (sedge), Poaceae, *Juniperus*, *Salix* and *Corylus* (hazel). These are clearly recognisable at Bramcote Grove, and this is then followed by a development of wood fen and finally alder carr in a *Quercus* (oak), *Ulmus* (elm) and *Tilia* (lime) dominated temperate woodland.

2.2 Mobile communities (*c* 9500 cal BC–*c* 2000 cal BC)

The Thames and its floodplain

For the purposes of this volume, the starting date of the archaeological survey has been taken as approximately ten thousand years ago. This is convenient both archaeologically and ecologically; there is only very limited evidence for Palaeolithic material in the study area, in the form of a handful of flint artefacts (Wymer 1968, 278–9). Ten thousand years ago is the approximate marker for the decay of the ice sheets and the beginning of climatic amelioration, which signals the transition from the Pleistocene to the Holocene.

Information is scarce for the river in the early period; it is thought that by 9500 cal BC, the Thames had developed to a multi-channel form, as mentioned above (Sidell et al 2000), with the relict channels gradually filling with peats. However, the majority of known peats in the study area date from approximately 4000 cal BC and later, although a series of peat-filled channels from the Isle of Dogs (Wilkinson 1995), Silvertown (Wilkinson et al 2000) and upstream of the study area date from several thousand years earlier (see Wilkinson et al in prep). It may be that, owing to the northward migration of the Thames, the early material is either lost through erosion or deeply buried and has not yet been recovered in the study area, with the exception of the site at Bramcote Grove.

The topographic model (Fig 5), constructed from the borehole and other data reflecting the interface of gravel and the overlying strata, was created as an aid to studying this period. Although radiocarbon determinations are only available for this period from Bramcote, a series of peat horizons which have been dated to 3650–3030 cal BC (Beta 199787; 4630±100 BP), 2840–2230 cal BC (Beta 122928; 3970±70 BP) and 1890–1520 cal BC (Beta 119875; 3420±70 BP) from Joan Street (GAZ 51) and Union Street (GAZ 53) are all located altitudinally above the levels reflected on this plot. From this it is apparent that the course of the Thames was running significantly to the south of the present route, across north Southwark. The decrease in spring meltwaters following decay of the Devensian ice sheets would have restricted seasonal discharge into the upper Thames, and the limited tidal reach (which would have been significantly downstream of modern central London) would probably have meant that the river was at its least significant. However, the concentration of the course into a single channel may have been sufficient for it to act as a barrier to people attempting to cross it.

The sequences at Joan Street and Union Street confirm the northward migration of the river in this section, based on the dates

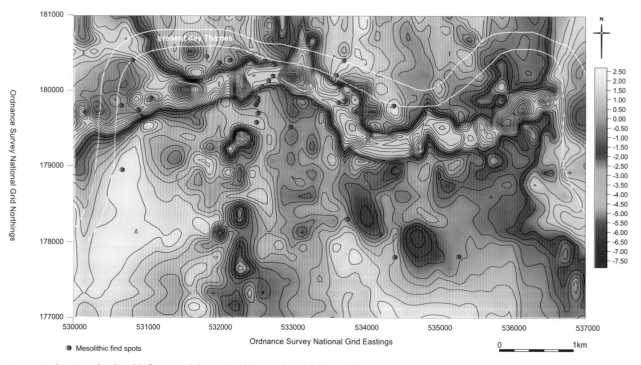

Fig 5 Map showing predicted model of Late Mesolithic Southwark/Lambeth with findspots (scale 1:50,000)

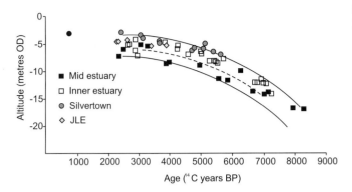

Fig 6 Sea-level age-altitude chart (after Long 1995 and Sidell et al 2000); the index points have been corrected to Mean Sea Level (MSL)

for the onset of organic sediment accretion. The earliest date obtained in west Southwark for this is c 3400 cal BC at −2.35m OD (Sidell et al 2000). The sequence at Union Street is very similar to that from Joan Street; however, there are several events, including one at c 2800–2550 cal BC, suggesting isolated inundations, submerging the southern floodplain margins. Limited diatom data indicate that these were tidal floods which represent the first evidence for the migration of the tidal head into central London. However, at this period the evidence indicates isolated flood episodes rather than continuous accretion of estuarine facies. Although there is no direct dating evidence for the formation of the sand dunes in Southwark and Lambeth, it does seem possible that dune accretion did continue after the Early Holocene, and therefore the configuration of the eyots and mudflats would have continued to be modified throughout this period in the study area, but this was probably mainly confined to the upstream reaches. The

radiocarbon date of 3082–2709 cal BC (Beta 122929; 4300±60 BP) obtained from the sands of Thorney Island on the opposing bank to the Lambeth foreshore may be a useful marker, and one equally relevant to the south bank.

The period approximately 5000–2500 cal BC is one of estuary contraction (Long et al 2000) which saw a reduction in the rate of relative sea-level rise and an expansion of the peatlands into the floodplain. Although RSL did continue to rise, this was not manifested in the study area in the form of estuarine microflora; nevertheless, it would have had an effect upon the relative altitude of the Thames. This would be through a lessening of the gradient the freshwater river had to cut in order to reach the levels of the estuarine waters. Current models for RSL suggest that mean sea level was at approximately −3.0m OD (Fig 6). The work of Woodbridge (1998) in Bermondsey led him to conclude that the tidal head was present at c 4400 cal BC at −3.5m OD. Although the data are suggestive, consisting of a brackish assemblage of diatoms in waterlain sediment, this information does not sit happily with the information contained in Devoy (1979; 1980), Long (1995) and Sidell et al (2000).

The environment

Detailed palaeoecological evidence from this period is scanty, with the exception of the results from Bramcote Grove (GAZ 215), which is taken as the type-site for early Southwark in this study. Unfortunately, it appears that an erosional event removed much of the Early Holocene stratigraphy at this site (Thomas and Rackham 1996). A lake (the Bermondsey Lake) formed in a relict channel dominated the site and the microflora indicates that the environment in the early period consisted of birch and pine

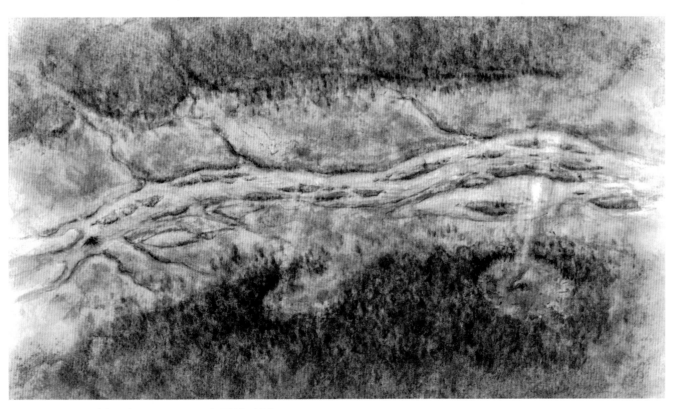

Fig 7 Reconstruction of the study area at approximately 7000 cal BC

woodland with the first appearances of *Alnus* (alder), *Corylus* (hazel) and *Tilia* (lime). This may reflect the ecology of wider areas of Southwark and it is on the basis of this evidence and the sedimentological information from the river that Fig 7 has been created. It is hoped that this reconstruction presents an image of what the area might have looked like, with the floodplain of a multi-channelled river fringed with a birch and pine woodland, which provided shelter and food for bands of people and other species such as *Cervus elaphus* (red deer) and *Bos primigenius* (aurochs).

The hiatus caused by channels cutting across Bramcote Grove appears to have removed sediments dating to between approximately 8000 and 7000 cal BC. The data subsequent to this event suggest that the local ecology had changed and fenland began to develop here, which gradually transformed into an alder carr fringed with a mixed *Quercus* (oak), *Ulmus* (elm) and *Tilia* (lime) woodland. This persisted until approximately the end of the 5th millennium cal BC, although conditions on site suggest a change away from dominance by *in situ* peat formation to inundation of the site by waterlain sediments with some intermittent periods of organic accretion. The alder carr is more likely to reflect local conditions dictated by the low-lying topography specific to the area of lacustrine basin than the previous woodland conditions. However, much of north Southwark and Lambeth is likely to have been low-lying and influenced by relict channels, particularly with the gradual northward migration of the main channel. Therefore, the alder carr prevailing at Bramcote may reflect quite accurately conditions across much of the study area. Unfortunately, there is no evidence in the record here for the exploitation of natural resources; in fact there is no evidence of direct human activity on the site until the late 3rd millennium cal BC.

A site with good environmental evidence from the middle of this period is located on the eastern side of Rotherhithe, across the river from the Isle of Dogs loop. This is Bryan Road (GAZ 230; Sidell et al 1995), where a relatively short sequence was sampled. The radiocarbon dates place the initiation of peat formation at 3940–3510 cal BC (Beta 68576; 4910±80 BP) and 3970–3700 cal BC (Beta 68577; 5040±80 BP). No impact of forest clearance is recorded in the pollen spectra at the base of the sequence, which may simply represent asynchronous clearance across the region. The picture available suggests that the drier land away from the river was dominated by mixed oak woodland with alder, elm, lime and hazel. The alder probably reflects the wetter conditions in the floodplain. This phase was rapidly succeeded by the elm decline, which is generally taken to reflect the first forest clearance by human communities. Initial opening up of woodland is thought to have enabled the elm bark beetle (*Scolytus scolytus*) to penetrate the woods and devastate elm trees (Girling 1988). This was succeeded by a short-lived *Landnam* clearance phase (see Iversen 1941) with Poaceae (grasses), *Plantago lanceolata* (ribwort plantain), *Rumex* (dock) and *Pteridium aquilinum* (bracken); all typical species found in association with cereal cultivation. Unfortunately, the rest of the sequence is not dated absolutely and it seems likely (by consideration of the litho- and biostratigraphy) that the end of the 3rd millennium cal BC saw a secondary regeneration of woodland with the re-establishment of lime and elm.

The evidence from the molluscs recovered from Bryan Road suggests low energy aquatic conditions (ie *Lymnaea truncatula*), with local channels (*Valvata piscinalis*) and also slum conditions (*Segmentina nitida* and *Vertigo antivertigo*). In addition, pools of standing water in local woodland/shaded conditions are also thought to be present (*Bathyomphalus contortus*, *Discus rotundatus*). One particular species of interest is *Trichia striolata*, which was thought to inhabit Early Holocene forests but then became locally extinct as a result of deforestation (Evans 1972). It would appear that it survived here, possibly because the initial clearance was not very extensive, as is suggested by the secondary regeneration that could have provided a *refugia* (Sidell et al 1995).

A rare find from this period comes from the modern foreshore, generally neglected archaeologically because it is a zone which tends not to be commercially developed; nevertheless, it is constantly under threat from erosion and river traffic. During a survey adjacent to Bankside Pontoon (GAZ 67), material dated to 3350–2750 cal BC was recovered (Beta 114003; 4370±70 BP) showing the contemporary floodplain environment to be of alder carr, recorded at c −1.9m OD, indicating that contemporary freshwater river levels were to be found below this.

Several other key sites which have been studied in Southwark provide detailed palaeoecological sequences. Joan Street and Union Street (Sidell et al 2000) have organic sequences that commenced formation in the 4th millennium cal BC, but slightly later than Bryan Road. The environmental evidence from the early levels indicate that, initially, both sites are likely to have been located on mudflats on the edge of the floodplain which became colonised by vegetation following the migration of channels (possibly those of the Thames) away from the sites. The basal levels suggest that they formed subsequent to the elm decline and that, therefore, this area of west Southwark had probably already been opened up, to an extent, by the local human community. The pollen suggests similarities with the Bryan Road spectra, with mixed oak forest on the drier ground to the south but marshy local floodplain environments with alder carr and other species such as *Rhamnus catharticus* (Buckthorn), *Salix*, and *Caltha* type (Kingcup). Cereal pollen and *Plantago lanceolata* were found in the basal zone from Joan Street and it is possible that these reflect early agricultural activity in the local region. Interestingly, only limited evidence for human activity was recovered from nearby Union Street, suggesting that the agricultural activity indicated by the pollen from Joan Street may well have been very small scale at this early period. Furthermore, there is no direct evidence for cultivation at this time, in the form of ard marks, field systems or macro-remains.

The sediments at Bramcote show a continuation of these alder carr environments, with additional evidence for oak, alder, lime and hazel woodland, presumably on the drier ground on the gravels to the south. Channels are thought to be migrating across the site for much of the conventional Neolithic. However, at the end of the period there is tentative evidence for the construction of a wooden structure, possibly a trackway or consolidation zone, suggesting that the area became waterlogged and artificial aid was required to traverse the wet areas between the eyots. This appears (within radiocarbon accuracy) to be roughly contemporary with a lime decline between 2190 and 1750 cal BC. It is possible that the final removal of woodlands (following the earlier records of the elm decline) either led to the base levels being raised, or to increased run-off causing waterlogging of the alder carr. Alternatively, the increased waterlogging may be associated with the gradual re-expansion of the estuary at the end of the 3rd millennium cal BC. Whatever the reason, Bramcote provides important evidence of human activity in the floodplain at this date.

The evidence from the B&Q Depot, Old Kent Road (GAZ 208), and Marlborough Grove (GAZ 204)

The best evidence for an early human presence within the study area comprised three flint scatters excavated adjacent to the Old Kent Road, in south Bermondsey (see Fig 1; Fig 3). Firstly, excavations at the B&Q depot during 1991 revealed two apparently *in situ* flint scatters located some 40m apart in trenches B and C (see Fig 8). The trench B scatter contained over 1500 worked flints focused on two hearth settings, defined on concentrations of burnt flint, and lay within a weathered sand deposit between 0.80m and 1.20m OD. A number of features, including a gully, several ditches and some postholes, were also identified, although their contemporaneity with the artefact scatter remains doubtful. The trench C scatter was much smaller, consisting of some 300 flints resting on a weathered sand deposit between 0.90m and 0.95m OD. This scatter had been sealed by makeup layers associated with the construction of Roman Watling Street. The third flint scatter was found at Marlborough Grove, some 200m to the north-west, during excavations in 1995. Close examination of the retouched tool elements within the three assemblages suggests that they can be dated to the conventional Early Mesolithic (see Chapter 6.1), a period for which, as we have seen, little local palaeoenvironmental data are currently available.

The local topography consists of weathered sand overlying Thames gravels, in this case the Upper Floodplain or Kempton Park/East Tilbury Marshes Gravel (Gibbard 1994, 89–94), with sedimentary evidence for the Bermondsey Lake, identified by Wilkinson at Bramcote Grove (Thomas and Rackham 1996) and also at the Bricklayers Arms (GAZ 191; Merriman 1992). The recorded heights of the gravel surface indicate a gradual sloping from north and west down to the south and east, ie towards the Thames. However, the slope of the gravel need not necessarily accurately reflect the Early Holocene land surface, which may have been a sandy soil of varying thickness. It is likely, however, that the general conformation of the gravel influenced the surface morphology. The weathered appearance of the overlying sand suggests it was exposed to sub-aerial processes.

The topography in the immediate vicinity of the three sites would have been dominated by the so-called Bermondsey Lake, which lay a short distance to the north and north-east. One of a number of lakes of probable Late Glacial origin situated along the Thames valley, the basin was likely to have been more than 200m (and possibly up to several kilometres) in length east to west and about 4m in depth, though at the time of the activity described here it had been silting up for several millennia. The three flint scatters lay on its southern shore and looked across the lake to the higher ground of what was later to become Bermondsey island, beyond which lay the multi-channel Thames river system. Evidence from Bramcote Grove just under a kilometre to the east indicates that the river system was unlikely to have exerted any influence on the lake basin itself at this period. Indeed it is likely that the contemporary river levels were below the water levels being maintained within the basin (Thomas and Rackham 1996).

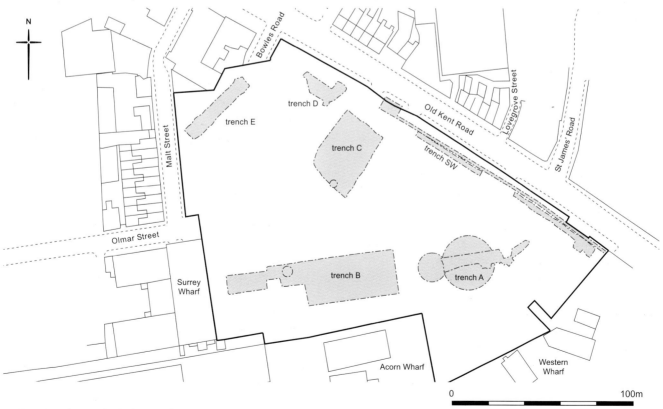

Fig 8 B&Q site location plan (scale 1:2000)

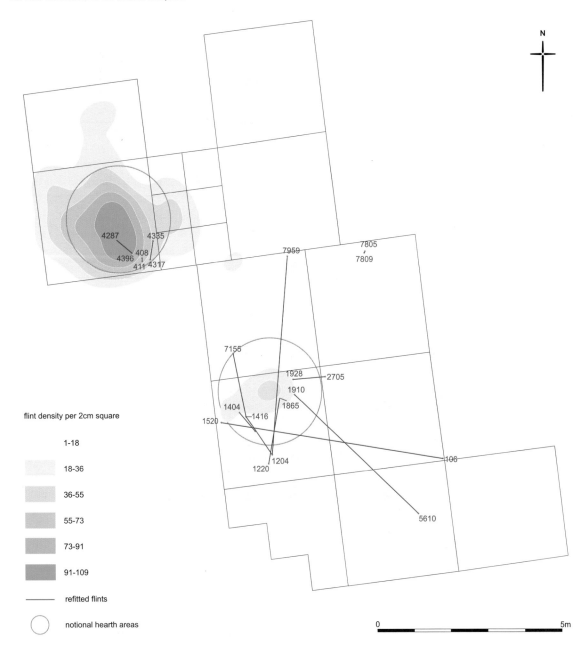

Fig 9 Plot of refitted flints, B&Q site, trench B (scale 1:100)

flint density per 2cm square

1-18

18-36

36-55

55-73

73-91

91-109

refitted flints

notional hearth areas

0   5m

If the trends observed in the local micro-topography can be relied upon, the two B&Q flint scatters were strewn across a low ridge that fell away to the north and to the south and east. By contrast, the Marlborough Grove scatter was situated closer to the lake and in the lee of higher ground to the north. This would have allowed an approach to be made to the lake margins without disturbing feeding game or wildfowl (eg Barton et al 1995, 108). Detailed evidence for the contemporary vegetation is limited, owing to the hiatus in the relevant part of the pollen sequence at Bramcote Grove referred to earlier. Nevertheless, it is likely that the lake edge was dominated by various sedges, reeds and dwarf willow, with birch and pine woodlands set further back (Thomas and Rackham 1996, table 3), though clearly there would have been little advantage in occupying a lakeside location if access to the lake itself was not relatively unimpeded (Mellars and Dark 1998, 226).

A wide range of animal resources would have been seasonally available in the locality at this time, encompassing large fauna such as deer, Alces alces (elk), aurochs and Sus scrofa (wild pig), together with wildfowl and fish. However, a single fragment of burnt 'deer-sized' (cf Capreolus capreolus, roe deer) metapodial from B&Q trench B apart, direct evidence from the three flint scatters is entirely lacking. Plant resources would probably have encompassed reeds, timber, birch bark, pine resin and nettle fibre alongside seasonally available edible tubers, nuts and fruit. Apart from one serrate with use-wear characteristic of herbaceous plant cutting (see Donahue, Chapter 6.1), there was no direct evidence for their exploitation either.

In addition to game animals and plants, the other resource available in abundance was flint, in the form of river cobbles. There was also limited evidence for the utilisation of quartzite/micaceous sandstone pebbles (for use as hammerstones and/or rubbers). It is likely that the bulk of

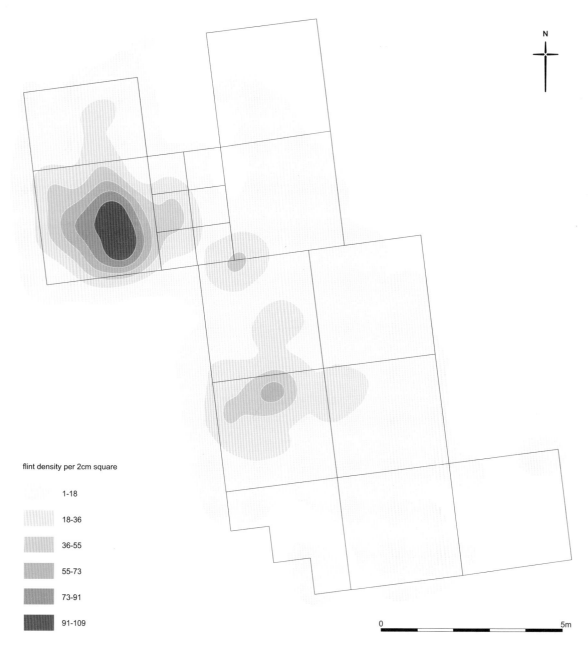

flint density per 2cm square

1-18

18-36

36-55

55-73

73-91

91-109

Fig 10 Burnt flint density plots, B&Q site, trench B (scale 1:100)

these raw materials were obtained very locally from the lake shore and from the gravel bars of the adjacent Thames river system. There was some evidence for the collection, caching and testing of suitable nodules at two of the three locations (Marlborough Grove and B&Q trench C), possibly for the preferential selection of the fine orange/yellow/brown flint utilised on the third (B&Q trench B).

The relatively tight distribution of the artefacts close to the top of the sediments in all three locations implies that they were largely *in situ*, with little post-depositional disturbance. There was no marked difference here between B&Q trenches B and C, despite the fact that Roman Watling Street sealed the latter, suggesting that any movement down the profile had already occurred by the Roman period. The broad contemporaneity of the two scatters was initially thrown into doubt by the presence of a single leaf arrowhead of earlier Neolithic date from trench C, but statistical analyses conducted

by Peter Rauxloh on the complete unmodified blades from the three scatters suggest that this could well have been intrusive. Furthermore, a limited refitting exercise (see Fig 9) carried out on the material from B&Q was successful in identifying both dorsal-ventral refits and straight conjoins, particularly within the trench B scatter.

This optimistic view of three *in situ* and broadly contemporary flint scatters is tempered by Donahue's study of the wear preserved on a range of lithics from B&Q (see Chapter 6.1), suggesting that the site had been affected by a range of post-depositional processes. Some appeared to be ancient, involving burning, human and animal trampling and gentle shifting of the matrix; others were more likely to be modern and connected with the excavation and subsequent storage and handling of the artefacts.

Taphonomic problems aside, activity at B&Q seems to have centred around two hearth settings located in trench B (see Fig 10).

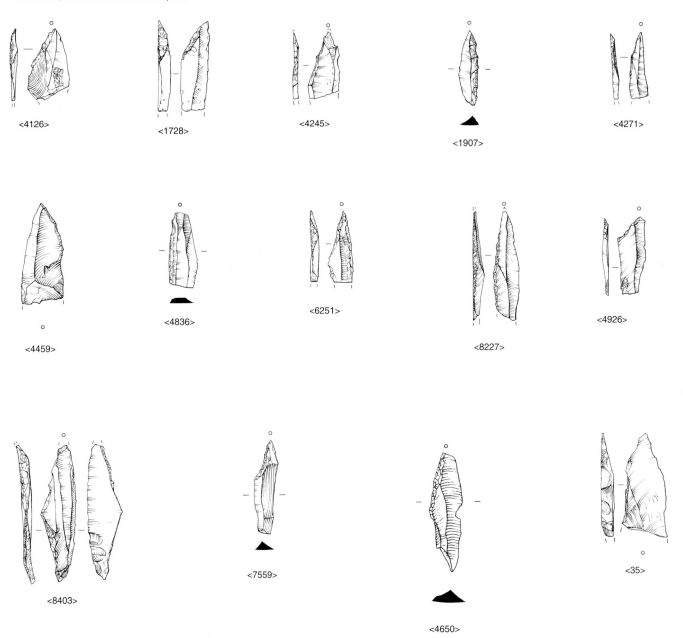

Fig 11 Microliths and microburins from B&Q, trenches B and C (scale 1:1)

These lay about 6 or 7m apart but rather towards the western periphery of the excavated area, which somewhat compromises our ability to interpret the activities carried out around them. Both settings were defined during post-excavation analysis only, using localised concentrations of burnt flint, both worked and unworked; ie no deposits of charcoal, stone settings or fire pits were noted during excavation. The densest concentration of flint artefacts centred on the northern hearth; that around the southern hearth was more diffuse. There was no way of determining whether the hearths were in contemporary or successive use, though it is possible that they marked seasonal reoccupation of a favoured place in the local landscape. No unequivocal evidence for the existence of any associated wind-breaks or shelters survived, either in the form of features such as stakeholes or pits or abrupt breaks in the distributions of the struck flint.

Attention has already been drawn to the possible caching and testing of suitable flint nodules in trench C 40m or so to the north, and to similar activity at Marlborough Grove a further 200m north-west. Although the reduction of selected nodules certainly took place at both locations, knapping activity was focused on the hearth settings in B&Q trench B. Here the full reduction sequence was present. This encompassed tested nodules, complete and fragmentary cores and preparation flakes (eg core tablets, core rejuvenators and crested pieces), large numbers of unmodified flakes and blades, and a range of retouched tools (principally microliths, scrapers and burins) and tool waste (microburins, sharpening flakes and burin spalls). The knapping activity was clearly geared to the manufacture and repair of flint tool kits, the best and most diagnostic evidence for which related to hunting equipment in the form of microliths and their waste

<12>

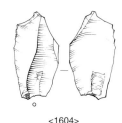

<1604>

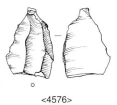

<4576>

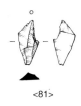

<81>

<7957>

<4248>

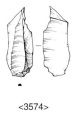

<3574>

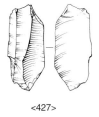

<427>

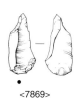

<7869>

<4704>

components (microburins). A majority of the microliths from B&Q trench B (12 out of 15) had been broken and four bore traces of impact fractures (these included two of the three complete pieces). Significantly, none of the microburins could be matched to any of the surviving microliths. Taken together this indicates two separate ways microliths reached the site (see Figs 11–13). The first comprises microliths manufactured elsewhere and brought to the site attached to arrow shafts or embedded in animal carcasses; the second comprises those made on-site to replace them and carried off to other locations. Close examination of the surviving microlith assemblage suggests that it is dominated by slender obliquely blunted and straight-backed pieces of Reynier's 'Deepcar' type, currently thought to span the period *c* 8500–7700 cal BC (eg Reynier 1998, 174–5). The microliths on Fig 11 comprise Early Mesolithic obliquely blunted points (Clark's Type A), <4126>, <1728>, <4245>, <4271>, <4459>, <6251>, <4926>, <7559>, <4650> from trench B, and <35> from trench C; backed points (Clark's Type B), <1907>, <4836> and <8227> from trench B; and a Late Mesolithic geometric point (Clark's Type D) <12> from

trench C. All of the microburins were recovered from trench B. Microliths <1907>, <7559>, <4650>, <4836> and <12> display evidence of impact damage; microburin <81> bears invasive fracture scars suggestive of wedging (Fig 11).

In addition to the maintenance and replacement of flint tool kits, there is good evidence for a range of other activities having taken place around the hearths. Direct evidence for cooking is limited to the single fragment of burnt 'deer-sized' metapodial bone mentioned above. However, the recovery of three burnt microliths suggests that these may have been lodged in carcasses and accidentally incorporated in the cooking process. Use-wear identified upon a number of the other retouched pieces such as scrapers and burins points to the organised processing of cached animal products. These comprise (Fig 14) end and side scrapers used to scrape dry hide, <3579>, <8603>, <6664>, <4538>, <7771>, <4589>, <2730>, <4588>, <4230> and <4615>; end scrapers and a flake used in hide working, <4648>, <8627>, <7358> and <58>; a crested piece used to pierce dry hide, <1903>; a blade used to cut

15

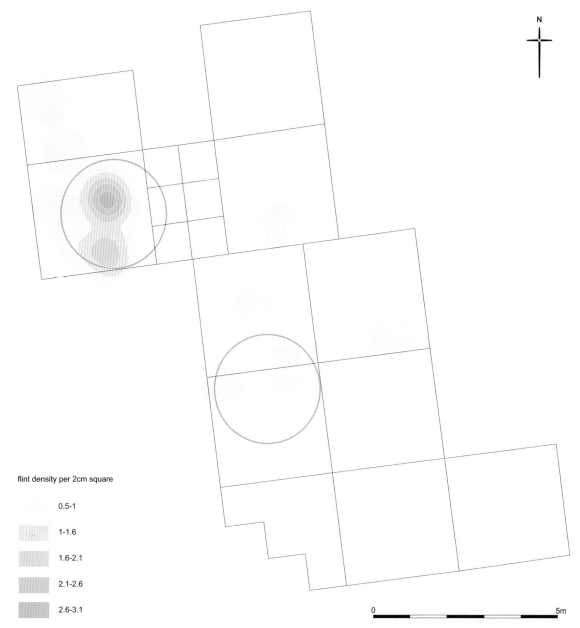

N

flint density per 2cm square

0.5-1

1-1.6

1.6-2.1

2.1-2.6

2.6-3.1

0   5m

Fig 12 Microlith density plots, B&Q site, trench B (scale 1:100)

hide/meat, <146>; a burin used to work antler, <88>; a
blade used for soft whittling (? of wood), <4526>; a serrate
used to cut soft plant material, <132>; a retouched blade
with undetermined 'hard' wear, <150>; a notched piece with
undetermined 'soft' wear, <6653>; and an Early Neolithic
leaf arrowhead displaying evidence of impact fracture,
<5701>.

The single serrate used to saw through herbaceous plant
material is potentially illuminating, although it was recovered
early in the excavation and from a context whose integrity is
therefore questionable. Evidence for plant exploitation need
cause no particular surprise, however, and 'cutting soft' use-
wear traces have been taken to indicate plant utilisation at
Thatcham in the Kennet valley further upriver (Healy et al
1992, 58–9). The working of dry (presumably stored) hide
is particularly interesting and, together with the numbers
of microliths, may carry implications for the season of

occupation and function of the site. Donahue (this volume)
suggests dry hide working is likely to have been an
autumn/winter activity, while Keeley (1988) notes the
dominance of dry hide over fresh hide scraping at residential
bases. Moreover, the number of scrapers recovered may carry
implications regarding the presence of women on the site
(as Clark 1954, 11).

The numbers of people engaged in these various activities
and the length of their occupancy remains singularly difficult to
quantify, particularly as so little of the area to the west of the
hearth areas was examined. On current evidence, the flint
scatters in B&Q trench C and at Marlborough Grove could
perhaps best be interpreted as the remains of short-stay primary
resource procurement sites. By contrast, the larger flint scatter
and hearth settings within trench B appear to represent (part
of) a multiple resource processing and maintenance activity site
(conventionally referred to as a 'home base'), perhaps revisited

N

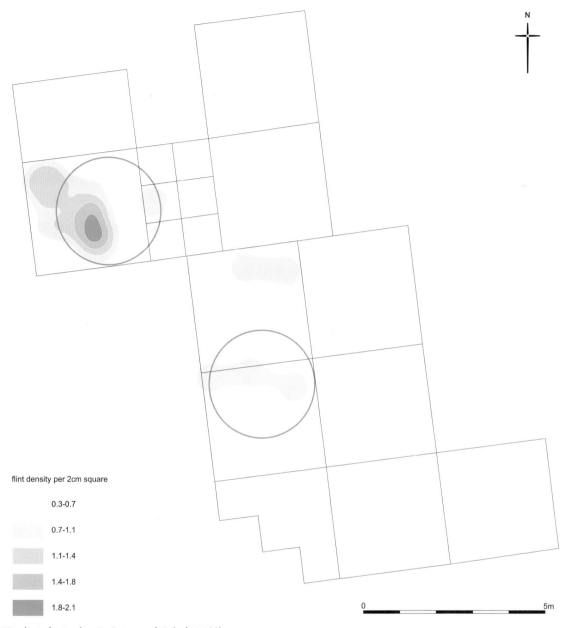

flint density per 2cm square

0.3-0.7

0.7-1.1

1.1-1.4

1.4-1.8

1.8-2.1

0   5m

Fig 13 *Microburin density plots, B&Q site, trench B (scale 1:100)*

on a seasonal basis (see Smith 1992, 28–9). However, the greatest interpretative pitfall would be 'to force a complex, repeatedly occupied and spatially extensive site…into an overly simple functional model' (Mellars and Dark 1998, 225). The conclusion is that the silting lake basin would have furnished a seasonally rich suite of resources for exploitation by mobile groups of humans, and other sites undoubtedly await discovery along its shoreline.

The information gathered from this project has enabled a reconstruction to be created (Fig 15), with the activities illustrated based on the evidence gleaned from the lithic analysis in association with the three-dimensional records of where each flint was discarded. The environmental and topographic information is derived from contemporary data recovered from Bricklayers Arms and Bramcote Grove. Some extrapolation, however, was required for the types of clothing and the number of individuals represented.

The evidence from isolated findspots and chance artefact recovery

The early flint assemblages fringing the southern shoreline of the Bermondsey Lake can be complemented by smaller collections of artefacts scattered across the study area and along the present Thames and its foreshore. Diagnostic finds, particularly of microliths, suggest that much of this activity is likely to post-date *c* 7500 cal BC, however. Characteristic narrow bladed microliths of geometric form occur on a number of sites, including an important collection of eight from Addington Street near Waterloo (WSC90) (GAZ 33) (see Fig 16), with others at Southwark Street (GAZ 91; Cowan 1992, 63 and fig 17, nos 2–4), 29 Addington Street, Waterloo (WSB90) (GAZ 34), Bermondsey Abbey (GAZ 159), Whites Grounds (GAZ 154) and Hopton Street (GAZ 54). A single Late Mesolithic point (and a Neolithic arrowhead) from B&Q trench

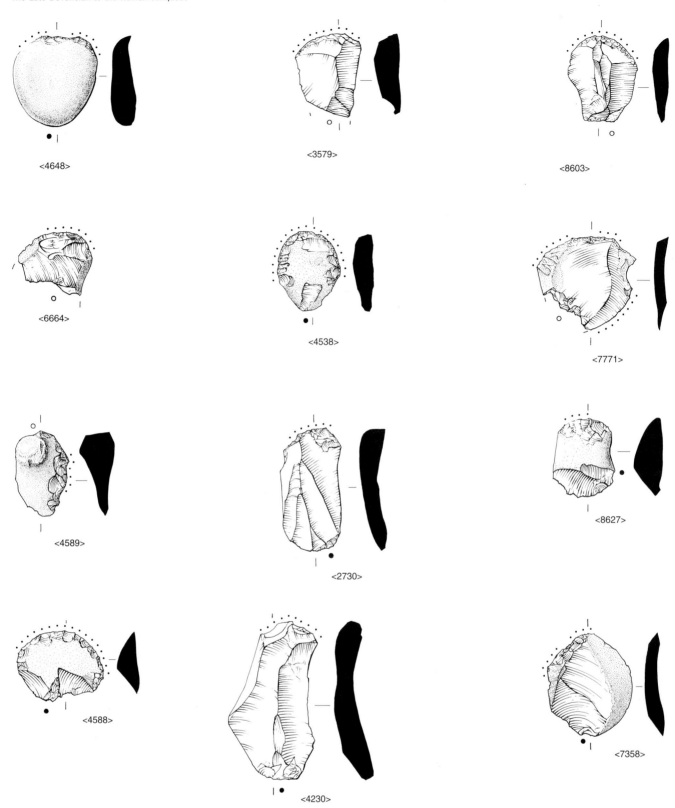

Fig 14 *Selection of Early Mesolithic artefacts from B&Q displaying traces of microwear (scale 2:3)*

C and possibly a second from trench B suggests that the Bermondsey Lake continued to exert an influence (albeit declining) in these later periods too (see below).

Heavy duty flint tools such as axes and adzes have been recovered from the Thames and its foreshore but not, so far, during excavations further inland. However, stray adze-sharpening flakes, removed to renew the cutting edges of such tools, have been recorded on a number of sites, as at Coronation Buildings (GAZ 9), Bermondsey Abbey, Courage's Brewery bottling plant (GAZ 81), Fennings Wharf (GAZ

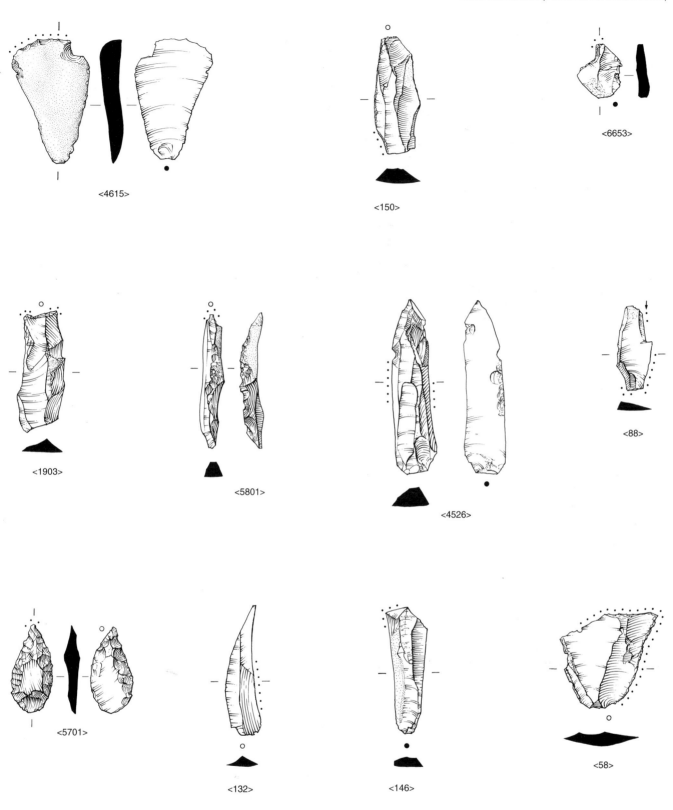

<4615>

<150>

<6653>

<1903>

<5801>

<4526>

<88>

<5701>

<132>

<146>

<58>

130), Southwark Street and Hopton Street. Bone and antler tools have a markedly riverine distribution (eg Lacaille 1966), which may simply reflect the conditions suitable for their preservation. Few direct dates are available for these (Smith 1989; Bonsall and Smith 1989), although a broken uniseral barbed antler point from Wandsworth has been dated to 8550–7950 cal BC (OxA-3736, 9050±85 BP) (Clive Bonsall, pers comm). This confirms anticipated Early

Mesolithic affinities. A second example was recovered from the river at Battersea.

Diagnostically Neolithic material is not well represented anywhere in central London (eg Merriman 1987), but the study area has produced some important small collections of struck flint and pottery together with several possible groups of cut features. These are complemented by a range of other artefacts collected from the present Thames and its foreshore

Fig 15 Reconstruction of task-specific areas around hearths at B&Q

and material (including two flint axes) recovered from the silts of the Bermondsey Lake at Bricklayers Arms. Earlier Neolithic material in the area is scarce and comprises a handful of broken leaf arrowheads (Fig 17) and the occasional fragment of pottery. To what extent this under-representation is a product of misidentification is hard to assess, for there does seem to be a genuine absence of such material within the excavated assemblages examined as part of the present study. With the exception of a single sherd from the foreshore at Chambers Wharf, Bermondsey (GAZ 207), and a few dubious scraps from Hopton Street, the pottery is almost exclusively Peterborough

Ware and, where identifiable, predominantly of Mortlake type. Although traditionally considered Late Neolithic, a recent project to obtain high-precision radiocarbon dates for Peterborough vessels has produced dates in the range 3400–2500 cal BC, indicating that a Middle Neolithic date may be more appropriate (Gibson 1995, 30; Gibson and Kinnes 1997). A number of the flint arrowheads of transverse type recorded from the study area may be so dated too, although there were no direct associations.

At the Bricklayers Arms site, excavated in October 1987 (Jones 1991), 11 evaluation trenches were opened along the

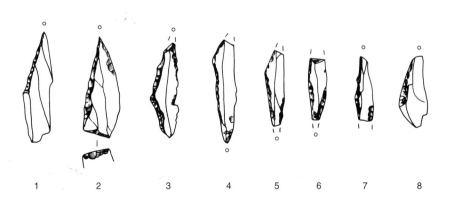

1   2   3   4   5   6   7   8

Fig 16 Narrow bladed microliths from Addington Street (scale 1:1)

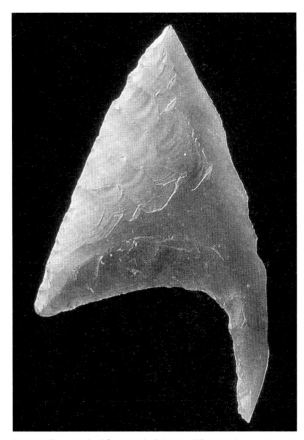

Fig 17 *Flint arrowhead from Lambeth (max width 25mm)*

edge of the Bermondsey eyot and out in the adjacent lake basin. Two Neolithic flint axes were recovered from the lake silts, the first comprising the blade of a ground artefact and the second a somewhat rough chipped axe of cherty material (see Fig 27). A collection of horizontal interlaced timbers, interpreted as a laid platform and considered to be broadly contemporary with the axes, was revealed at the edge of the eyot and the lake, stratigraphically between the freshwater lake silts and a subsequent peaty horizon thought to be evidence of gradual lake-infilling. The platform, therefore, seems to have been used while the lake was still extant. It was of interlaced timbers, consisting of a mixture of alder, willow and birch with some cut marks still identifiable. A second platform was found in another of the trenches overlying a ditch that might reflect early land division or drainage. Several hearths were located adjacent to the platform, associated with much fire-cracked flint. Two horse bones were found in this area, close to the hearths, and may be an indication that horseflesh was eaten, but no butchery marks were recorded and so this cannot be stated conclusively. Also the bones were articulated but truncated by a later feature, so there may once have been an entire skeleton deposited here. Details of the platform construction were lost; it was thought that it might have been held together by withies (Jones 1991). A series of utilised flakes (including a possible serrate and blade) were found enmeshed with the structure, which is likely to have represented a lakeside jetty or platform between the dry ground on the eyot and the boggy area adjacent to the lake. It is possible that the tools indicate that this was very

much a working environment, collecting resources from the lake, such as reeds and possibly fish; however, the deposition of the two axes may indicate a ritual connotation in addition to the practical aspects. No artefacts or structural evidence were found within the peats and it seems likely that when the lake began to fill with peat, the lakeside activity ceased as it would have become increasingly difficult to reach the dwindling lake across a boggy marsh.

Small groups of features of possible Neolithic date have been located on two sites near Waterloo Station (GAZ 34 and GAZ 33). Features included a ditch terminus, three pits (of which two had posts burnt *in situ*), a linear slot with associated postholes and various other postholes. It is possible that the postholes and linear features form part of a structure. The features were associated with a reasonably large but mixed flint assemblage and some sherds of pottery. One pit at WSB90 produced a total of 15 sherds, which included rim fragments <P1> and <P2> from two Peterborough bowls (Mortlake type) (Fig 18) and also a collection of body sherds with impressed decoration and incised lines. These sherds are in poor condition and only patches of decoration are visible so, while the styles of decoration are comparable, they could not be attributed to Peterborough vessels with certainty. Another decorated sherd from this context is from a collared vessel <P4>, possibly a Collared Urn, which may be of slightly later date. A further sherd of Neolithic Peterborough bowl <P3> was recovered from St Thomas Street (GAZ 117).

At present these few sites comprise the only direct evidence for Neolithic activity within the study area. It may be

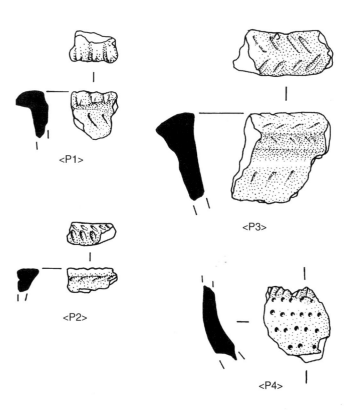

<P1>

<P2>

<P3>

<P4>

Fig 18 *Peterborough Neolithic bowls (Mortlake type) <P1>–<P3>; decorated sherd <P4> (scale 1:2)*

significant that some of the best evidence for clearance and cultivation in the form of cereal pollen and *Plantago lanceolata* was located at Joan Street, which lies roughly midway between Waterloo and St Thomas Street.

Discussion

Predictive modelling

The topographic model for the Early Holocene indicates a cluster of findspots along a south–north linear feature, presumed to be a relict channel draining from the higher ground to the south into the Thames. Observation elsewhere in London suggests that Early Holocene activity is often to be found adjacent to watercourses, including the tributary valleys such as the Lea, Colne and Wandle (see Wilkinson et al in prep). Furthermore, a site was recently uncovered in Erith on what appeared to be a relict foreshore (Bennell 1998). However, it seems unlikely that, in the central zone at least, locations on the floodplain would have been attractive, because of the general instability of the muds, sands and gravels. The Thames itself would have been coursing through several channels, particularly in the early period, and although it would have been quite easy to traverse, owing to the channels being relatively shallow and divided by sand bars, the floodplain might have appeared unstable for anything other than fairly short-term activity. It is on the higher ground where sites are more likely to be found, so well exemplified by the B&Q flint scatters, and the margins of the Bermondsey Lake may well contain further, early, material. Therefore defining the extent of the lake should be a priority for the future.

The topographic plot also indicates that the Thames ran in a course to the south of the modern river (Fig 5). It is possible, then, that the northern bank of the Thames, which is steeper than the southern, may also be a good area to look for early material, as it would have been elevated above the river. Unfortunately, the northward migration of the Thames is likely to have eroded these riverside locations but, as with the B&Q site, possibly preferred locations were a little removed from the foreshore itself. Furthermore, the City is not traditionally

known for its prehistory, and in such cases, a self-perpetuating myth can be created; no prehistoric evidence is known, *ergo* none is searched for. It is important to collect better information on the Early Holocene route of the Thames and so this too should be a future priority.

For younger sites, a similar scenario may be envisaged. The formation of the sand islands, possibly in the 4th millennium cal BC, is likely to have made this area difficult for any kind of seasonal or semi-permanent activity and, again, more stable ground is likely to have been preferred. Furthermore, the processes involved in eyot formation are likely to have eroded evidence. Therefore gravel terrace margins should be targeted for future work. The final silting of the Bermondsey Lake would probably have ruled out this area for occupation. The reduced dataset of Neolithic material (and from the early period in particular) suggests that, although evidence may still await recovery, there really was either a perceived aversion to the area, or simply a preference for other regions.

Mobile communities within the study area and beyond

Some of the best evidence for early prehistory recovered from the study area, indeed from the London region as a whole, is from the B&Q site and Marlborough Grove. Now represented only by flint scatters, these sites appear to have been geared around the exploitation of a Late Glacial lake basin. This lakeside location is a classic one for hunter-gatherer activity, and can be matched elsewhere within the greater Thames valley and beyond. Moreover, the existence of further sites, such as that at the Bricklayers Arms, fringing the contemporary shorelines of the Bermondsey Lake and the developing river system to the north can be anticipated with some confidence.

The flint assemblages (see Fig 19) are directly comparable with those from Three Ways Wharf, Uxbridge (Scatter C west; Lewis 1991 and 2000) and West Heath, Hampstead (Collins and Lorimer 1989), though there is evidence for a substantial Late Mesolithic presence at the latter. Assemblage composition is broadly similar in each case, with large quantities of debitage (well in excess of 90%) and smaller percentages of tools and tool waste; however, tool type percentages vary across the site.

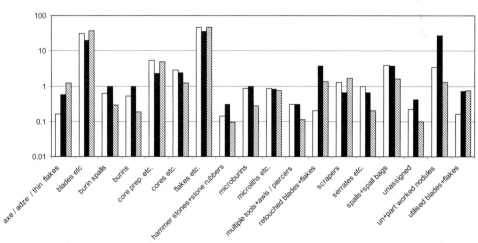

Fig 19 *Comparison of flint assemblages from B&Q/MAG with Uxbridge Scatter C west*

Detailed examination of the microliths from each of the sites has shown that all broadly conform to assemblages of Reynier's (1998, 174–5) 'Deepcar' type, currently dated to between c 8500–7700 cal BC (conventionally dated from 9300 to 8700 BP). The strong correlation between these 'Deepcar' assemblages and major river valleys across southern Britain suggests that the pattern of settlement and exploitation may represent a specific adaptation to this particular physiographic zone (Reynier 1998, 181).

There are further points of comparison to be drawn, particularly between the sites at B&Q and Three Ways Wharf. Both were set on low ridges adjacent to water: open water in the case of B&Q and an active stream channel at Three Ways Wharf. Both appear to have exploited these favoured locations on a possibly seasonal basis and both appear to have utilised hearth settings as the focus for a wide range of social activities, including the cooking of meat. Finally, both produced evidence of the caching of raw materials for later processing: dry (as opposed to fresh) hide working at the B&Q site and the extraction of red deer bone marrow, fat and grease at Three Ways Wharf (Lewis in prep).

It would be prudent not to be too dogmatic about matters such as site function, duration and season of occupation and numbers of individuals involved, particularly in view of the fact that relatively small areas of the local landscape have been examined. Nevertheless, the wide range of activities undertaken around the Bermondsey Lake encourages the view that it provided a rich and possibly stable focus for human groups during the Early Holocene. In wider terms, the dispersal of these sites within the landscape can be compared with the situations in the Kennet valley (eg Healy et al 1992) and particularly the Vale of Pickering in Yorkshire (Schadla-Hall 1989). In both areas targeted fieldwork has successfully located a range of Mesolithic sites and begun to explore some of the complexities of specialised resource procurement and social organisation that move the argument beyond the simple 'home base' model.

Compared to the early period, the evidence relating to the Late Mesolithic in the study area is less well focused, which reflects the wider regional situation (Lewis 2000). The Bermondsey Lake appears to have exerted a declining influence, while the Thames became increasingly influential, as the distribution of various artefact types demonstrates. Rising sea levels out in the Thames estuary at this time may even have led to the inundation and abandonment of traditional hunting grounds, which would presumably have placed greater pressure on resources inland (Wilkinson and Murphy 1995, 212). Certainly there is some evidence for Late Mesolithic activity further up the tributary valleys in the London region, on valley slopes and around the headwaters of tributary streams. This includes traces of the widespread firing of late Boreal woodlands in the upper Colne and Lea valleys (eg Lewis et al 1992, 244–5) possibly to create browse for game.

On the basis of the evidence currently to hand, the pattern of activity does not appear to change much in the Early–Middle Neolithic. Pollen apart (see above), direct evidence for human

intervention in the landscape is currently restricted to the presence of a few diagnostic flints and sherds of pottery. This need not indicate much more than the traversing of the area by mobile groups or individuals in the course of their daily or seasonal routines. However, evidence from other floodplain and marginal inter-tidal zones (eg Allen et al 1997, 123; Wilkinson and Murphy 1995) suggests that this picture is not necessarily untypical. Indeed, given the serendipitous nature of the fieldwork and the usually restricted areas available for examination within an overwhelmingly urban study area, it is perhaps surprising that we are able to say anything meaningful about this period at all.

2.3 A ritual riverscape (c 2500–c 1000 cal BC)

This section deals with a group of sites, river finds and placed deposits gathered here together under the umbrella term 'ritual riverscape'. The sites comprise a ring ditch from Fennings Wharf, close to the southern approach to London Bridge; a boiling pit and burnt mound from Phoenix Wharf, close to London Bridge on the Horselydown eyot, and a substantial piled structure from Nine Elms, Vauxhall. Dated to the first half of the 2nd millennium cal BC (the conventional Early Bronze Age), these various interventions along the floodplain can perhaps be seen as the floodplain equivalent to the earlier 'ritual landscapes' on the west London terraces (see Cotton 2000 and Andrews et al 1998).

The Fennings Wharf ring ditch (GAZ 130)

During 1984, excavations were carried out in advance of redevelopment at Fennings Wharf, close by the southern approach to modern London Bridge (Watson et al 2001) (see Fig 1). These revealed a small ring ditch and other prehistoric features dug into the natural subsoils of a riverside spur. The sandy subsoil had formed on the terrace gravels between 0.85–1.18m OD. Excavation of the same subsoil horizon further east at Toppings Wharf (GAZ 132) revealed undatable flint blades and abraded prehistoric pottery (c 1000–400 cal BC) (Sheldon 1974).

Victorian foundations truncated the ring ditch, but the surviving portion had a narrow V- or U-shaped profile and was over 1.0m deep with the upper portion of the sides widened by erosion. The ring ditch had an internal diameter of 7.0–7.4m (see Fig 20). The primary fills of the ditch consisted of redeposited natural sand/gravel and at least one possible cremation spread located within the primary fill with evidence for in situ burning. The secondary fills of the ditch consisted of silty sands and contained another four spreads of charcoal and cremated bone; all the cremations were deposited within the eastern portion of the ring ditch. The nine radiocarbon dates from these spreads confirm that the ring ditch was in use during the early 2nd millennium cal BC (see below). An area of 'compact silty loam' may represent the last remains of a mound covering this central feature. The angle of the tiplines within the ditch fills suggests that natural processes had probably largely levelled the mound (presumably formed from the ditch spoil) even before the rising river deposited a band of flood clay.

The eastern side of the ditch was subsequently recut and its backfill contained another three spreads of charcoal and cremated bone which were probably derived from the dumping or scattering of material from nearby pyres, as there is little evidence of in situ burning. However, the monument appears to have acted as a focus for activity for a longer period of time, potentially up to a thousand years (including

the reuse of the central feature), on the basis of the associated pottery (see below). The central feature was an oval cut measuring 2.04m by 0.8m filled with silty gravel, cremated bone and pottery. It is interpreted as a secondary cremation, on the basis of the pottery dating from its fills (c 8th–5th century cal BC). The feature also contained some plant remains (Giorgi 2001), including Anthemis cotula (stinking mayweed), Papaver sp (poppy), Juncus spp and Eleocharis palustris/uniglumis (rushes), Carex spp (sedge) and one grain of Triticum spelta (spelt wheat). The sample was rather small and cannot be overinterpreted, but it seems possible that the grain and weeds may be part of an assemblage that was burnt with the body, perhaps as fuel. The wetland plants are likely to reflect the local conditions,

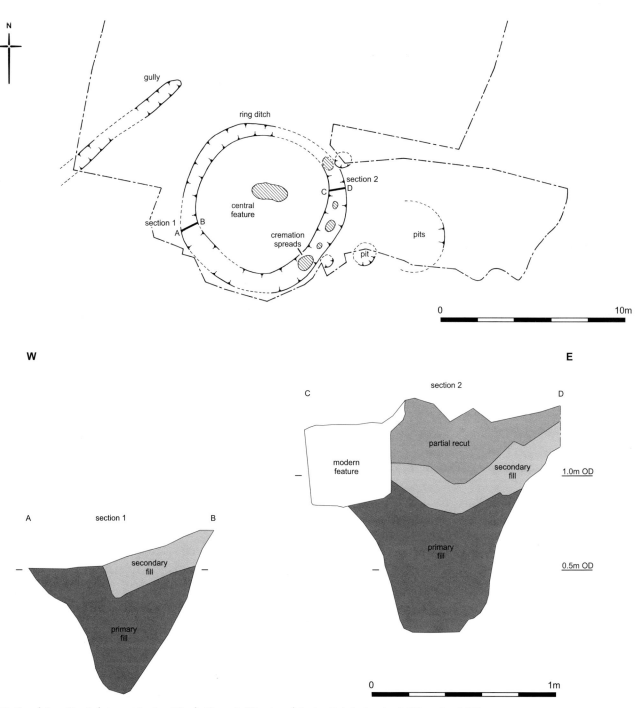

Fig 20 Plan of the prehistoric features at Fennings Wharf with two E–W sections of the ring ditch (scales: plan 1:200; sections 1:20)

as the site would have been within a boggier environment (owing to rising base levels) than when the monument was first constructed.

In the vicinity of the ring ditch, but not stratigraphically related, were several other prehistoric features, dated to the later Bronze Age by a few sherds of flint-tempered pottery and three fragments of perforated clay slab. Immediately to the west was a narrow 7.5m long gully, aligned north-east to south-west. To the east was a group of four small pits filled with gravels, sands and sandy silts, as well as an area of later subsoil. All these features were undated and of uncertain function. However, as a group they are interesting, demonstrating activity on the edge of the river in an area that was subsequently inundated. It can be assumed that the builders of the ring ditch did not consider this area marginal, although it is unclear how far away the river bank lay because of extensive erosion in the post-Roman period (Watson et al 2001). A conservative estimate would locate the contemporary foreshore somewhere near the northern edge of the site, at least 15m away, but it could have lain considerably further out into the modern river.

The cremation deposits

Radiocarbon dating of the charcoal within the ring ditch shows that the primary fill incorporating cremated remains can be ascribed to the early 2nd millennium cal BC (see below and Chapter 6.3). Four more cremation spreads were located in the secondary fill of the ring ditch and a further three in the backfill of the recut eastern side of the feature (see Table 2). A secondary cremation was found within the oval feature in the centre of the ring ditch. The cremations include mature and immature persons.

The human bone was recorded in accordance with MoLAS standard procedures for the analysis of human skeletal remains. Observations recorded for cremations included: weight free of inclusions, colour, the presence and size of identifiable fragments of cremated bone and an age estimate for the deceased. Cremated human bone was recovered from eight contexts (potentially involving nine individuals) from the ring ditch. There were no cremation vessels nor admixed animal bone. With the exception of context [1104] there was no evidence of more than one individual in any cremation sample. They are listed below and details are summarised in Table 2.

The extreme rarity of human remains of this date in this part of the lower Thames valley makes this site particularly important. Several of the cremations were highly fragmented but the bone was usually well preserved and allowed at least a coarse ageing of the remains. Some of the material from the cremation of immature individuals was eroded. It has been pointed out that cremation burials from the Early to Middle Bronze Age are substantially small *samples* of the human bone burnt elsewhere on site (McKinley 1998).

The simple picture of seven child and one adult cremations distributed about a single child cremation burial is complicated by the fact that burials of this date are difficult to distinguish from deliberate spreads of 'pyre debris', as found recently at Twyford Down (McKinley 1999). Redeposited pyre debris consists of a mixture of fuel ash, burnt stone, burnt clay, slag, bone and fragments of pyre goods (ibid, 19). Hence, the small quantities of burnt bone found in the secondary fill of the ring ditch may be residues of pyre debris. If this consideration were taken seriously it would have the effect of reducing the number of individuals to six, with cremation burials of four children and one adult surrounding the burial of a child.

Table 2 Summary of cremations from Fennings Wharf

Context	Weight	Colour	Maximum size of fragments (mm)	Age group	Comment
[1020]	525g	grey-brown	30 × 22	child	Cremated bone from backfill of the partial recut eastern side of the ring ditch; absence of epiphyseal union showed this was an immature individual
[1082]	115g	grey-brown	35 × 26	child	Cremated bone from backfill of the recut side of the ring ditch comprised the partial remains of an immature person
[1098]	680g	white	32 × 20	adult	Cremated bone from the backfill of the ring ditch recutting included a molar tooth from the only adult found in the group; the fragments of bone were too small for the assessment of sex and precise age
[1100] UB4431	10g	grey	10 × 5	child	The primary fill of the ring ditch contained only a small quantity of human bone. The identifiable material was from a child
[1104]	5g 5g	grey black	25 × 3 10 × 5	child ×2?	Two very small samples of human cremations found in the secondary fill of the ring ditch were sufficiently unburnt to suggest the remains of two children
[2046]	5g	grey	5 × 5	child	Sufficient recognisable fragments remained in this sample of cremated bone from the secondary fill of the ring ditch to show that a child burial had been involved
[2078]	5g	grey	15 × 5	child	The primary burial in the grave in the centre of the ring ditch was of a child
[2142]	10g	white	20 × 8	child	The sample of cremated bone from the secondary fill of the ring ditch represented a child

Table 3 Fennings Wharf radiocarbon determinations

Laboratory no.	Sample reference – context	Radiocarbon age (BP)	δ¹³C (λ)	Material	Calibrated date range (95% confidence)	Probability density estimate (95% probability)
OxA-8763	FW84 435a [1020]	3360±40	−22.7	charcoal, *Quercus* sp sapwood	cal BC 1750–1520	*cal BC 1740–1600*
OxA-8764	FW84 435b [1020]	3400±45	−22.6	charcoal, *Quercus* sp sapwood	cal BC 1880–1610	*cal BC 1740–1610*
OxA-8765	FW84 546a [1104]	3345±45	−22.6	charcoal, *Quercus* sp sapwood	cal BC 1750–1520	*cal BC 1750–1640*
OxA-8766	FW84 546b [1104]	3425±40	−22.9	charcoal, *Quercus* sp sapwood	cal BC 1880–1640	*cal BC 1860–1840 (1%) or cal BC 1820–1790 (2%) or cal BC 1780–1650 (92%)*
OxA-8767	FW84 547a [1104]	3420±40	−22.7	charcoal, *Quercus* sp sapwood	cal BC 1880–1630	*cal BC 1810–1790 (1%) or cal BC 1780–1650 (94%)*
OxA-8768	FW84 547b [1104]	3490±40	−22.5	charcoal, *Quercus* sp sapwood	cal BC 1930–1690	*cal BC 1830–1680*
OxA-8769	FW84 573a [1104]	3430±45	−22.7	charcoal, *Quercus* sp sapwood	cal BC 1890–1630	*cal BC 1860–1840 (1%) or cal BC 1820–1790 (3%) or cal BC 1790–2650 (91%)*
OxA-8770	FW84 573b [1104]	3545±40	−22.8	charcoal, *Quercus* sp sapwood	cal BC 2030–1750	*cal BC 1850–1730 (64%) or cal BC 1720–1680 (31%)*
UB-4431	FW84 607 [1100]	3407±33	−23.5–0.2	charcoal, *Quercus* sp sapwood	cal BC 1860–1620	*cal BC 1880–1840 (24%) or cal BC 1830–1790 (11%) or cal BC 1780–1690 (60%)*

The radiocarbon dating

In 1999, nine charcoal samples (Table 3) were processed for radiocarbon dating. Eight of the samples consisted of single fragments of oak sapwood selected from the spreads of charred material in the silts of the ditch. These were dated at the Oxford Radiocarbon Accelerator Unit, processed according to methods outlined in Hedges et al (1989), and measured using Accelerator Mass Spectrometry (Bronk Ramsey and Hedges 1997). The other sample consisted of bulked fragments of oak sapwood from a concentration of cremated remains in the primary fill of the ring ditch. The dating of a bulked sample was considered valid in this instance because the material consisted of a discrete spread in a primary context, which appeared to be functionally related to the cremation of a single individual (Bayliss 1999; *pace* Ashmore 1999). This sample was dated at the Queen's University, Belfast Radiocarbon Laboratory, processed according to methods outlined in Pearson (1984), McCormac (1992), and McCormac et al (1993) and measured using Liquid Scintillation Counting (Noakes et al 1965).

There are four pairs of replicate measurements on different fragments of charcoal from the same sample. Each pair is statistically consistent (T'=0.4, OxA-8763–4; T'=1.8, OxA-8765–6; T'=1.5, OxA-8767–8; T'=3.6, OxA-8769–70; T'(5%)=3.8; n=1; Ward and Wilson 1978). This suggests that the samples are homogeneous and supports the interpretation of the charred material as fuel from the cremation pyres. The ranges quoted in italics are *posterior density estimates* and derive from the mathematical modelling described below. These estimates are shown in black in Fig 21; those in outline are simple calibrated radiocarbon dates and have been calculated according to the method of Stuiver and Reimer (1993). In this case, however, the simple calibrated radiocarbon dates do not provide the most realistic estimates of the dates of the cremations, as additional relative dating information is available from the stratigraphic sequence of deposits. This evidence has been integrated with the radiocarbon results using a Bayesian approach to the modelling of the chronology of the site (Buck et al 1996). This has been implemented also using OxCal (v3.5). The algorithm used in the model described below can be derived from the structure shown in Fig 21.

In this analysis it was decided to impose a uniform prior distribution on the spread of dates, while assuming that the dated samples represent independent events and a random sample of a relatively constant level of human activity; see Bronk Ramsey (in prep) for further details of its implementation. Such an approach has been used because when radiocarbon dates are constrained by relative dating information, it has been shown that there is a danger that the posterior density distributions may be spread evenly across a plateaux in the calibration curve, irrespective of the actual age of the material dated (Steier and Rom 2000). This is due to the fact that the statistical weight of a group of measurements naturally favours longer overall spans.

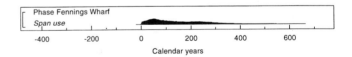

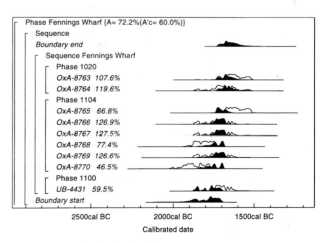

Fig 21 Fennings Wharf radiocarbon determinations

Fig 22 *Pottery from Fennings Wharf central feature <P7>–<P8> (scale 1:4)*

The posterior density distributions of the individual radiocarbon samples are shown in black in Fig 21. This model also estimates that the construction of the ring ditch occurred in 1920–1690 cal BC (95% probability) and that the last cremations occurred in 1740–1530 cal BC (95% probability), spanning a period of 1–360 years (95% probability; Fig 21). This distribution is heavily skewed towards a shorter period of use and it is certainly possible that the cremations were deposited by a few generations during the first half of the 2nd millennium cal BC.

The lithics

A small assemblage of 125 struck flints was recovered from a range of contexts across the site. The majority of material came from the secondary fills of the ring ditch, although smaller groups were recovered from its primary fill and from the central feature (12 and 14 pieces, respectively). Diagnostic finds were few: a convex scraper from the primary ditch fill, and a small core and an axe- or adze-sharpening flake from the secondary fills. Finds from other contexts included a second convex scraper and a core fragment.

The ceramics

The pottery assemblage from Fennings Wharf totalled 165 sherds (576g), the majority of which are in poor condition with highly abraded surfaces. One vessel, from the central oval feature is particularly fragmentary, with a light, soft, friable fabric that has suffered badly from leaching due to adverse soil conditions (Fig 22). Only four sherds were recovered from actual fills of the ring ditch and these are all highly abraded body sherds of indeterminate date. The oval feature within the ring ditch contained fragments of two vessels. The first vessel <P7> is a cup with an upright rim and slight carination at the shoulder. The only decoration consists of two poorly executed incised lines above the shoulder. The fabric is hard with fine flint temper (moderately well sorted) in a silty matrix. The second vessel <P8> is in a light, soft vesicular fabric, oxidised on the exterior surface. The fabric was originally shell-tempered but only voids remain in a sandy matrix. There appears to be an external bevel or applied cordon below the rim but this is so abraded it is impossible to determine the full extent or whether it was originally decorated. There is no trace of decoration on the rest of the vessel but in general the surface is so worn that this is not surprising. One hundred and two very fragmentary pieces in a similar fabric are present without association to a context, but probably relate to <P8>.

The general style of the cup suggests a date within the Late Bronze Age–Early Iron Age transition period as its closest parallel is with vessels of the Darmsden-Linton group, of 8th–5th century cal BC date. The second vessel is harder to place, although it should be noted that the appearance of shell-tempered fabrics seems to date from the early 1st millennium cal BC in the London region. The rim form finds some parallel with a published bowl from Kingston Buci (Barrett 1980, 304, fig 5 no. 10) but the condition of the sherds makes it unwise to put much weight on this. Activity of Late Bronze Age–Early Iron Age date is more clearly evidenced by the presence of perforated clay slabs in the overlying ploughsoil (see Fig 43) and from other negative features not associated with the ring ditch.

The association of the pottery with the central feature appears to be good, suggesting that it may be more appropriate to see the pit as a later insertion into an existing burial monument. Conversely, the presence of the cremated remains of children from both the central feature and the ring ditch may indicate that these deposits are part of one episode of burial but this could equally be coincidence. Brück lists the Fennings Wharf ring ditch in her gazetteer under category D: cremation burials/deposits apparently unassociated with settlement evidence (Brück 1995, 274). Clearly until the radiocarbon dating was obtained the ring ditch, the central feature and all the cremation deposits were thought to relate to the same broad phase of activity. The site, therefore, provides increasingly important evidence of burial practices for both the Early and later Bronze Age and should be considered against the wider evidence for contemporary burial practices in Surrey and the Thames valley.

The Phoenix Wharf burnt mound (GAZ 189)

In 1988, an excavation at Phoenix Wharf, downstream of Tower Bridge (see Fig 1; Fig 23) revealed an Early Bronze Age boiling pit, burnt mound and stake line. Evidence for agricultural activity was also recovered and is discussed below.

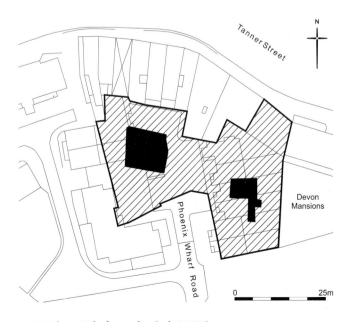

Fig 23 *Phoenix Wharf site outline (scale 1:1000)*

Fig 24 *The burnt mound, Phoenix Wharf (2m scale)*

Several similar features have been found in the London area (for instance in Rainham) but this is the only one found within the study zone (Bowsher 1991). At Phoenix Wharf a distinct spread of burnt material lay on the natural sand underlying a ploughsoil layer. It comprised white patinated and fissured flint, charcoal (mostly from *Salix/Populus* sp (willow/poplar)) and cinders. The burnt spread covered some 3.5m² although truncated by modern foundations to the south (see Fig 24). Excavation of the spread revealed that it covered and filled a straight-sided flat-bottomed rectangular pit 0.5m deep, measuring 1.85m (E–W) by 0.95m (N–S). A charred cattle-sized radius was present within the fill.

Adjacent to the large pit were several smaller pits or depressions, including areas of reddened sand and ash. At the eastern edge of the burnt spread was an irregular line of stakeholes. All of these depressions and stakeholes were filled and sealed with the same burnt material. To the south-east of the pit was an east–west small channel, which ran for 3.3m before being truncated by the trench edge. The basal fills of the channel were waterlain and included animal bone fragments. If the line of this channel is projected westwards it can be seen that the pit could not have extended more than about a metre further south, thus bringing it to a maximum of about 1.95m. This suggests that the pit may have been square and in alignment with the northern bank of the channel. Samples of wood charcoal (willow/poplar) from the basal fill of the Phoenix Wharf boiling pit produced a radiocarbon determination of 1690–1490 cal BC (BM 2766; 3310±40 radiocarbon years BP). The overlying ploughsoil

contained flints and pottery dating, primarily, to the mid 2nd millennium cal BC, which provides a *terminus ante quem* for the sealed burnt material. It would seem that the pit was only used once or twice before the decision to cultivate the land was made.

The depressions and pits around the trough were probably hearths for heating the stones. The line of stakeholes at Phoenix Wharf indicates a revetment containing the eastern edge of the 'mound' as at Cob Lane (Barfield and Hodder 1980, 17), although a similar feature at Cullyhanna was interpreted as a wind break (Hodges 1958, 9). At Buckenham Tofts there appears to have been piles of unburnt flints awaiting use (Layard 1922, 485); indeed, it was also postulated by Layard that the collected flints were reduced to a uniform size before heating (ibid, 486), and that many had been reused in subsequent burnings (ibid, 490). The flints from Phoenix Wharf were mostly gravel pebbles and their probable origin is from the foreshore or the gravel band a metre below the surface.

The interpretation of burnt mounds has mostly related to boiling or dry roasting of meat. The boiling troughs have usually been located in low-lying marshy areas or moorlands, but always close to streams. Recorded measurements of (maximum) extent range from 2.5 to in excess of 24m (for instance the Reading Business Park; Moore and Jennings 1992) with an average of 20m or just less. Heights are recorded from 0.25 to nearly 2m. The presence of a possible stream just to the south of the Phoenix Wharf example would suggest that this trough utilised a boiling technology. Patches of clay found might indicate that it had been clay lined, thus allowing for water retention in the sand. The heat-shattered flints had a freshness to their fracture and a white colour rather than a bluish tinge that does not suggest immersion in water whilst hot, or even reuse after heating. An apparent contemporaneity with the stream would therefore appear to be coincidental and unrelated to the usage of the pit, although perhaps not to settlement.

The Vauxhall piled structure (GAZ 6)

In August 1993 the remains of a substantial piled structure (Fig 25) were identified on the Thames foreshore at Nine Elms, Vauxhall, at the site where Jake Rylance discovered two side-looped copper alloy spearheads (Fig 26). The structural remains were planned and their condition subsequently monitored at appropriate low tides by a team from University College London directed by Gustav Milne for the Thames Archaeological Survey (1995–9), then based at the Museum of London under the Survey Officer, Mike Webber (see Haughey 1999).

This part of the Thames foreshore is subject to continuing and accelerating erosion: many of the sand, silt and peat deposits which must be broadly contemporary with the feature have already been washed away, as have large segments of the wooden piles themselves. Two samples taken from the piles provide a broad chronological context for the structure, with dates of 1770–1520 cal BC (Beta-122970; 3380±40 BP) and 1620–1260 cal BC (Beta-122969; 3180±70 BP) (see Chapter 6.3). The surviving feature comprised the bases of over 20

earthfast piles that were set in two irregular rows some 4m apart, extending riverwards down the exposed foreshore for a length of at least 15m. The majority of the piles were some 0.4m in diameter, although some were significantly smaller, being between 0.2m and 0.3m in diameter. The differing pile size may reflect different load-bearing functions or phases of repair, or even that more than one structure is represented. Few of the surviving piles were set vertically, but the angle and direction of the inclination varied markedly from pile to pile. The ensuing pattern is therefore unlikely to be a constructional attribute as might be anticipated, for example, with the basal members of an A-framed trestle structure; the pattern is arguably more consistent with the possible deformation of the structure (or structures), either by river action or by a deliberate act of demolition.

The surviving tops of the most 'southerly' (landward) piles are currently exposed on the foreshore at a level of *c* −1.30m OD. As part of a joint Museum of London/University College project, one of the timbers [1538] in this row was partially excavated in April 2001. It extended at least 1.25m below the present-day foreshore level, tapering very gradually. Much of the bark and sapwood had been hewn away using a tool with a 20–30mm-wide blade that left a very clear series of facets.

A limited programme of survey, fieldwalking and geoarchaeological study accompanied the excavation, and analysis of the results is continuing. A provisional interpretation suggests that the piles represent the foundations of a substantial causeway, jetty or platform structure, rather than a building,

Fig 25 The Vauxhall piled structure

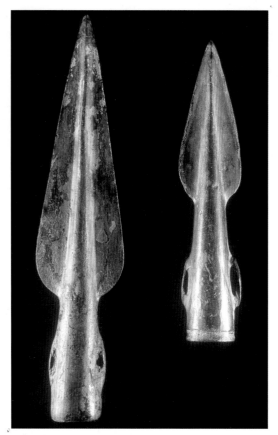

Fig 26   The spearheads associated with the Vauxhall piled structure (max lengths 164mm and 123mm)

and could conceivably be part of a bridge to an eyot (now lost) that may have occupied part of what is now the dredged deep water channel of the Thames. Possible parallels for such features are discussed below.

River finds and 'placed deposits'

The phenomenon of river finds has been touched on several times already and now needs to be considered further if we are to address the possible significance of other information recorded within the study area. The latter include a small number of 'placed deposits', here taken as the inland equivalent of river finds. It is acknowledged that not all of the objects recovered from the present river need have been deposited directly in its waters: they could include material deposited in midstream eyots, sand bars or channel foreshores.

The lower Thames valley is justly famous for the spectacular sequence of objects dredged from the Thames (eg Lawrence 1929). Virtually no distribution map of any artefact type would be complete without its quota. Indeed, until quite recently such finds provided the main source of evidence for the region's later prehistory. Variously interpreted as marking the sites of battles or fords, boating accidents or the flooding of riparian settlements, recent research has focused more narrowly on the potential status of these objects as prestige offerings made during funerary and other ceremonies (eg Bradley 1990). Compared with the prolific west London stretches, however, fewer pieces are known from the areas downstream of

Westminster. The reasons for this are broadly twofold: firstly, the early introduction of mechanised dredging beyond London Bridge and the rapid disposal of the dredged material as ballast on sea-going ships (Cotton 1999, 62); secondly, the natural widening of the estuarine floodplain and the consequent increase in the number of subsidiary channels and backwaters available to receive offerings, as at the Bricklayers Arms (GAZ 191).

While the river finds reported from the study area reaches cannot compare in numerical terms with those from further upriver, they include some equally prestigious objects, such as two circular Bronze Age sheet bronze shields (Smith 1854, 80, no. 359; Coles 1962, 187) and the famous Iron Age horned helmet from the Thames near Waterloo Bridge (Franks 1864–7). Furthermore, these finds can be related directly to the results of the archaeological work conducted within the study area and along the inter-tidal zone. For example, the finds recovered during dredging campaigns associated with the construction of new London Bridge (opened 1831) and Tower Bridge (opened 1894) lay off areas of high ground (the main north Southwark island and Horselydown/Jacob's Island, respectively) that have produced compelling evidence for prehistoric land use of various kinds (see above and Chapter 2.4 below). Moreover, the two Neolithic flint axes recovered by chance from the Bermondsey Lake at Bricklayers Arms (see above and Fig 27) clearly relate to the series of axes dredged from the present river channel (eg Adkins and Jackson 1978).

In situ deposits on the modern foreshore provide a further and still more direct link between the river finds and the study area. The timber structure and adjacent peat sequences recorded at Nine Elms, Vauxhall (see above and Haughey 1999), perhaps best illustrate this. Here a pair of side-looped copper alloy spearheads, similar to others recovered from the river, had been pushed down into the foreshore between two of the wooden piles (Cotton and Wood 1996, 14–16). Comprising a 'personal arms hoard,' to use Needham's term (1990, 138), the spearheads probably represent a deliberate 'placed deposit' and can be compared with several others from the study area. Of most note is the complete Beaker bowl buried in a small pit at Hopton Street, 170m inland from the present channel, along with a flint core and a blade (Ridgeway 1999, 74). This vessel has been interpreted as being deliberately placed as part of a

Fig 27   The Bricklayers Arms chipped flint axe (max length c 150mm)

ritual deposition, possibly to prepare the land in advance of agricultural use (Ridgeway 1999, 72–6). Given other circumstances, this could have entered the river as a result of soil erosion; likewise the small group of three flint scrapers and a flake knife recovered from a second Beaker feature at Southwark Street (Cotton 1992, 65), now 300m inland on the southern edge of the main north Southwark island.

Other Beaker pottery findspots, aside from river finds, are restricted to the assemblage from 15–23 Southwark Street (Swain 1992, 67–8), a single sherd from 106–114 Borough High Street (Barrett 1978, 197–9) (GAZ 90) and two sherds from Cromwell Green, Westminster (Needham 1987, 101; Rayner in prep). The Beaker material from Southwark Street, comprising both pottery and worked flint, came from three discrete features including a truncated gully or slot and a large posthole or pit. Although clearly a 'domestic' assemblage, the largest group of material from the posthole or pit includes four flint tools and is highlighted as a possible 'structured' deposit rather than general rubbish disposal (Cotton 1992, 65).

Discussion

When considered together, this disparate group of sites, river finds and 'placed deposits' comprise a notable dataset, particularly when the serendipitous nature of the work and the modern urban context are taken into account. Indeed there is evidence to suggest that they can be located within an increasingly wet landscape articulated ever more explicitly on the Thames, whose locally fluctuating tidal head may have lain within the study area throughout much of this period (Sidell et al 2000). Furthermore, it is difficult to avoid the conclusion that the enactment of non-utilitarian 'ritual' observances invariably underpinned a wide range of activities occurring within this low-lying liminal riverscape. In this context, ritual can be seen to embrace the river, its margins and the diminishing expanses of higher, drier sand islands, and to encompass both personal as well as social observances. It is inextricably bound up with the construction and maintenance of earthen and wooden structures, with episodes of feasting/bathing and with the carefully structured deposition of human remains, ceramics, lithics and metalwork.

The ring ditch at Fennings Wharf represents the truncated remains of a small circular earthen barrow, used and subsequently reused for up to a thousand years after its construction. Situated on a local eminence overlooking the Thames close to modern London Bridge, it is unlikely to have been an isolated feature; the small barrow group adjacent to a contemporary river channel at Eton Rowing Lake offers a plausible parallel (Allen and Welsh 1996, 127). Whether or not it formed part of such a group, the monument clearly provided a focus for ceremonies involving the deposition in both primary and secondary contexts of token amounts of pyre debris comprising the unurned cremated remains of one adult and between five and eight children. It is possible that other deposits were placed on the original ground surface or were inserted in a central mound, though neither survived.

Although few comparable sites have been examined within the London region, cropmark surveys have identified a number of ring ditches flanking the Thames in north-west Surrey (eg Longley 1976; see also Andrews and Crockett 1996, 61–4) and further downstream, as at Mucking in Essex (eg Clark 1993, 18). Moreover it is likely that other barrows lie sealed beneath the alluvium in the Thames floodplain, well beyond the reach of air photography (eg Needham 1987, 133). The recovery of a fine ogival dagger from the river off Horselydown/Jacob's Island (GAZ 201; Gerloff 1975, 101, no. 158), an artefact type invariably accompanying burials under barrows, may hint at the whereabouts of another within the study area. Redeposited pyre debris has been excavated from the ditches of several Bronze Age barrows in the region – for instance Prospect Park, Harmondsworth and Fairlop Quarry, Redbridge (Cotton 2000) – including perhaps the site of a pyre itself sealed beneath the large barrow in Sandy Lane, Teddington (Akerman 1855). Token deposits involving children as at Fennings Wharf may reflect their perceived lower status in contemporary society (eg McKinley 1997, 142).

The 'boiling pit' and burnt mound at Phoenix Wharf comprise one of a number of similar complexes now known from the London region (Brown and Cotton 2000), including several excavated in Rainham, East London. While the exact function of these sites remains a matter of debate (ie whether they are cooking areas or sweat-lodges (O'Drisceoil 1988)), their topographic siting is usually low lying and adjacent to a water source. More significant in the present case, perhaps, is the positioning of the Phoenix Wharf example close to the edge of an area subsequently taken into cultivation (see below). In this sense it could, like the Fennings Wharf ring ditch or the burial of the Beaker bowl in a pit at Hopton Street, represent a phase of 'land grab', by which areas of 'wildscape' were staked out and incorporated into an expanding and increasingly socialised landscape. This could relate to agricultural intensification following a possible earlier period of restricted cultivation in the Hopton Street area (see below). A similar sequence of events has been identified elsewhere on the west London gravels at about this time (John Lewis, pers comm).

The range of river finds and 'placed deposits' from the study area and its environs are of particular interest, and can be fitted into the wider picture of 'non-utilitarian' observance. The Neolithic flint axes recovered from the silts of the Bermondsey Lake at Bricklayers Arms connect directly with the river finds and, like the Beaker 'placed deposits' located at Hopton Street and Southwark Street, probably represent examples of personal observance. By contrast, the piled structure recently identified within the inter-tidal zone at Nine Elms, Vauxhall, is a substantial piece of construction likely to have had a more than local significance. Whether this 4m-wide structure comprised part of a bridge to a mid-channel sand island, a jetty or indeed some other structure, is likely to remain speculative until more detailed research is undertaken, although repeated dredging of the present river channel will have removed the evidence for its northern extent. Nevertheless, assuming that it supported some sort of decking, the Nine Elms structure would have provided a platform suitable (amongst other things) for public display and for the deposition of offerings in the river at a point likely to have been close to the contemporary tidal head. The placing of a pair of copper alloy side-looped spearheads between two of the wooden piles may represent an example of private/personal observance or possibly some sort of event marking or foundation deposit. Intriguingly, a sequence of similar, though less substantial, structures thrown across a sub-channel of the Thames at Eton Rowing Lake appear to have been associated with the deposition of human remains (Allen et al 1997, 125). Although not accurately provenanced, it should be borne in mind that a skull of this approximate date (1200 cal BC) was recovered from the Thames between Battersea and Vauxhall (GAZ 1; Bradley and Gordon 1988).

2.4 Settled communities (*c* 2000 cal BC–cal AD 50)

This section analyses the evidence relating to more settled communities within the study area. It takes two forms; firstly the clearance and cultivation of the sand islands (Fig 28) of Horselydown and the area around Hopton Street in the early to mid 2nd millennium cal BC and, secondly, the direct evidence for settlement is addressed. The latter is limited and confined to a series of early 2nd millennium cal BC features identified on sites such as 15–23 Southwark Street (GAZ 91; Cowan 1992), Hopton Street (GAZ 54; Ridgeway 1999) and Three Oaks Lane (GAZ 176; Proctor 2000). This evidence is not dealt with in detail here as it has either been published elsewhere or awaits analysis. Rising base levels rendered subsequent cultivation difficult and later settlement activity

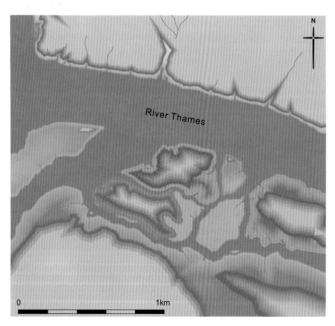

Fig 28 Map showing predicted model of Southwark/Lambeth at c AD 50 (scale 1:25,000)

is also restricted but comprises material from Bermondsey Abbey (GAZ 159) (Steele in prep), Courage's Brewery bottling plant (GAZ 81) and Coronation Buildings (GAZ 9). This can be related to previously published material from 201–211 Borough High Street (GAZ 88) and Park Street (GAZ 70; Tyers 1996).

The Thames and its floodplain

It is in the later part of this period that the river shows the first signs of permanent tidal conditions within the study area. Although there is an isolated event evident at Union Street and Joan Street indicating inundation by estuarine waters in the 3rd millennium cal BC, it is not until c 1100 cal BC that a permanent positioning of the tidal head has been positively identified on the Southwark/Lambeth stretch of the Thames. Recent work on the Jubilee Line Extension (Sidell et al 2000) has looked at this question in detail and although some of the best evidence comes from Thorney Island, the data can be applied to the study area.

Previously, the peat horizons in this area have been termed 'Tilbury IV' after the work of Devoy (1979; 1980), who proposed a model of sedimentation now known as the Thames/Tilbury model. The extrapolation of the model to locations significantly outside the original study area is bad practice when the analogy has been made purely on the basis of recovered peat, often poorly dated, if indeed dated at all. Generally, the detail of the biostratigraphy has not been considered either, which is a significant problem in that reanalysis has indicated that some of these peats may have formed under periods of rising RSL (Haggart 1995). This would appear to be the case in Southwark and Lambeth, although the data collected from Thorney Island and Joan Street/Union Street suggest that the movement of the tidal head was not a uniformly upstream progression; it was characterised by intermittent oscillations of positive and negative tendencies of sea level movement.

By c 1100 cal BC the west Southwark sites are exhibiting the accretion of estuarine sediments, submerging the peat horizons that formed during the preceding period of estuary contraction. The best data come from Union Street where the diatom flora changes from fresh to brackish water assemblages (including species such as *Paralia sulcata*, *Cymatosira belgica*, *Rhaphoneis* spp and *Thalassionema nitzschiodes*) (see Fig 29). This occurs at approximately −1.0m OD, and a limited tidal range could be bracketed around this figure. These changes are not reflected at Joan Street, which may have been protected from Thames flooding by some form of barrier like a gravel bar, or been fed by a freshwater channel from the south. This date is confirmed by deposits on Thorney Island, and so will be comparable with the Lambeth bank. Extrapolation from Devoy's sites such as Crossness (Devoy 1979), Silvertown (Wilkinson et al 2000) and the Isle of Dogs (Wilkinson 1995) suggests an upstream migration of the tidal head in this renewed phase of estuary expansion of c 5m per year (Sidell et al 2000; Wilkinson and Sidell in prep).

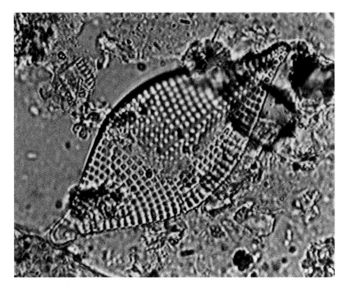

Fig 29 The diatom Rhaphoneis amphiceros (length c 50μm)

The sequence from Union Street does suggest that, rather than the tidal head continuing to migrate further upstream in the late 2nd and into the 1st millennium cal BC, the marine influence does in fact decline in this area. This is shown in the diatom assemblages where the dominance of marine species declines throughout the profile following the initial incursion of estuarine deposits. The data suggest (and this is confirmed by evidence from Thorney Island), that there is a progressive downstream migration of the tidal head, which cannot satisfactorily be explained at this stage but may be associated with changing estuary geometry or differential crustal subsidence. There are a few instances where the situation is reversed, ie marine dominance increases, but these may be extremely short-lived events, for instance, storm surges.

Unfortunately, there are only limited data available on the developing river and environment of north Southwark and Lambeth in the 1st millennium cal BC. However, the majority of substantial peat units dated in the study area were submerged c 1000 cal BC, which could simply be an artefact of later erosion giving the appearance of a significant change in floodplain sedimentation. Owing to the relative difficulties of dating inorganic sediment, the minerogenic sediments overlying the organic units have not been dated so in turn it is not easy to ascribe a date to these underlying layers. Certainly there is a period when, often substantial, silt-clay facies are being deposited with no inclusions, but at sites such as Joan Street and Union Street there is nothing that can obviously be dated to the Roman or Saxon periods. Therefore it is possible that, rather than a change in sedimentation in the mid 1st millennium cal BC, the trend of downstream tidal head migration and concurrent peat formation continued into the Roman period.

The environment

It is from the 2nd millennium cal BC that much of the data on the palaeoecology of the study area are derived. This is primarily as a result of the large expanses of the contemporary

peat beds on the foreshore, at the eyot margins and in relict channels that have been targeted for examination. A major synthesis was produced in 1988 summarising the findings to that date (Tyers 1988). This indicated that the upper surface of the peat had been eroded as a result of Thames flooding and that the base of the peat had filled underlying features, which meant that the thickness of the peat strata was highly variable across Southwark. Tyers concluded that the general pattern of vegetation development was of alder/fen carr forming on the margins of the eyots with oak/hazel woodland on the higher ground. Evidence for agriculture was identified in the pollen record from Wilson's Wharf (GAZ 148) just off Tooley Street and the Southwark Leisure Centre (GAZ 55) by the Elephant and Castle. Since then, many more peat sites have been examined and in fact produced much of the topographic data that have been used in plotting the maps which illustrate this volume.

The site of Stamford Street (GAZ 43) in north Lambeth produced a sequence overlying the Shepperton Gravel of sands sealed by waterlain silts, presumably a result of flooding from the main channel cutting the corner of the Lambeth bend. This was sealed by an organic sequence dating from 1670–1515 cal BC (Beta 85223; 3320±60 BP) (just above the initial organic muds) to 980–830 cal BC (Beta 85222; 2770±60 BP) shortly after which the site was once again inundated by the Thames. Significantly, there is evidence for cereal cultivation (cereal pollen plus associated species, including plantain and Asteraceae (daisy family)), throughout this sequence following earlier clearance. There is a decline in lime just above the base of the sequence, but an earlier clearance must have taken place to free up land for the cultivation that is indicated as occurring contemporaneously with the lime decline. Subsequent to this, in the middle of the sequence there is evidence for an expansion of the woodland elements. This may indicate that less land was required in the later parts of the Bronze Age; however, it is very probably only a localised phenomenon as there is a general consensus for expansion of settlement density in London at this date (Merriman, pers comm). Whether this was a result of initial over-clearance or movement of local peoples to other parts of the region is unclear.

From west Southwark, again the best information comes from Joan Street and Union Street. Evidence for further waterlogging comes in the form of an expansion of species such as *Typha angustifolia* (lesser reedmace)/*Sparganium* type, Cyperaceae, and *Alisma* type (water plantain) replacing the alder carr conditions of the previous period. This is likely to be a result of a combination of factors such as clearance, reduction in evapotranspiration and rising relative river levels, this latter caused by positive trends in sea-level combined with regional subsidence. The process did not continue unchecked: some evidence exists for the re-emergence of alder carr with oak woodland on the higher ground to the south. However, the general trend of inundation and waterlogging persisted throughout the Bronze Age. Further evidence for cereal cultivation was recorded at Joan Street with cereal pollen and associated species such as ribwort plantain. There is, for the

Fig 30 Reconstruction of the Bramcote Grove trackway looking north

first time in the study area, evidence for likely cereal cultivation in the form of ard marks cut into the sandy eyots and buried beneath the cultivated soils, in turn sealed under the waterlain sediments that are the evidence for the gradual inundation of the area. Some of the best-preserved marks come from the area around Tooley Street, on the Horselydown eyot, from sites such as Phoenix Wharf (GAZ 189), Wolseley Street (GAZ 199) and Lafone Street (GAZ 179; Bates and Minkin 1999). They appear as dark lines criss-crossing the sands, and are extremely important survivals, showing that the sand islands of the floodplain were cultivated. These grooves are created by the tip of a traction implement being pulled through the overlying ploughsoil. The best-dated marks are from Lafone Street where it was possible to date the organic soil through which the marks were cut. This gives a date of 1520–1220 cal BC (Beta 107981; 3100±60 BP). The other sites around Tooley Street are thought to be contemporary and presumably form part of one field system, which links well with the evidence in the pollen record from Wilson's Wharf (GAZ 148; Tyers 1988).

There are also data from west Southwark, where ard marks have been recovered from Hopton Street (Ridgeway 1999), dated to the Early Bronze Age. This site is approximately 300m from Joan Street, and it is possible that the pollen from this site originated from an extensive field system of which the remains at Hopton Street form a part. However, Union Street is as close to Hopton Street as Joan Street is, yet the pollen evidence is negligible. One possibility is that the crops producing the cereal pollen recorded at Joan Street were located further to the west and that a link can be made between the Joan Street and the Stamford Street data. There is an area to the south of Stamford Street and Waterloo Station known as the north Lambeth eyot, and it seems possible that this area could have been cultivated as was the Bermondsey eyot and, apparently, Thorney Island,

Westminster, where ard marks have also been tentatively identified (Chris Thomas, pers comm). The presence of a possible timber structure in the peat at Waterloo, just south of Stamford Street (GAZ 43) and north of the Lambeth eyot, may strengthen this argument for contemporary use of the area.

The record from Bramcote Grove is captured in an organic sequence submerged by the Thames at approximately 1000 cal BC. The alder carr from earlier phases persists, but the sequence reflects a greater dominance of fully aquatic forms towards the end of this period. This is also borne out by the evidence from sites such as Canada Water (GAZ 221; Mason 1991; Sidell et al 2000) and Bryan Road (Sidell et al 1995) in Rotherhithe. Although these sites were very marshy, wet and apparently inhospitable, the artefacts and pollen from Canada Water indicates that people were present in the area. The site is relatively close to the edge of the Bermondsey eyot and approximately a kilometre from Bramcote Grove, where there is also evidence for further woodland clearance and cereal cultivation. There is a substantial trackway present in this phase, dated to 1740–1530 cal BC (Beta 70410; 3350±60 BP; Beta 70411; 3410±70 BP; Beta 70412; 3370±60 BP (T'=0.4; v=2; T'(5%)=6.0; Ward and Wilson 1978) (Fig 30), constructed as a means to traverse the marshy area between the gravels to the south and the edge of Bermondsey eyot to the north (Thomas and Rackham 1996). This suggests that the base levels of the late 3rd millennium cal BC continued to rise. Unfortunately, it is not possible to establish whether the trackway was needed in summer or just for the wetter seasons. The timbers recorded at Canada Water were possibly worked, and may be the traces of a makeshift structure on an east–west alignment. This was never conclusively resolved, but if this were the case, it strengthens the evidence for contemporary activity in the wetlands adjacent to the eastern edge of the Bermondsey eyot.

Fig 31 *The ard marks from Phoenix Wharf (scale 1:40)*

0   2m

The inability to date the later minerogenic sediments makes the reconstruction of contemporary ecological conditions extremely difficult. At Bramcote Grove, waterlain silt-clay dates from *c* 1000 cal BC–17th/18th century and represents seasonally flooded wet meadow/pasture (Thomas and Rackham 1996). Limited pollen data are available from the Jubilee Line sites (Sidell et al 2000), suggesting that dryland oak and hazel cover was present, but probably as background regional vegetation, possibly scattered trees rather than actual woodland, and it is likely that vegetation cover continued to be reduced as cereal cultivation increased.

The Phoenix Wharf field system (GAZ 189)

Evidence for cultivation was recovered at Phoenix Wharf, Lafone Street and Wolseley Street (sites 45, 42 and 47 on Fig 1). The two latter sites have been published in a limited fashion (Bates and Minkin 1999; Drummond-Murray et al 1995) and are included here to draw out the wider significance of the area. Similar evidence from recent excavations at Hopton Street (Ridgeway 1999), south of Blackfriars Bridge and Three Oaks Lane, off Tooley Street (Proctor 2000) is also drawn upon. A series of dark criss-crossed lines on the natural sand bed were recovered at Phoenix Wharf, which were interpreted as ard marks (see Fig 31; Fig 32).

35

Fig 32 *Ard marks from Phoenix Wharf (1m scale)*

The sites are all close to the modern river and thus probably closer to the edge of the main prehistoric channel. They all lie on raised ground and the sand horizon was fairly level in each case. All the ard marks are fairly closely aligned, on a north–south/east–west axis. There are also a few diagonal marks at each site. The north–south ard marks at all of the sites are roughly at 90° from the southern bank of the (modern line of) the river. The marks at Lafone Street covered just over 12m² and were generally fairly sparse, with a minor concentration in the centre. The largest area was that at Phoenix Wharf, covering 21m² , whilst Wolseley Street was the smallest at just under 5m². There were no traces of ard marks in sands 5m farther north of Lafone Street, or 25m west of the ard marks at Phoenix Wharf. The underlying burnt mound at Phoenix Wharf does not seem to have been used more than two or three times and its basal fill has provided a radiocarbon date of 1690–1490 cal BC (BM-2766; 3310±40 BP). The soils at Lafone Street and Phoenix Wharf were sealed by fluvial deposits suggesting that cultivation in the area was abandoned, probably as a result of flooding. The soil at Lafone Street dates to 1520 to 1220 cal BC (Beta 107981; 3100±60 BP). The dating evidence suggests, therefore, that cultivation in this area

lasted for a comparatively short time in the mid 2nd millennium cal BC. The (mostly flint-tempered) pottery is in very poor condition but may represent a chronological range from the 3rd to 1st millennia BC.

At Phoenix Wharf the distance between the north–south ard marks was between 0.3 and 0.6m and they were up to 1.4m long. The east–west ard marks were spaced, on average, about 0.25m apart, although some were as close as 50mm and were up to 2.4m long. At Lafone Street the north–south marks were an average of 0.7m apart and *c* 1m long whilst the east–west ones were an average of 0.25m apart and slightly shorter in length than the north–south marks, while at Wolseley Street the marks were between 0.2 and 0.3m apart but no complete north–south lengths were uncovered beyond the narrow 0.90m limits of the trench. Several spade or hoe marks were found in the sand at Phoenix Wharf and Lafone Street (see Fig 33). At Phoenix Wharf there were three at the northern, sparser, end of the trench. Reynolds (1981, 29) has suggested that the heavy rip ard would become stuck after short stretches and have to be dug out. Indeed, the three similar 'spade' marks at Lafone Street all occur at the ends of particularly thick irregular marks. Soil micromorphological analysis at Phoenix Wharf suggests that manuring took place (Macphail et al 1990, 65); however, botanical analysis on the ploughsoils failed to reveal what crops were being grown.

A recent excavation at Three Oaks Lane (Proctor 2000), directly adjacent to Lafone Street, has provided new information. Although no actual ard marks were present, several ditches were found, cutting into the sand of the eyot, which perhaps marked a field boundary. Other features were excavated, including many post and stakeholes interpreted as evidence for Late Neolithic to Middle Bronze Age settlement. The chronology is attributed on the basis of a single sherd of Grooved Ware, which has been assigned to approximately 2700–2000 cal BC, and a radiocarbon date of 1670–1430 cal BC (Beta 136117; 3270±50 BP) obtained from one of the stakes. The flintwork is also assigned to the Late Neolithic/Early Bronze Age. Interestingly, the radiocarbon date is statistically comparable with the dates from the burnt mound at Phoenix Wharf, 1690–1490 cal BC (BM 2766; 3310±40 BP) and from the soil through which the ard marks were cut at Lafone

Fig 33 *Spade mark from Phoenix Wharf (0.2m scale)*

Street, 1520–1220 cal BC (Beta 107981; 3100±60 BP). This may indicate that the Three Oaks Lane stakes are indeed closely associated with the cultivation observed at Lafone Street and the burnt mound and subsequent cultivation at Phoenix Wharf, representing an extensive field system in this area in the Mid Bronze Age. The fragment of Grooved Ware is enigmatic and may indicate Late Neolithic settlement on the eyot, but in the absence of other firm, contemporary, evidence in this location, this cannot be stated with certainty. The problems with establishing firm chronologies for the prehistoric period are extremely apparent in this area where we cannot resolve whether the various fields are contemporary or represent successive areas taken into cultivation.

In addition to the stakes and cut features, a fragment of a grinding stone was found; however, it is not certain what was being ground. The most remarkable find was a broken fragment of an ard share made from a split oak log. This had simply been discarded after breaking and reused in the stake line; however, the break is extremely neat and it could be considered a 'placed deposit' prior to the act of breaking the soil on new fields. Ard fragments are extremely rare in south-east England; the nearest parallel comes from Eton Rowing Lake, Dorney (Allen and Welsh 1996). However, this example appears to be slightly later in date than the Three Oaks Lane find.

The succeeding phase at Three Oaks Lane contains a series of artefacts, including some residual Mesolithic material. The pollen evidence indicates a terrestrial wooded environment, with limited evidence for clearance, but no firm evidence for cereal cultivation. Nevertheless, this phase of the site must be considered almost exactly contemporary with the Lafone Street field system next door. A transition to a wetland environment becomes manifest in the upper part of the sequence, culminating in a peat dating to 1050–790 cal BC (Beta 136118; 2720±80 BP). It is in this peat that evidence for large-scale clearance was recovered, along with some limited data suggesting that farming was taking place, in the form of pollen and high total phosphate concentrations. Additional information regarding phosphate levels (possibly relating to manuring fields or grazing livestock) comes from a contemporary site located close by, on Tower Bridge Road (GAZ 156) in the channel to the south of the eyot. Diatom assessment (Cameron 2000) indicated the presence of high levels of phosphate in the water, strengthening the case for a contemporary increase in total phosphate entering the peat/aquatic system. It is acknowledged that the material from the Tower Bridge Road site may well be completely unassociated with the information from Three Oaks Lane; nevertheless, the balance of probability is that manuring or stock raising took place over a wider area in the mid 2nd millennium cal BC.

Lithics from the ploughsoils

Phoenix Wharf, Lafone Street and Wolseley Street all produced small lithic assemblages from the soils over the ard marks (see Fig 34 and Chapter 6.1). A large proportion of the assemblage was composed of unretouched flakes and a few blades, nearly 40% of which were broken or had suffered edge damage, presumably as a result of the

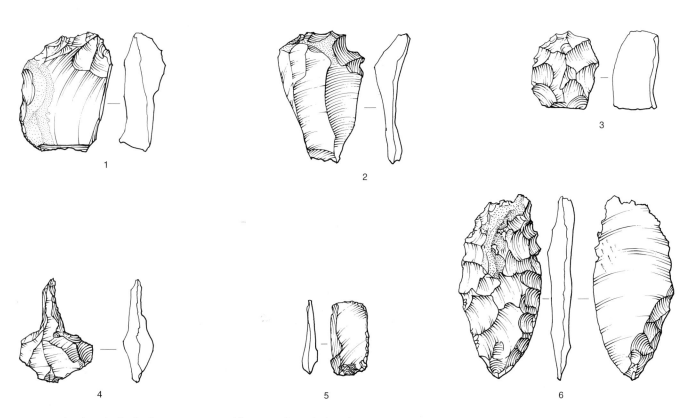

Fig 34 Lithics from the ploughsoils: 1–3 scrapers; 4 awl/borer; 5–6 knives (scale 2:3)

ploughing and general cultivation activity. Diagnostic finds were few: a plano-convex knife from Phoenix Wharf is likely to belong within the later Neolithic/Early Bronze Age, as is the single small scraper from Wolseley Street. Other pieces, for example a leaf arrowhead roughout, could be earlier. On the other hand, the numbers of broad, thick flakes and the high incidence of opportunistic nodule testing at Phoenix Wharf were interpreted as evidence of Bronze Age activity, perhaps linked to the use of the adjacent boiling pit and burnt mound (Merriman nd a). Taken together, it is likely that the material recovered from the soil horizons represents earlier episodic use of a locality subsequently disturbed by a series of cultivation phases. The occurrence of an adze butt and an adze-sharpening flake in the humified peats sealing these soils at Lafone Street can also be noted. The presence of these artefacts, usually regarded as Early Holocene, serves to underline the amount of disturbance to which this low-lying area was later subjected and the ease with which notionally earlier finds came to be redistributed across it.

The Courage's Brewery bottling plant and related sites (GAZ 81)

A series of excavations took place within the area of the former Courage's Brewery bottling plant, and in its vicinity, in north Southwark between 1984 and 1990 (see Fig 35). These have generally been considered together, as the Courage's study area, for the purposes of publication (see Cowan in prep and Hammer in prep for recent synthetic analyses). The main body of evidence recovered from the sites dates to the Roman period, but there is also an earlier phase of activity which is outlined here.

The topography of the area appears to be one of the reasons for the existence and recovery of prehistoric material. The brewery bottling plant was situated on a relatively high area of sand which may be a feature associated with the Shepperton Terrace or be part of the later eyot formation, the so-called 'northern island'. The relative altitude of the eyot surface (+1.55m OD at the highest point) meant that the prehistoric levels were less deeply buried than elsewhere in Southwark and therefore more easily accessible.

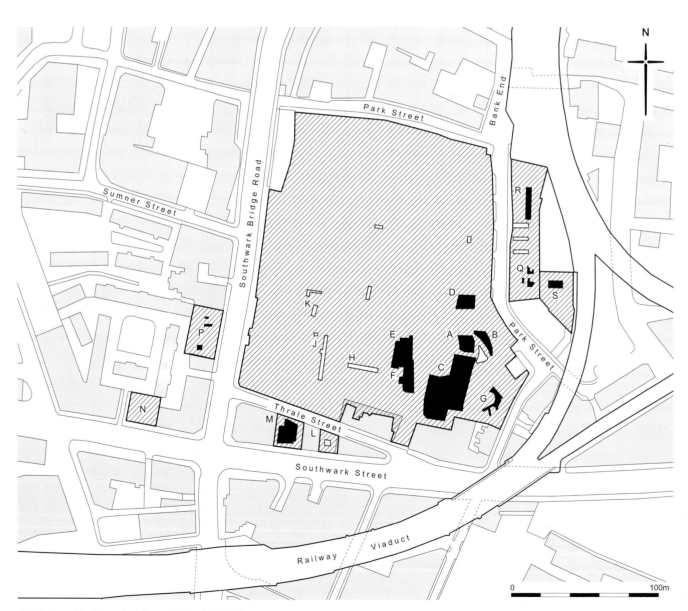

Fig 35 Plan of the Courage's study area sites (scale 1:2500)

There have been significant problems in accurately dating
the features from the sites (no radiometric dates were
obtained); therefore, the individual area sequences are
described rather than giving an overall chronological
discussion, which could not be attempted without a cross-area
chronology. In general terms, the majority of the diagnostic
pieces from the sites (convex scrapers, knives, the blade of a
polished flint axe and two arrowheads) are of Neolithic–Bronze
Age type, although the odd piece could be earlier, for example
the single Mesolithic adze-sharpening flake from CO88 site E.
Only sites D and F provided evidence for pre-Roman activity in
the form of cut features and other deposits, though
disappointingly few diagnostic artefacts could be directly
associated with any of them.

Site D

A handful of struck flints were recovered from the early
'foreshore gravels' (group D1) and from the various small
features that cut into them (group D2). For the most part the
flintwork comprised small flakes and pieces of nodular shatter.
The D2 features, interpreted as 'possible hearths', produced 11
unretouched flakes and nodule fragments. A broadly
Neolithic–Bronze Age date has been ascribed to the flintwork.
It seems unlikely that the cut features are indeed hearths but
rather pits which have been filled with a mixture of waste,
including ash and flint.

The various 'flood clays' (group D3) which sealed the
foreshore gravels contained the bulk of the struck and burnt
flint from site D. Again, the majority of the worked material
comprised unretouched debitage in the form of flakes and
nodular fragments. However, the deposits also produced two
diagnostic pieces, including the mid-section of a bifacially
worked arrowhead of probably leaf-shaped type and a broken
unretouched flake/blade knife with localised traces of
utilisation. The former piece is probably Early Neolithic. The
clays were sealed by a thin peat with some fine-grained clastic
horizons (group D4) containing further amounts of
unretouched debitage as did the more substantial clay silt (D5)
sealing the D4 group. The debitage was concentrated within
the layers and was not associated with the few cuts and stakes
present. These stakes were truncated but formed two
approximately north–south alignments and may have formed
part of a trackway or platform on the damp ground. The peat
was most productive of artefacts, almost certainly a factor of its
more terrestrial nature. Forty-eight flakes, flake fragments and
nodular shatter of broadly Neolithic–Bronze Age were
recovered from this horizon. Similar peats have been recovered
in the area (Tyers 1988; Sidell et al 2000), generally forming
in the Mid Bronze Age, and are likely to be part of the wider
estuary contraction that took place in the Thames in the
Neolithic/Early Bronze Age (Long et al 2000). Although the D4
peat at the Courage's study area has not been directly dated, it
is certainly comparable with the wider environmental picture
and may indicate that the flintwork dates to the latter end of
the range ascribed, on typological grounds.

Site F

A very few unretouched undiagnostic flints were recovered
from the various contexts considered to be of prehistoric date
(groups F2–F6). These included several from within the
weathered sand (group F2) that directly overlay (or formed
part of) the surface of the eyot. In addition to the flints,
undiagnostic prehistoric pottery was recovered from the same
horizon, identifiable only as Neolithic or later in date. There
were several cut features in the weathered sands, previously
interpreted as hearths but there is no firm evidence to support
this and, as with the site D cut features, they may simply be
pits. They are recorded as having been filled with sediment,
stone and charcoal flecks and may therefore be cooking pits.
Some pottery sherds were also recovered, of bowl-shaped form
with slashed decoration, ascribed to the Mid–Late Neolithic. A
single undatable flint flake was also present within one of the
pits.

The key find from this site was a double row of postholes,
previously interpreted as a possibly Bronze Age round house or
post-built structure (see Fig 36 Building 1) recorded at 1.6m
OD (Dillon et al 1991). Only part of an arc was recovered, but
much of the site was truncated and so the full extent could not
be revealed to confirm the theory. A projection shows that if
the postholes continued, they would enclose an ellipse 10–11m
in diameter. The dating is highly tenuous because the only
artefact recovered in direct association was a Roman sherd (AD
55–120) from a stakehole cluster (group F6) which is thought

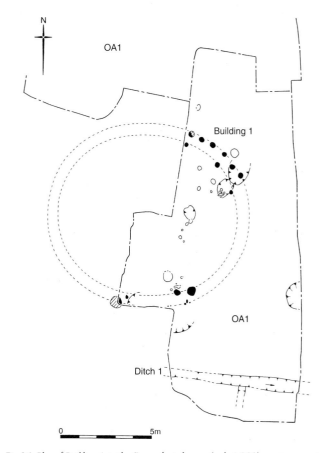

Fig 36 Plan of Building 1 in the Courage's study area (scale 1:200)

to be intrusive (as indeed may be the stakehole cluster itself). However, the surface that the postholes were cut from was lost, making it impossible even to locate the structure accurately within the stratigraphy of the site. Certainly it is later than the weathered sands at the base of the sequence, but these can only be dated to the Neolithic or later. The posthole traces were covered by homogeneous sandy silt, although they may have been cut through it. This again cannot be accurately dated, and therefore the construction of the structure can only be estimated as being at some time between the Neolithic and early Roman periods. However, if the remains are part of a 10–11m diameter post-built structure, on morphological grounds it may be of Late Bronze Age date.

There were some unretouched pieces of flint and some prehistoric pottery recovered from the fill of an east–west ditch (group F5) some 3m to the south of the structure at approximately the same level as the posts were recorded. The ditch is thought to be a boundary marker, also acting as a drainage ditch and, as such, in combination with the post-built structure, could indicate low-level domestic settlement here. In the southern area of site F, another weathered sand (group F12) was rich in artefacts with several convex scrapers, a core and part of a ground axe blade, the latter of Neolithic date. Pottery was also recovered from this deposit, including a weakly carinated shoulder sherd. The fabric is sandy with iron oxide inclusions, a fabric type also recorded from sites in west London, such as Caesar's Camp, Heathrow (Grimes and Close-Brooks 1993, 350), the Late Bronze Age–Early Iron Age assemblage from Snowy Field Waye, Isleworth (Timby 1996, 46–7) and Jewsons Yard, Uxbridge (Barclay et al 1995, 10). Neck sherds from a small, Late Bronze Age, fineware vessel were also recovered. Unfortunately, no relationship could be established with the possible round house.

The lithic material from the various Courage's study area sites conforms in all respects with that recovered from other sites examined across north Southwark, both in terms of the artefact types represented and the restricted range of contexts from which they were recovered. Typically, therefore, there are three main context types containing lithics. Firstly, isolated prehistoric features cut into the natural eyot surfaces; secondly, the flood clays and/or weathered natural deposits overlying the eyot surfaces; and lastly various Roman and later contexts. The lithic data recovered are indicative of low-level (possibly seasonal) riparian activity within the Mesolithic and particularly the Neolithic–Bronze Age periods. The quantities of material recovered from the various 'flood clays' (eg within the low-lying site D) also highlight the amount of post-depositional disturbance that early land surfaces are likely to have undergone.

The pottery falls into two broad chronological ranges: Mid to Late Neolithic and Late Bronze Age/Early Iron Age, which reflects the evidence recovered elsewhere in Southwark. It seems apparent that the relationship of finds to stratigraphy reflects a partial dependence upon environmental conditions. The early deposits on the surfaces of the eyot may possibly be tied to the Neolithic period (and perhaps Late Mesolithic) when river levels were relatively low and the islands were

habitable. The expansion of the wetlands and consequent formation of peat, seen here at the Courage's study area, also provided surfaces that could be traversed. It is notable that the majority of material from the sites comes from layers/land surfaces rather than cut features, suggesting that although the 'north island' was of some importance, it was not central to settlement. Peat formation probably continued into the later Bronze Age, when additional artefacts were incorporated into the deposits before estuarine clays sealed the peats. Such an environment would have been inhospitable and this is seen in the drop-off in artefacts recovered from these later deposits.

Bermondsey Abbey (GAZ 159)

The 1984 excavations at Bermondsey Abbey (Fig 37) yielded features dating to the historic period only (Steele in prep). Nevertheless, significant prehistoric activity occurred on this site, on the basis of the ceramic and lithic finds contained within later features. This assemblage is the largest single artefact group from the 1st millennium cal BC in the study area and it is extremely unfortunate that prehistoric features were not located. There was additional evidence for earlier communities traversing the area, in the form of a microlith, adze-sharpening flake and the arrowheads.

Lithics

In total, 277 struck flints were recovered, including both prehistoric and later (possibly medieval) dressing of flint for building purposes. The latter comprised large fresh flakes detached by a hard (probably metal) hammer. The prehistoric material ranged from Early Holocene to 2nd/1st millennium cal BC in date. All appeared to have been recovered from later contexts. Diagnostic early pieces included a single bi-truncated

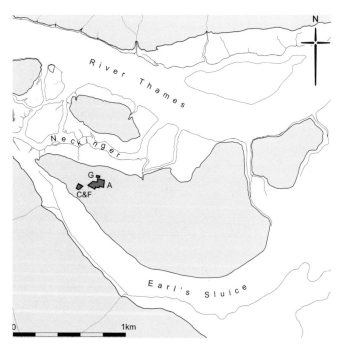

Fig 37 *Early topography of Bermondsey with site outline*

microlith and an adze-sharpening flake. No fewer than three Neolithic/Bronze Age arrowheads were recovered, of leaf, transverse and barbed and tanged form. Other finds included a small series of cores, scrapers, serrates and several flake knives. Even allowing for the post-prehistoric flints, the assemblage is a large, if mixed, one for the study area. This can be attributed to two key factors: the topographic position of the site on the higher ground of Bermondsey island and the extensive nature of the excavations conducted on the abbey site.

The ceramics

The assemblage is characteristic of 'decorated assemblages' of the Late Bronze Age–Early Iron Age transition period, *c* 8th–6th century cal BC (Barrett 1980, 305–8, fig 6). The most diagnostic vessels are the jars, of which carinated, rounded and slack-shouldered types are present, frequently with finger-tip decoration on the rim and/or the shoulder (Barrett Class I; ibid, 302). Fineware bowls are also present but decoration is limited to burnished surfaces and inscribed lines. One example <P13>, with single incised grooves on the upper edge of the carination and at the base of the neck, is closely paralleled by a vessel from Heathrow (Canham 1978, 27, fig 17 no. 59). The range of decoration recorded includes finger-tip and fingernail impressions, impressed dimples, and one example of a plain applied cordon and a single sherd with a red iron-rich coating (see Fig 38, <P12>).

There are also a number of vessels of Middle Iron Age and Late Iron Age–early Romano-British date (Fig 39). The Iron

Age sherds mark an increased use in sandy fabrics and a move away from coarse flint-tempered wares, which dominate the Late Bronze Age–Early Iron Age assemblage. The most complete vessel of this period is a Middle Iron Age jar <P28>. It is similar to vessels from Little Waltham and fits into the Little Waltham type-form F3 (Drury 1978, 53, fig 37). The other rims identified are either upright or everted and probably also derive from jars or bowls. There are no decorated sherds assigned to this period, although the majority of sherds have burnished surfaces.

From the Late Iron Age/early Roman assemblage the most common form is the bead-rimmed jar, although necked and everted-rim jars are also recorded. Sherd <P37> is from a carinated bowl with a tall rim and double cordon, but is the only example of this type. The sherd <P38> is from either a jar or bowl with a rippled zone on the shoulder (Thompson type B2 or more likely D2-4), a type that emerges in late pre-Roman Iron Age assemblages and continues to occur post-Conquest (Thompson 1982, 329). One other example of this form has been found previously in London from a pre-Flavian ditch fill at 201 Borough High Street, Southwark (GAZ 88; Tyers 1996, 140, fig 17.1 no. 5). It has not occurred in any other early Roman assemblages from either the City or Southwark, which may give support to a pre- AD 50 date for the Bermondsey material. A number of decorated body sherds are present with incised decoration. This is seen on the globular-necked jar <P40>, which has a band of decoration on the shoulder.

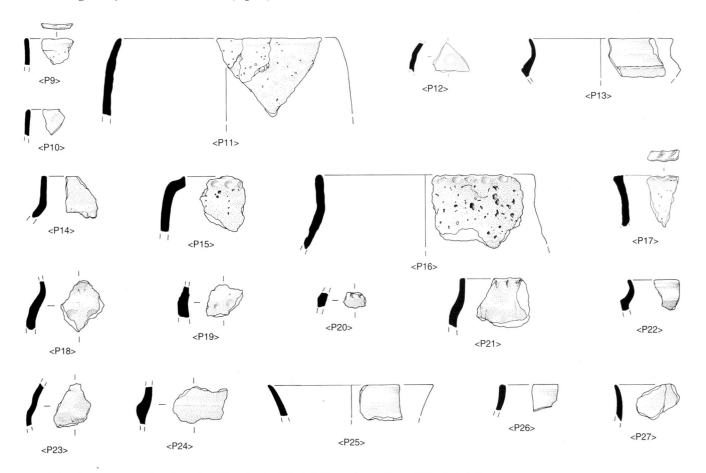

Fig 38 Later Bronze Age pottery from Bermondsey Abbey, Fennings Wharf, St Thomas Street <P9>–<P27> (scale 1:4)

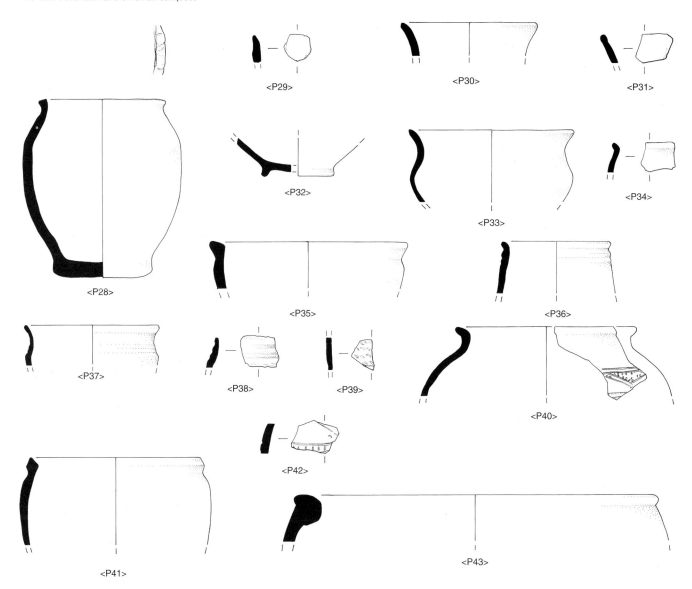

Fig 39 Middle Iron Age vessels: <P28>–<P32> Bermondsey Abbey; <P33>–<P34> Coronation Buildings, Late Iron Age–early Romano-British from Bermondsey Abbey <P35>–<P43> (scale 1:4)

Of great interest and importance is the triangular (with rounded corners) clay weight (Fig 41). It is the most complete example of a triangular-shaped weight recovered from the central London area and has three perforations, one across each corner, comparable with examples from Danebury (type 1) (Poole 1984, 403). Such weights are commonly called loomweights but other uses such as thatch, door or gate weights have also been discussed (ibid, 406). Whatever the exact function, the recovery of the weight is a good indicator of contemporary settlement in the Bermondsey area.

Coronation Buildings (GAZ 9)

The site was excavated in 1989 and is located on floodplain gravels at 2.70m OD. Riverlain sands sealed the gravel and it was on this surface that the prehistoric features and artefacts were recovered. The sand horizon would therefore appear to have been exposed to subaerial weathering and consequently transformed into a terrestrial surface. A channel recorded in trench B (see Fig 40) was cut through the sand and gravel and

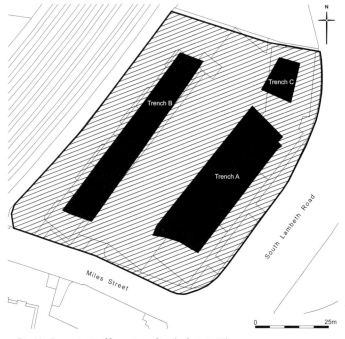

Fig 40 Coronation Buildings site outline (scale 1:1250)

had subsequently filled with fine-grained waterlain sediment. The sand horizon was cut by a number of Mid–Late Iron Age features including eight pits, three possible postholes/pits, two hearths, a terminal of a boundary/enclosure ditch, and a possible four-post structure. One of the pits/postholes may be a hearth/oven and flue. A reasonable quantity of pottery was recovered (see below), which has dated these features to the later part of the 1st millennium cal BC. Flint tools, burnt daub, iron objects, polished stone objects and carbonised seeds were also recovered.

The ceramics

A small assemblage of Middle Iron Age pottery was recovered from the excavated features (see Fig 39). There are no decorated sherds, but many have smooth, burnished external surfaces. From the fill of one of the pits, a large fragment from a wide everted-rimmed jar was recovered, distinctive in terms of its size and condition in comparison with the rest of the assemblage <P33>. The fabric is glauconite-rich with a distinctive highly burnished, oxidised surface, with the horizontal tool marks evident. This vessel is very similar in shape to examples from the Iron Age settlement at Little Waltham, Essex (form F13), which also occur in glauconite-rich fabrics (Drury 1978, 54–78, fig 48 no. 202 and fig 50 no. 250). A number of fired clay objects were also recovered; many were too fragmentary to be identified but several have finished edges and one has a central perforation, and these possibly come from weights (see Fig 41).

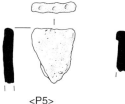

Fig 42 *Deverel-Rimbury sherds <P5>–<P6> (scale 1:4)*

Ceramics from elsewhere within the study area

Much of the prehistoric pottery examined from the project was recovered from contexts described as subsoil, ploughsoil or flood/waterlain deposits. The material from these layers, which is often of mixed date, marks an increase in the quantity of ceramic evidence dating from the Middle and Late Bronze Age. Sherds from Middle Bronze Age Deverel-Rimbury urns have been identified from 11 St Thomas Street <P5> (GAZ 125) (Fig 42). There are also flint-tempered body sherds from St Thomas Street and Lower Marsh, Lambeth (GAZ 39), with no diagnostic features or decoration, but which, from the fabric type and wall thickness, are likely to derive from Deverel-Rimbury type urns.

Evidence for the Late Bronze Age and Late Bronze Age/Early Iron Age transition was identified from Lower Marsh, Lambeth, and 11 St Thomas Street. From the latter site sherds and fragments of perforated clay slab were found on the natural gravel, which also produced Peterborough Ware. Three joining rim sherds are from a plain hooked-rim jar <P11> (Fig 38), a type first defined at Rams Hill (Barrett 1975). This 'plain ware' form has been recovered associated with Deverel-Rimbury vessels, suggesting it occurs early in the development between the two ceramic traditions. Parallels for this vessel can be found at other Late Bronze Age sites, such as Aldermaston Wharf, which is dated either to the end of the 2nd or the beginning of the 1st millennium cal BC (Barrett 1980, 306). Fragments of base with densely gritted undersides are also present, as noted at other contemporary sites (Adkins and Needham 1985, 29; Longley 1980, 65).

Excavations at Brockham Street, Southwark (GAZ 72) produced a fragment of clay slab with a double perforation and a small assemblage of Late Bronze Age pottery, including a slack-shouldered jar (see Yeaxlee 1998). All of the perforated clay slabs found in the study area are coarsely flint-tempered and oxidised in colour (see Fig 43). The fragments show no signs of burning or sooting, despite suggestions that these

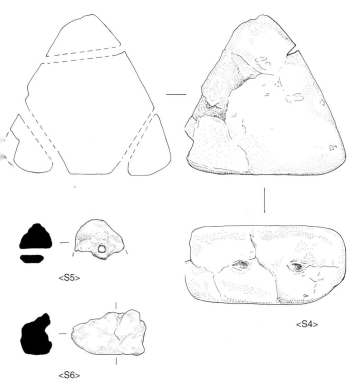

Fig 41 *Fired clay objects: Bermondsey Abbey triangular weight <S4>; fragments of possible weights from Coronation Buildings <S5>–<S6> (scale 1:4)*

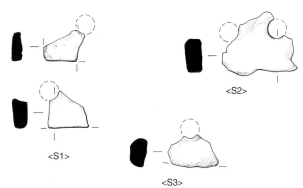

Fig 43 *Fired clay objects: perforated slabs from Fennings Wharf <S1>–<S3> (scale 1:4)*

plaques were used in kilns or domestic ovens. As discussed by Champion (1980, 237–8) perforated clay slabs have been recorded at a number of Late Bronze Age sites in the Thames valley, including Heathrow, Yiewsley and Carshalton and on sites in Essex and Kent, but doubt still remains regarding the function of these objects.

Discussion

The evidence discussed in this chapter has very much focused on two discrete types of activity. The first of these, the cultivation identified in the field systems and the environmental record can be classed as extremely rare, and perhaps unique within a British context. Not only are the ard marks present, but the identification of spade and hoe marks and indeed the ard itself makes this group of sites extremely significant.

The field systems appear to represent two distinct phases of activity. The earliest of these is centred on low-lying land, typified by sites such as Hopton Street and reflected in the pollen record at sites such as Canada Water and Joan Street. This phase would appear to start at approximately 2200–2000 cal BC and is noticeably altitudinally lower than the second phase of cultivation which is observed on the Horselydown sites centred around Phoenix Wharf, dating from c 1500 cal BC. Rising water levels observed through the lithological record indicate that the second phase of cultivation may in fact reflect a seamless transition from the early through the mid 2nd millennium cal BC, led by the same group but simply relocating to higher, drier, ground. A further possibility comes from the, admittedly limited, evidence for enriching the soils. Possibly the earlier sites became nutritionally exhausted after several centuries of cultivation and new, virgin, sites were required to generate good crop yields. The evidence for the addition of fertilisation is small and comes from total phosphate measurements at Three Oaks Lane and Tower Bridge Road (GAZ 144) and the soil micromorphology from Wolseley Street. However, Hopton Street has yet to be fully analysed and it may be the case that soil enrichment also occurred here. However, if there was a 'second phase' which was simply a relocation, then what was originally considered to be an expansive co-axial system may just reflect a temporal change of focus. Indeed, there is no contemporaneity

between the outer sites (Hopton Street, Canada Water environmental record) and a small Horselydown cluster. This would also make sense with the two associated 'ritual' finds that have been associated with the practice of 'land grab'. The 'placed deposit' at Hopton Street and the burnt mound at Phoenix Wharf could then be seen as preparatory 'rituals' to each of the two phases of cultivation.

There is much less hard evidence with reference to settlement and this in itself is enigmatic. With so much evidence for the field systems presumably supporting the community, it is strange that so few traces of contemporary settlement have been found. This is undoubtedly a factor of the 'keyhole' approach of the archaeology fieldwork in the urban environment. There are material remains and the occasional feature, such as those identified at Three Oaks Lane, but little that may be conclusively interpreted. It seems likely that some of this problem arises from truncation: Bermondsey Abbey has such a significant group of 1st millennium cal BC material that it seems almost certain to have been reworked from underlying deposits rather than representing casual loss. Again, it is possible that the lack of settlement evidence may also be cultural and this area was only sparsely used, whilst elsewhere in the London region the Iron Age is well recorded at places such as Uphall Camp (Greenwood 2001).

The information on the evolution of the Thames has shown that, in the late 2nd millennium cal BC, there was a significant upstream progression of the tidal head which would have had an effect on the floodplain topography, with substantial lateral flooding further exacerbated by the twice daily fluctuation of the tide itself. It has been shown that this led to the submersion of the field systems identified around Phoenix Wharf. Once these had been abandoned, what reason might there be to occupy the area? It seems possible that with the end of cultivation potential, the local communities chose to cut their losses and relocate to a less marginal, more stable area. Ironically, if the evidence from the river is to be believed, the tidal head did not continue the upstream migration, but in fact reversed to a downstream migration shortly after the initial incursion into the study area, which would have perhaps re-exposed the sand islands and once again provided a fertile zone to cultivate.

3

Themes

3.1 The changing environment and its effect on developing human habitation

This study has synthesised disparate palaeoecological information gathered from often extremely small archaeological interventions in Southwark and Lambeth. Using these data, it has been possible to construct a picture of the developing ecological systems across the study area and to attempt to gauge how the local prehistoric community interacted with their environment (ie the Thames, the sand eyots and the marshes).

Early warming

The transition from the Devensian to the Holocene saw a significant improvement in climate as well as the change in vegetation outlined above. This culminated in the Climatic Optimum (Atlantic period), when mean summer temperature was several degrees higher than today (Evans 1975, 71). This improvement in the climate would have made the London basin much more attractive to the transient people of the Early Holocene and the early settlers. This would not only be a result of increased temperature but the changes associated with it. Pine and then mixed oak woodland developed, populated by forest dwelling animals such as red deer and aurochsen (see Fig 44). Admittedly, the changing climate and replacement of tundra by forest did push north some previously used resources such as reindeer, which are thought to have been followed and hunted on their migration paths. Evidence for reindeer has been recovered from Three Ways Wharf, Uxbridge (Lewis et al 1992).

This climatic change is best shown within the current study area at Bramcote Grove (Thomas and Rackham 1996), where the lake of the Late Devensian (Lake Windermere Interstadial and Loch Lomond Stadial) was fringed with cold climate species of willow and birch, probably in an open landscape. However, the early Postglacial period saw this develop to an infilling lake with pine woodland and gradually the colonisation by lime, alder and hazel in a less open, less cold landscape. Unfortunately, there are few traces of contemporary human activity in north Southwark and Lambeth, although there is the evidence from Bermondsey and a cluster of findspots shown on the topographic plot (Fig 5).

Deforestation I (elm decline)

The next major change in environmental conditions after climatic amelioration would have been the opening and gradual deforestation of the landscape. The earliest concrete evidence for this comes with the so-called elm decline. Other sites in London, for instance Hampstead Heath, have shown slight evidence for pre-elm decline clearance at the very beginnings of the Neolithic (Greig 1992) with rare cereal pollen grains. However, Greig indicates that no evidence for such early clearance was present in the floodplain, where changes to local ecology were likely to be a result of fluctuating

Fig 44 *London woodland 8000 years ago (after Merriman 1990)*

water levels. There is certainly no evidence from Bramcote for any type of clearance prior to the elm decline. The elm decline here is dated to after 4770 cal BC (Thomas and Rackham 1996) and at Bryan Road to after 3900 cal BC. At Joan Street and Union Street, evidence for the primary elm decline is lacking, although at the base of the Union Street profile there is a sharp drop in elm, but it is thought (Sidell et al 2000) that this may be a secondary decline after a phase of Mid Neolithic regeneration. The same is the case for Joan Street, where the basal samples suggest that the primary elm decline has not been preserved here because it took place prior to the beginning of peat formation. However, there is some evidence for clearance; ash is present which can be viewed as a secondary component subsequent to the elm decline. Although the date of the elm decline is not accurately recorded, ie after 4770 cal BC at Bramcote and before 3500 cal BC at Union Street, it is possible that it was asynchronous across the study area, being earlier in the east. This indicates that the eastern side of the study area appears to have been settled earlier than the west, a suggestion supported by recent fieldwork in east London, particularly north Woolwich and Rainham where several Early Neolithic sites have been found. However, it should be noted that preservation tends to be better in east London.

The information from Southwark and Lambeth may be seen within the broader London context as generally comparable and part of an overall trend in the Early Neolithic. To the east, out in the estuary, Wilkinson et al (2000) recorded an elm decline dating to 3960–3660 cal BC (Beta 120960, 5010±70 radiocarbon years BP) whilst Devoy (1979) obtained a record of the elm decline at Stone Marsh dating to 3970–3380 cal BC (Q-1336, 4930±110 radiocarbon years BP). The Mar Dyke,

Essex, has a similarly dated sequence (Wilkinson 1988), of 3640–3100 cal BC (HAR 4523, 4650±90 radiocarbon years BP). It seems possible that there is a trend here with areas further downstream being cleared earlier. Hampstead Heath has already been mentioned and is not accurately dated, whilst, sadly, the intensive work at Runnymede (Needham and Longley 1980; Needham 2000) did not recover any evidence for an elm decline and suitable deposits are rarely preserved in west London. The pattern for south-east England is similar (Scaife 1988) with an average date for this occurrence of c 3600 cal BC, which falls towards the end of the span for Britain calculated by Smith and Pilcher (1973). Nevertheless, the available evidence suggests that the eastern half of London is opened up fairly consistently from the Early Neolithic. This is unlikely to have been absolute: there are continued records of arboreal species throughout the prehistoric period in pollen spectra from the area. What seems more likely is that small areas were initially cleared and later expanded, leaving extant areas of woodland which could have been exploited for timber and other resources, such as the animals that lived there, for example deer.

Initial development of agriculture

The elm decline has been seen as the precursor to the introduction of farming by opening up the landscape to allow room for better hunting, pasture, arable fields and actual settlements. However, the decline has been attributed not only to clearance by the contemporary population, but also elm disease *Ceratocystis ulmi* carried by the elm bark beetle *Scolytus scolytus*. This is thought to have taken place after initial opening

Fig 45 Clearing the wildwood (after Merriman 1990)

up of the woodlands, which allowed massive expansion of *Scolytus scolytus*. Therefore, deforestation is likely to have been more widespread, initially at least, than could be attributed to the first farmers. This seems to be the case at Bramcote, where there is no direct evidence of cereal cultivation until the Bronze Age. However, the presence of an earlier trackway indicates that the area was used, although it is not possible to say for what purpose. It may be that palaeoecologists have allowed themselves to concentrate on cereal cultivation and look for associations of elm decline followed by the immediate appearance of cereal pollen. It is possible that substantial clearance in areas lacking obvious settlements may have been for pasture, and that the area around Bramcote may have formed seasonal pasture for livestock.

Joan Street, however, has good evidence of cereal cultivation in the pollen record following the secondary clearance phase here after 3500 cal BC, consisting of cereal pollen and that of associated weeds, including ribwort plantain. This is likely to have been local to Joan Street, but probably on slightly drier ground, such as one of the sand islands. The same may be true of Bryan Road, where the evidence for cereal cultivation comes hard on the heels of the elm decline, in the early 4th millennium cal BC.

The removal of woodland cover (see Fig 45) would have transformed north Southwark and Lambeth into a relatively open landscape, probably interspersed with intermittent woodland on the higher ground to the south, with some arable fields and pastures (probably in the river margins in summer). The foci of settlement were probably on the gravel terrace

margins. As well as opening up the landscape for the fundamental aspects of life such as building huts and ploughing fields, there may have been other reasons for clearance that are more difficult to interpret. The sight lines that were opened up would possibly have allowed large areas to be viewed from any one place and may have focused on areas such as burial centres like the Fennings Wharf ring ditch. The 4th and 3rd millennia cal BC are the periods of monument building in areas such as Heathrow (Andrews et al 1998). It is possible that the gravel terraces and sand ridges of the central London region also had monuments that could be viewed with ease in an open landscape. Nevertheless, the evidence from the pollen spectra which have been studied to date does not indicate total clearance; rather there appear to have been patches of woodland fairly consistently throughout the prehistoric period and, therefore, a patchy rather than entirely deforested landscape should be envisaged with stands of trees that would have been encroached upon as the need for land grew. There is likely to have been regeneration of woodland in the 1st millennium BC (see Joan Street, Sidell et al 2000) when the archaeological evidence indicates a lower human presence than in the preceding millennium.

Deforestation II (lime decline)

Although significant amounts of land are thought to have been cleared by c 2500 cal BC (Merriman 1990, 22), there is a further event in the pollen record which indicates that there is likely to have been remnant woodland or perhaps isolated

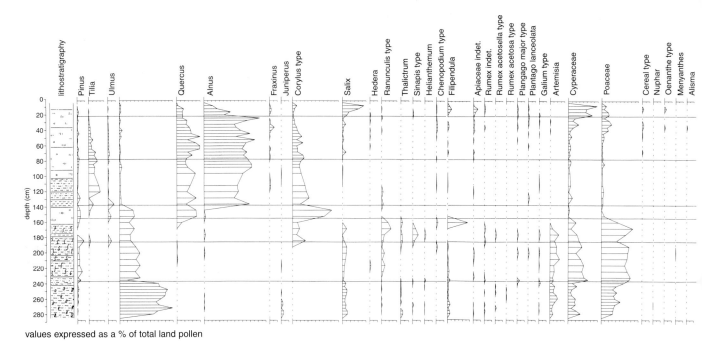

values expressed as a % of total land pollen

Fig 46 Bramcote Grove pollen diagram (from Thomas and Rackham 1996)

copses present in the region. This event is the lime decline, where the native species disappear or are drastically reduced in the pollen record. This was originally attributed to climate change (Godwin 1956) thought to have taken place following the end of the Climatic Optimum, as conditions gradually deteriorated. This theory was succeeded by a suggestion that the lime decline may have been associated with prehistoric clearance, because of the increase in agricultural weeds that were found in combination with the lime decline (Turner 1962). This appears to be asynchronous across southern England, ranging from c 4000 cal BC onwards, but mainly occurring in the 3rd/2nd millennia cal BC. There are other suggestions, however, for the decline, which are significant in a wetland context. Waller established that expanding wetlands (paludification) could kill off local lime (Waller 1994) and certainly there is ample evidence for developing wetlands with the mass peat accumulation in the Bronze Age in the study area.

The earliest evidence for the lime decline in Southwark and Lambeth is from c 2500 cal BC from Union Street, where pollen percentages drop from approximately 40% to 10% (Sidell et al 2000). There is no evidence for associated cereal cultivation, however, and there is a subsequent re-expansion of lime at c 2000 cal BC. It is difficult to establish whether this decline is a result of waterlogging or human clearance. Nevertheless, the result would have been more open space for a limited period, available for seasonal pasture of livestock if not settlement. At the nearby Joan Street site the lime was declining at the same time that it was regenerating at Union Street, which shows that it is possible to pick up quite local fluctuations in the pollen record which may show how different areas were being manipulated by the local population.

The next (chronological) evidence for the lime decline comes from east Southwark, at Bramcote (Fig 46), where it is

dated to between 2190 and 1750 cal BC, and Canada Water where it is contemporary with that at Bramcote and is dated to c 2295–1742 cal BC (Beta 122968; 3650±100 BP). The probability distribution shows the date is more likely to be in the middle of the range, c 2200–1900 cal BC rather than the earlier part of the range, roughly comparable with the regeneration of lime at Union Street and the first decline at Joan Street. However, this appears to be the lime decline proper at both sites; there is no evidence for subsequent regeneration. At Canada Water, there is a sharp increase in cereal pollen and associated weeds concomitant with the lime decline, strongly suggesting that people requiring land for the expansion of arable farming caused the lime decline here. However, there is still no evidence for cereal cultivation at Bramcote until a succeeding phase of alder carr has passed (up to a thousand years later). Therefore, either clearance took place by the peoples building the trackways, or possibly this is evidence of paludification, which would fit with the need for trackways to cross an increasingly marshy area close to channels cutting the floodplain. This difference between Canada Water and Bramcote, which are less than a mile apart, is significant and may be a factor of relative OD height. The lime decline at Canada Water has been recorded at c −1.19m OD, whilst at Bramcote, it is at least 0.2m lower, possibly as much as 0.7m lower. Although differential compaction may be affecting the sequences on these sites, it seems likely that the contemporary surfaces at Bramcote were relatively lower than at Canada Water, subsequently wetter and therefore less suitable for cultivation. This opens up possibilities for human activity in the central zone of Rotherhithe, previously considered to be wet and uninhabitable.

The second lime decline at Union and Joan Street, although not specifically dated, is estimated to have taken place roughly contemporaneously c 1500–1000 cal BC and

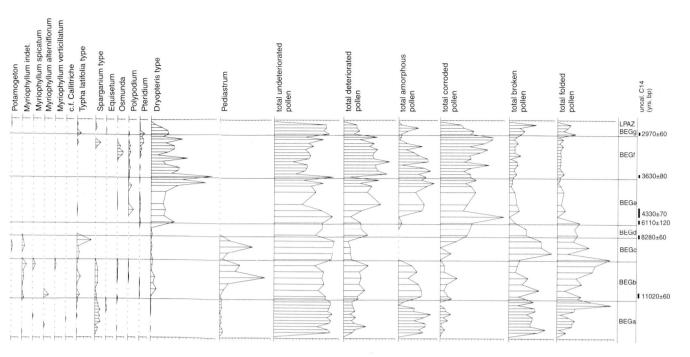

both are associated with an expansion of cereals, evidenced in the pollen record. The date is similar to that for the introduction of cereal farming at Bramcote and suggests that there were several phases of lime removal in the study area. Some initial clearance of lime (although possibly a result of waterlogging) took place in the later Neolithic (for instance Union Street). This was then followed by further clearance (Joan Street first event, Bramcote and Canada Water) that coincided with the evidence for cultivation at Canada Water. A further lime decline then occurred in the late 2nd millennium cal BC (Union Street/Joan Street) and coincided with the first appearance of cereals at Bramcote. It is possible that this was a seamless process with initial Late Neolithic lime clearance in the west, then transitional period clearance in the east, followed by a final thrust in the west with additional increased cultivation in the east.

The river

The River Thames has been a dominant feature in the central London region for probably all of the period of human occupation. In the raw, Late Glacial/early Postglacial landscape of north Southwark and Lambeth it must have been an impressive feature. The available data suggest that in the last ten thousand years, the river has undergone several fundamental changes that are manifested in the study area. These would have affected the local inhabitants at the different periods and, depending on the location, these changes could either have enhanced life or made it insupportable.

At the beginning of the time period this study is concerned with, the Late Glacial/Postglacial transition, the Thames would have pursued a braided form, with relatively shallow channels separated by sand/gravel bars. This is likely to have been relatively easy to traverse when compared with later river forms. However, there followed a change to a single channel river, which would have been deeper than the previous braided system. This probably occurred as a result of lower flow competence due to a reduction in spring ice melt, consequent on the retreat of the Devensian ice sheets. The river deposited sands in this new form and it is in this period that the initiation of dune or eyot formation is thought to have taken place.

The effect of this on the human population lies in several areas. Firstly, the appearance of the floodplain would be significantly altered over a relatively short time. In addition to the concentration of the river into a single channel, the levels are likely to have been raised. Although the increase in RSL which can be attributed to the Early Holocene (Devoy 1979; Long 1995) would not have sent the tidal head into the study area, nevertheless the downstream expansion of the estuary is likely to have affected flow dynamics and also the gradient of the river further upstream. This made the river a much more effective barrier.

One aspect of this change that may well have impinged upon any local people relates to the new course. The topographic plot (Fig 5) suggests that, within the study area, the river has shifted significantly northward from the Early Holocene onwards. This will have redefined the floodplain and exposed new areas of previously submerged land which would have become available for exploitation, even if only seasonally. In addition, on the north bank of the river, it is likely to have swamped and/or eroded what was earlier dry land. The north bank of the central stretch of the river is quite steeply shelving, unlike the southern floodplain that is much flatter. This may have made the southern floodplain of Southwark and Lambeth more attractive for exploitation of, for instance, reeds/rushes and waterfowl, and almost certainly influenced the local

Fig 47 *The estuarine diatom* Cocconeis placentula *(length c 50 μm)*

3.2 Early human communities within the study area

Turning from the physiographic and environmental setting to the human communities themselves, the project has brought together a wide range of evidence for their activities within and across the study area. Broadly, these activities encompass aspects of mobility and/or habitation, subsistence and belief. However, direct traces of the people themselves within the study area are few and generally poorly dated. They comprise individual bones (including skulls and long bones) recovered from the river and its modern foreshores (eg Bradley and Gordon 1988; Richard Hill, pers comm); small deposits of cremated bone from the early 2nd millennium cal BC ring ditch at Fennings Wharf; and a single possibly early Roman inhumation burial from 124 Borough High Street (not dealt with here; see Cowan and Wheeler in prep). Details regarding gender, age at death and pathology usually elude us, although the number of earlier 2nd millennium cal BC juveniles represented at Fennings Wharf is of note.

No physical remains of the early hunter-gatherers who ranged along the valley floor have been found. Yet their lifestyle was sufficiently well attuned to available floodplain resources to have endured for millennia. This is best demonstrated by the small group of sites probably dating to the centuries either side of c 8200 cal BC on the south side of the Bermondsey Lake, where evidence for a subsistence strategy based on the hunting and processing of large fauna was obtained. Typified by slender obliquely blunted flint projectile points of Reynier's 'Deepcar' type (1998, 181) found in other low-lying river valleys, it is conceivable that the human groups responsible for their manufacture had adopted a less nomadic existence and were exploiting this physiographic zone on a year round basis. Though without parallel in central London, the assemblage from B&Q (trench B) in particular can be compared with others from Hampstead Heath and the valley of the River Colne at Three Ways Wharf, Uxbridge (Scatter C west). By contrast, hunter-gatherer activity post-dating c 7500 cal BC within the study area is less well focused, though a small collection of eight flint points, including an asymmetric 'Horsham' point and two narrow scalenes from Waterloo site C, is worthy of note. The reasons for this apparent diminution in activity remain to be determined, but could relate to the inundation of traditional hunting grounds by rising sea levels (eg Lewis et al 1992, 244–5) and/or later erosional and taphonomic processes.

community. Currently, there is more evidence for Neolithic occupation in Southwark than there is from the City of London, although this may be a factor of varying degrees of urbanisation and excavation between the two areas.

The migration of tidal waters (identified through the diatom record) into the study area was the next change of riverine conditions that impinged on the local groups. This occurred in the mid–late 2nd millennium cal BC, when the pollen evidence suggests that significant amounts of woodland clearance and the introduction of cereal cultivation had taken place. Even if the earliest tidal ranges were very small, the encroachment of the intertidal zone may have led to uncertainty about available dry land and potentially caused problems through flooding. A limited amount of flooding would probably have been useful for farming; however, substantial amounts of estuarine floodwater would almost certainly have been damaging. It seems likely that in fact this was a relatively rapid event, with an initial strong estuarine influence that decreased as the tidal head migrated (erratically) downstream, shown by the diatom evidence from Union Street and Joan Street (Fig 47). The stratigraphic sequences from sites such as Lafone Street show that some of the cultivated sand islands were indeed submerged in the later prehistoric period. Unfortunately, it has not been possible to date this event accurately; however, a mid–late 2nd millennium cal BC date is likely, and corresponds to the end date of many of the peat sites such as Bramcote. Obviously the inundation of the floodplain field systems exemplified in the ard mark sites may have rendered the floodplain useless for settlement and cultivation and forced the population back to the gravel terraces. This would have been a significant disruption to a farming tradition that seems to have been present in the study area since at least the 4th millennium cal BC, and indeed appears to have prompted the general abandonment of the area by the prehistoric groups.

Subsequent progressive rises in sea level resulted in the eventual establishment of a very different estuarine regime within the study area by the mid–late 2nd millennium cal BC (Sidell et al 2000). The dynamic nature of the resultant riverscape, ultimately dominated by a locally fluctuating tidal head and episodes of flooding, may have lent itself to the continuance of a mobile lifestyle, perhaps seasonally geared around pastoralism with some localised cereal cultivation. As such, exploitation of the floodplain was always likely to have been 'well below the level of a maximising economy', to borrow Needham's (1991, 372) description of the situation at Runnymede in the 4th millennium cal BC. According to the pollen data, human interference in the landscape (natural causes such as beaver and elm disease notwithstanding) appears to have been locally if asynchronously influential from around 3900 cal BC, although direct evidence in the form of features or artefacts is slight until the currency of impressed Peterborough Wares and transverse arrowheads in the centuries either side of c 3000 cal BC. The slightly later, beaker-dominated, ceramic assemblage from Hopton Street (Gibson 1997), which includes a complete bowl, is of particular interest here, and can be compared with another small beaker assemblage from Southwark Street (Cowan 1992, 67–8). There is as yet no evidence for the construction of communal monuments within the study area prior to the Fennings Wharf ring ditch, though this is hardly conclusive in view of the generally restricted areas examined hitherto.

Situated on a local eminence a few tens of metres south of the Thames channel (Watson et al 2001, fig 8), the small Fennings Wharf ring ditch appears to have provided a focus of interest for perhaps the best part of a millennium. Successive token deposits of cremated bone, principally children or juveniles, were buried within the eastern arc of the ditch between c 1900–1600 cal BC, with a further deposit placed within an offset central pit. Late 2nd millennium BC activity is attested by the presence of diagnostic ceramics. The successive use of the eastern arc of the ditch for the deposition of cremations is of particular note and may hint at a wider traditional cosmology, reflected in the positioning of other human remains within the eastern sections of earlier monuments in the region, as at Yeoveney Lodge, Staines (Robertson-Mackay 1987, 36) and Staines Road Farm, Shepperton (Jones 1990).

The ring ditch itself, perhaps, along with the Phoenix Wharf boiling pit and the careful burial of a complete beaker bowl with a flint core and blade in a pit at Hopton Street (Ridgeway 1999), could also be regarded as acts intended to denote ownership of land by local communities. For these activities preceded phases of clearance and ard cultivation on several of the higher sand islands with, it would seem, an earlier (Beaker) phase at Hopton Street and a somewhat later, mid 2nd millennium cal BC, phase on Horselydown further east. Paradoxically, while the ard marks etched into the sands appear to point to the establishment of more settled subsistence regimes, their clarity is likely to indicate that the actual cultivation phases were relatively short-lived and probably ultimately curtailed by rising base levels. Furthermore, it is tempting to link the oak ard tip found in a ditch at Three Oaks Lane with the ard marks located at Lafone Street close by (Bates and Minkin 1999). The deposition of the ard tip could be interpreted as a deliberate ritual act, perhaps intended to be emblematic of the physical act of tillage (eg Rowley-Conwy 1987). In wider terms, the close agreement in orientation of the various cross-ploughing episodes (all within a few degrees

of N–S and E–W) hints at the existence of field systems set out according to the prevailing 'lie of the land' (Pryor 1998, 78–9) and perhaps aligned on the Thames. This provides an interesting counterpoint to the broadly contemporary field systems now coming to light on the wider expanses of the higher terrace gravels elsewhere within the region (eg Barrett et al 2001, 222–4), many of which appear to have been geared to the needs of stock raising rather than arable agriculture (Yates 1999, 167; 2001).

The increasing influence of the tidal Thames may be reflected in the growing numbers of prestige artefacts offered to its waters from this time (eg Rowlands 1976; Bradley 1990). Mapping the distributions of the products of successive metalworking phases has provided an indication of changes in patterns of activity along the river between Ditton and Woolwich from c 1200–600 BC (Needham and Burgess 1980, 452–7 and fig 7), some of which could conceivably relate to fluctuations of the tidal head. The construction of various timber trackways in the floodplain is a further tacit acknowledgement of the river's influence (Thomas and Rackham 1996; Meddens 1996) and presumably reflects an attempt to formalise and maintain traditional routeways in a rapidly changing world. The most substantial of these floodplain structures are the paired oak piles currently interpreted as the foundations of a jetty or 'bridge' located within the modern inter-tidal zone at Nine Elms, Vauxhall. Though the full implications of this structure have yet to be addressed pending further fieldwork, it is likely to have fulfilled a variety of functions, both utilitarian and non-utilitarian, affording access to spiritual as well as physical resources. It certainly acted as a focus for at least one 'placed deposit' of metalwork (a pair of side-looped spearheads) and, later in the earlier 1st millennium BC, as an anchor for a lighter, slighter wooden structure currently interpreted as a fish trap (Mike Webber, pers comm).

This latter feature apart, evidence relating to the centuries after c 800 cal BC within the study area is restricted, as indeed it is across much of central London. At Thorney Island, Westminster, this may have been the result of a major erosional episode connected with the River Tyburn (Sidell et al 2000, but see Andrews and Merriman 1986). However, the evidence available from the study area, though scrappy, indicates activity on a number of the higher sand islands in the period leading up to and beyond the Roman Conquest. The western end of the large Bermondsey island has furnished a relatively wide range of data (Heard 1996, 77–8), for example, including features and artefacts comprising pottery, fired clay and worked antler, and appears to offer the most promise for future work. Other sites closer to the later Roman bridgehead have produced features containing pottery and small metal objects (Cowan 1992, 137; Drummond-Murray et al 1995; Tyers 1996, 143–4), while stray finds from the river and its modern foreshore include occasional pieces of harness and parade gear (eg Franks 1864–7; Cotton and Merriman 1991, 52–3).

3.3 The character of prehistoric Southwark and Lambeth in a regional context

The evidence presented here relates to the prehistoric development and utilisation of a part of the lower Thames valley floodplain sealed beneath later alluvial deposits and a modern urban landscape occupied more or less continuously for the last two thousand years. Only in the last decade or so has this buried prehistoric landscape begun to receive the attention it deserves from archaeologists (eg Merriman 1992), despite a long history of casual observation and discovery dating back to at least the 17th century AD (summarised in Bates and Barham 1995, 88–9).

In range and preservation, if not spatial extent, the evidence from the study area bears comparison with that recovered from elsewhere within the Thames valley floodplain and the estuarine intertidal zone (eg Allen et al 1997; Needham 1991; 2000; Wilkinson and Murphy 1995). Locally, broadly comparable evidence has been glimpsed at the Tyburn/Thames confluence at Thorney Island, Westminster (Thomas et al in prep), for example, and has been examined in rather more detail in the north-east London wetlands (Meddens 1996), most recently along the line of the modern A13 (Ken Whittaker, pers comm). Taken together, this body of evidence now stands comparison with that recovered from other alluviated lowlands elsewhere in the country (Noort et al 2001, fig 1) and the lithic scatters, cut features, and especially the wooden structures and ard marks, allow important, sometimes even startling, insights into the ways in which human communities utilised a dynamic landscape over a period of some eight millennia. Furthermore, these discoveries have provided a much needed and long overdue contextual setting for the often magnificent objects casually dredged from adjacent stretches of the Thames and collected since the early years of the 19th century (Cotton 1999).

In wider regional terms, the evidence from the study area assembled here can also be considered in the context of that emerging from the higher gravel terraces in areas such as west London. In the Heathrow region in particular, large-scale excavations have begun to shed light on the ways in which the local landscape was occupied, worked and transformed by human communities during the same time-frame as that studied in this volume. Not surprisingly, there are a number of interesting points of comparison and contrast. The monument-dominated 'ritual landscapes' of the higher terraces in the west, broadly datable to the mid–late 4th millennium BC to the early–mid 2nd millennium BC, for example, find no immediate parallels within the floodplain, apart from the presence of late round barrows and ring ditches such as that located at Fennings Wharf. Equally, however, the prestige artefacts (including beaker pots) that are such an increasingly noticeable component of the river and adjacent floodplain are absent from the monumental landscapes. It may well be that the two zones

formed separate parts of a loosely integrated landscape utilised by the same groups of people, 'who simply drew clear distinctions between the most appropriate settings for particular actions' (Cotton 2000, 24). If so, it also rather implies a relatively low population and a less than maximising subsistence economy.

For reasons which still elude us, but which may revolve around an increasing population competing for finite land and metal supplies during a phase of rising base levels in the floodplain, the situation changed markedly from the mid to late 2nd millennium BC, both in the floodplain and on the terraces. Following initial claim-staking of land commemorated by episodes of feasting, vast areas of the Heathrow terrace were laid out as co-axial field systems served by droveways and water holes, while ards were put to work in the floodplain. (This distinction, of arable in the floodplain and pastoralism on the terraces, may prove to be more apparent than real once further work has been completed.) Production and consumption intensified as new settlement types emerged and river deposition of fine metalwork, particularly weaponry, steadily increased (eg Yates 1999; 2001). The latter phenomenon has attracted much attention, and connections between funerary rites, river burial and weapon deposition have been sought (eg Bradley 1990, 135–42). Other factors could be relevant, however, in particular the shifting nature of the tidal head – an elemental and untameable force that required suitable placatory offerings at propitious times and tides. The structure at Vauxhall is of special interest in this context, for not only does it offer a fresh perspective on the dynamics of human movement within the floodplain (and perhaps into or across the river channel itself), but also on the means by which offerings were physically deposited in the waters of the Thames.

The mid–late 2nd millennium BC represented something of a high water mark in the region's fortunes. Thereafter renewed climatic deterioration coupled with the sudden dislocation of long-established exchange networks forced a period of retrenchment and consolidation, though river deposition continued but on a reduced scale. The paucity of evidence for the ensuing centuries within the floodplain contrasts with the picture that is starting to emerge on the terraces from around the middle of the 1st millennium BC (eg Wait and Cotton 2000, 106; Merriman 2000, 44–5; Barrett et al 2001, 225–7), and it may be that erosional and taphonomic processes provide one explanation for the mismatch, as at Thorney Island, for example.

Taken as a whole, the evidence for the 1st century BC/AD suggests that the study area is likely to have lain on the periphery of the 'contact zone' of continental influence exemplified by richly furnished burials, Mediterranean imports and oppida. The general absence of such essentially exceptional phenomena from the London area, however, encourages the assessment of the local evidence on its own terms (as Hill 1999, 186–9), and the traces of small farmsteads and continuance of river deposition noticed within the study area and beyond may ultimately prove to be the most important defining features of the region. Certainly, major centres are, so far, thin on the ground. Uphall Camp, overlooking the eastern (left) bank of the River Roding at Ilford, provides the best evidence within the metropolitan area to date (Greenwood 2001), though it appears to have fallen from use prior to Caesar's British expeditions in the middle of the 1st century BC. Reports of another heavily defended site on the Thames at Woolwich (Merriman 2000, 46) remain unconfirmed. On current evidence, other important settlement foci belonging to the period appear to have lain still further downstream on the Hoo peninsula at the Isle of Grain. It may be, as Millett (1990, 89) and others have argued, that it was precisely *because* there was no pre-existing major centre in the area that Londinium was eventually founded where it was. Other factors such as topography and, crucially, the position of the contemporary tidal head are, however, likely to have been equally influential.

4

Evaluation of the study and future research

This project was originally conceived with three relatively simple research questions (see Chapter 1.2) relating to the human presence, topography and environment of the study area. It was realised early on that the available data did not fit the traditional pattern of mobile groups of people manipulating their environment in the Mesolithic and developing into settled farming communities in the Early Neolithic, followed by intensification in the Bronze Age with a subsequent withdrawal to defended settlements in the Iron Age. As a result, the decision was taken to modify the structure of the analysis and publication to reflect the archaeology better and the interpretations that could be derived from the dataset. This study has, therefore, been an organic one: it developed and responded to the information available, even though this necessitated a change in the final project.

In terms of reconstructing environment and topography, the study has been extremely successful. It has been possible to draw together a complete narrative of vegetational development from the Late Devensian to the Iron Age, made possible by the inclusion of data from sites such as Bramcote Grove and the Jubilee Line. The pollen record has been especially important in establishing patterns of human modification of the area, and in bringing forward the discrepancies between, for instance, the early appearance of cereals in the palynological record which is not matched by any direct archaeological evidence for cultivation until much later. Although this is difficult to explain convincingly, it provides fascinating information on the nature and incompleteness of the archaeological record, and underlines the importance of a multi-disciplinary approach.

With regard to topography and, in particular, the Thames, there are still substantial gaps in our knowledge. For instance, although topographic modelling indicates that the Early Holocene river was significantly to the south of the modern course, our current information suggests that at this date the Thames was multi-channelled and it would be extremely interesting to know more about the location of the individual branches. Nevertheless, the data on river levels, formation of the sand islands and the incursion of the tidal head have provided an important context for the archaeology, and may help to account for the slim evidence for 4th–3rd millennia BC activity and the far-reaching developments of the 2nd millennium BC. The significance of the Bermondsey Lake has also become apparent through this study. Its existence was known previously but the exact relationship between it and sites such as B&Q and Marlborough Grove had never been fully established. Its extent is still not understood, or even if there is more than one lake. Nevertheless, there is great potential for locating further early sites along the margins of the lake (or lakes), and excavation in these areas is now required.

Through the present analytical programme it has been possible to draw together a number of pieces of work that would otherwise have been published in isolation or have languished in the archive. Although there have been many benefits from developer-funded archaeology following the introduction of PPG16, the difficulty of funding synthetic publication remains a significant drawback. This is exacerbated in large urban centres such as London, where the number and complexity of the sites and the number of competing contracting units make meaningful syntheses virtually impossible to contemplate. The present project, centrally funded by English Heritage, has attempted to square the circle and it is to be hoped that the resulting volume has added up to more than the sum of its parts. It remains to draw up a short, and by no means exhaustive, list of topics requiring further research.

1) Firstly, there is the fundamental need to study the prehistory of central London in its own right and not simply regard it as an optional prequel to the 'real' story: that of 'London-as-an-urban place'. By the same token the area needs to be related to its Thames valley, Greater Thames estuary and southern North Sea Basin context, as appropriate (eg Williams and Brown 1999).

2) Chronology is crucial. Greater resolution in dating specific human interventions is urgently needed across the board. At present the human interventions at the B&Q site are dated solely on the evidence of microlith typology, for example. Other key events, such as the apparently asynchronous clearance episodes and the appearance of cereal cultivation, also remain poorly dated. In order to achieve this, many more radiocarbon determinations will be needed. Other techniques should be exploited too, such as Optically Stimulated Luminescence (OSL), which can be used to date inorganic sediment, and even dendrochronology following the encouraging results obtained from a mid to late 2nd millennium cal BC site at Swalecliffe near Whitstable in Kent (Nick Branch, pers comm).

3) There is an urgent need for a new model addressing changes in relative sea level to update Devoy's model (1979; 1980), which has been widely misapplied. Associated with this is a need to date more closely the formation of the sand eyots within the Thames system and scrutinise the movement of the tidal range. The formation and extent of the Bermondsey Lake is a further research topic. Such an analysis then requires consideration in the light of the cultural data. For instance is the upsurge in 2nd millennium cal BC ritual activity linked to rising base levels?

4) The extent and effects of landscape clearance need to be assessed, as do the detailed chronologies, cultivation regimes and characteristics of the 2nd millennium cal BC fields within the study area. How large were these fields and how long were they in use? What crops were grown? Were there deliberate attempts to improve soil quality? The apparent mismatch between the ecological signal and the archaeological evidence here also requires further examination and this can only be achieved through higher resolution analysis and dating.

5) The ways in which human communities, with their inherited sense of place and mental mapping, reacted to fluctuations in river and sea level provides a further important focus for research and raises questions of mobility, seasonality and transhumance scarcely yet addressed in London. Human actions are not pre-determined but are adaptive and fluid: the construction of trackways during the 2nd millennium cal BC is a case in point, as local communities sought to maintain traditional access routes and adapt to rising water levels. It could be argued that the deposition of artefacts in the river is another 'coping mechanism' adopted in the face of elemental and uncontrollable flood hazards (as Bell 1992, 274–5), and the relationship between the shifting tidal head/flood episodes, metal deposition and structures such as the Vauxhall jetty or 'bridge' is of particular relevance and research potential.

6) No longer should London archaeologists be attempting to 'predict the unexpected' in the floodplain environment (Merriman 1992). Instead they should be modelling subsurface stratigraphy in a coordinated fashion, to determine potential locations for buried archaeology using an integrated borehole and geophysical programme of ground investigation (eg Bates and Bates 2000). Good results have already been achieved at Custom House (Nick Truckle, pers comm) and in the lower Ebbsfleet valley (Bates and Bates 2000, 854–6; Martin Bates, pers comm).

5

The gazetteer

This gazetteer has been compiled from the Greater London Sites and Monuments record and published and archive sources. The sites are ordered by National Grid reference using the National reference system of Great Britain. All the sites are in the 100km square referenced as TQ. It should be stated that, although every effort has been made to ensure the accuracy and completeness of the record, the gazetteer might not record every single find ever made within the study area. Additionally, more sites are being excavated and more finds are being made every week and it is likely that, by the time of publication, discoveries will have been made that could not be included. Therefore the data are stored (at the Museum of London – LAARC) in a manner that may be updated in future reviews. It has been designed in the hope that it will provide a useful and comprehensive tool for individuals interested in the prehistory of this area.

Publication references in the gazetteer can be found in the bibliography. However, the numerous site roundup references to *London Archaeologist* and *Surrey Archaeological Collections* in the gazetteer are summarised in the bibliography as single references under a general heading of 'Editors'.

Key

PA	Palaeolithic
ME	Mesolithic
NE	Neolithic
BA	Bronze Age
EBA	Early Bronze Age
MBA	Middle Bronze Age
LBA	Late Bronze Age
IA	Iron Age
PU	Prehistoric undated
‡	Refers to sites published in the archive guide (Thompson et al 1998)

GAZ no.	Address	Site code	NGR (TQ)	Period	Description	GLSMR no.	Bibliographical references
1	Between Vauxhall and Battersea Bridge	–	–	BA	Human skull		Bradley and Gordon 1988
2	Thames foreshore, Vauxhall	–	52970 17780	ME	Flint core of single platform pyramidal bladelet form		Cotton and Wood 1996
3	Thames foreshore, Vauxhall	–	52980 17782	PA	Flint side scraper		Cotton and Wood 1996
4	Thames foreshore, Vauxhall	–	53005 17790	EBA	Cast-flanged copper alloy axe		Cotton and Merriman 1991
5	River Thames, Vauxhall	FLM01	53010 17810	NE/BA	Flint axe, NE 'flat axe with pointed butt', BA copper alloy rapier blade and a BA copper alloy leaf-shaped sword	114000 114002 114016 114017	Webber 1999
6	Thames foreshore, Vauxhall	VXF93	53020 17800	BA/IA	Part of a prehistoric pile structure was recorded on the foreshore. Associated artefacts included a pair of MBA side-looped spearheads and a piece of worked red deer antler. A further timber structure was found, dated to the IA and thought possibly to be a fish trap.	092155	Haughey 1999 Cotton and Wood 1996 Webber 1999
7	River Thames, Tate Gallery	FLM02	53030 17850	NE/BA	NE flint knife, BA knife or dagger, NE polished stone or flint axe, BA copper alloy spearhead and a BA dagger blade.	114003 114025 114038 114011 114024	Webber 1999
8	River Thames, Vauxhall	–	53035 17835	BA	Copper alloy chisel.	114030	
9	Coronation Buildings and 30–60 South Lambeth Rd, Lambeth	COR89 30SLR89	53040 17777	ME/IA	Three hearths, two possible ditches and a large number of pits and postholes dating to the mid–late IA. Further possible prehistoric features (undated) were uncovered at the adjacent site of 30–60 South Lambeth Rd. The small flint assemblage (48 pieces) from COR89 included an adze-sharpening flake of ME type, one core tablet and a single side scraper. Mid IA pottery and triangular loomweights.	091253 091678 091679 091680	‡ Heathcote 1990 Bird et al 1990
10	Vauxhall, Lambeth	–	53040 17800	PA	Possible flint core.	090147	
11	36–48 Albert Embankment	EMB89	53043 17836	NE/BA	Flint implements.	091261	
12	River Thames, Westminster Bridge	FLM05	53046	BA	Three copper alloy socketed axes, three copper alloy swords and a copper alloy chisel.	114022 114026 114027 114031	Webber 1999
13	River Thames, Lambeth	–	53050 17900	NE	NE flint axe.	114020	
14	River Thames, Lambeth	FLM03	53050 17910	NE/BA	NE ground serpentine axe, polished black flint axe, diorite axe and axe with flattened sides, BA copper alloy sword blade, BA copper alloy flanged axe and two BA copper alloy spearheads.	114013 114014 114015 114029 114040 114019	Webber 1999
15	5 South Lambeth Rd, Unigate Dairy	UDL88	53054 17795	PU/NE/BA?	Residual finds recovered from a weathered sand horizon included flint implements and pottery mainly of late NE date, and a loomweight of possible BA date. Phase II of the excavation produced further flint tools and pottery and a possible Beaker period scraper. The small flint assemblage (12 pieces) included a single large backed blade and a circular scraper.	091117	‡ Girardon and Heathcote 1989
16	19 Albert Embankment	ALA88	53054 17862	PU	Blades and cores.	091101	‡ Girardon and Heathcote 1989
17	Randall Row/ Tinkworth St SE1	RAN88	53058 17848	PU	Residual flint flakes and burnt flint.	091113	‡ Girardon and Heathcote 1989
18	River Thames, County Hall, Lambeth	– 17980	53060	BA	EBA copper halberd blade.	114007	
19	River Thames, Lambeth	–	53060 17980	PU	Two deer antlers.	114006	
20	Millennium Wheel, Jubilee Gardens, Belvedere Rd	JUL97	53060 17990	PU	Prehistoric peats.		

GAZ no.	Address	Site code	NGR (TQ)	Period	Description	GLSMR no.	Bibliographical references
21	79–81B Vauxhall Walk, Vauxhall	VXH96	53062 17843	PU	Two pieces of residual worked flint.	092353	
22	County Hall, Belvedere Rd	–	53065 17980	ME/NE/ BA/IA	Three ME antler mattocks, NE flint axes, a human mandible, an EBA copper halberd, a LBA copper alloy sword, and two IA copper alloy dagger sheaths, one of which retained the blade of an iron dagger.	090151 090153 090154 090155 090156 090157 090159 090161 090169 0901 090158 090168	
23	129 Lambeth Rd	LAM12973	53066 17895	ME/NE	Two flint flakes.	090828	‡
24	Harleyford Rd, St Annes RC Primary School	SAP96	53068 17796	BA	Residual flints and a sherd from an EBA Collared Urn.	092279	
25	Norfolk House, 113–127 Lambeth Rd	NOR88 and 90	53070 17895	PU	Residual flints were recovered from later contexts. These included a single possible scraper and six or seven pieces likely to have resulted from the dressing of flint nodules for a later building.	091324	‡ Webber 1991 Bird et al 1991–2
26	River Thames, Waterloo Bridge	–	53070 18050	IA	A copper alloy horned helmet was recovered from the Thames some time prior to 1868.		Franks 1864–7
27	Lambeth Palace Kitchen Gardens, Lambeth Rd	L52585	53074 17906	PU/?NE/ BA	Two prehistoric pits were recorded. The small flint assemblage (69 pieces) included a single multi-platform core and four convex scrapers of end, side, end/side and thumbnail form, respectively. Nine sherds of pottery (probably LBA), abraded non-diagnostic flint-tempered ware.	090692	‡ Richardson 1986 Bird et al 1987
28	Lambeth Palace North Garden, Lambeth Palace Rd	L58286	53074 17931	NE/BA/IA	Two prehistoric features with flint and pottery. Two sherds of an IA bead-rim jar. The flint assemblage (237 pieces) was notable for the number of diagnostic NE/EBA pieces. These included two transverse arrowheads, a barbed and tanged arrowhead, two fragments of ground flint axes, a single adze fragment, a blade knife, three scrapers of end and thumbnail type, two single-platform cores and a quartzite hammerstone.	090808	‡ Richardson 1986 Bird et al 1987
29	River Thames, Waterloo	FLM06	53080 18040	ME/BA	A ME tranchet axe and a flint battle-axe.	114036 114041	Webber 1999
30	County Hall, Addington St Annex	ADD95	53088 17974	ME/NE	Flint artefacts and burnt flint debris on a raised sand eyot and a possible cut feature.	091723 091724	
31	Finck St	LAM 16778	53090 17957	PU	Flint implement/flake.	090829	‡ Hinton 1988
32	Waterloo Station, Upper Marsh St, Lambeth	WSD89	53091 17958	BA	Flint waste and LBA pottery from a weathered sand layer. The small flint assemblage (40 pieces) contained no diagnostic tools, although a number of the flakes were of generally later prehistoric type. The pottery could not be located for examination.	091752	‡ Filer 1991 Bird et al 1991–2
33	Addington St, Waterloo	WSC90	53091 17966	ME/NE	Evidence for ME and/or NE occupation and settlement. The evidence consisted of a number of features including pits, postholes and a ditch terminal of prehistoric date. The flint assemblage (439 pieces) included a small but important collection of eight Later ME microliths comprising: four rods, one scalene piece, one obliquely backed piece, one crescentic piece and one hollow-based point of possible 'Horsham' form. Also present were a number of cores and core fragments, a single burin spall, the butt of a triangular arrowhead of probably Later NE type, and a flake knife. The few sherds of pottery were in very poor condition: pinched fingernail decoration possibly NE.	091351	‡ Filer 1991 Bird et al 1991–2
34	29 Addington St, Waterloo	WSB90	53091 17970	ME/NE/BA	A prehistoric occupation horizon that produced a number of struck flints and prehistoric pottery. This horizon was cut by six pits dating to the NE which were sealed by a sand layer containing further flintwork together with pottery, burnt flint and animal bone. The relatively large amount of struck flint may indicate that knapping was taking place close by; the presence of animal bone and burnt flint suggests cooking activities. A natural channel present on the site was filled with a thin layer of undated peat. The flint assemblage (282 pieces) included a single small obliquely backed microlith of Late ME type, together with a single microburin, four cores of single and multi-platform type, three convex scrapers and a flake knife. Sherds of Peterborough NE bowl and a possible Collared Urn.	091730 091731 091308	‡ Filer 1991 Bird et al 1991–2

GAZ no.	Address	Site code	NGR (TQ)	Period	Description	GLSMR no.	Bibliographical references
35	Upper Marsh, Waterloo, site E	WSE90	53092 17952	PU	Several flints.	091312	‡ Filer 1991 Bird et al 1991–2
36	Carlisle Lane, Waterloo, site F	WSF90	53095 17936	PU	Several flint flakes and tools.	091352	‡ Filer 1991 Bird et al 1991–2
37	126–156 Westminster Bridge Rd	–	53100 17950	PU	Possible prehistoric ditch with fire-cracked flint and several waste flakes.		Jackson et al 1999
38	Waterloo Rd, Waterloo Station	–	53105 17990	ME	A ME tranchet axe.	090711	
39	Lower Marsh	WBR88	53106 17956	NE/BA	Flint tools and pottery assemblage (?residual) The small flint assemblage (36 pieces) included a naturally holed bifacially worked triangular arrowhead of probably Later NE or EBA form. MBA? and Later BA decorated sherds.	091107	‡ Girardon and Heathcote 1989 Bird et al 1990
40	126–156 Westminster Bridge Rd	WBG96	53109 17953	PU	Burnt flint and waste flakes were found in the base of a Roman ditch. The flintwork could not be located for examination.	092322	
41	Coin St, site B	–	53110 18030	BA/IA	Prehistoric peat.		Howe et al 2000
42	Savoy Arches, Mepham St	MEP93	53112 17999	PU	Prehistoric peat.	091604	
43	127 Stamford St	SMF95	53117 18017	BA	Peat horizons with pollen showing evidence for nearby land clearance and cereal cultivation.	091751	
44	Kennington Park Rd, Kennington Church, Prima Rd	–	53120 17750	PA	Flint flake.	090053	
45	River Thames, Waterloo Bridge	FCY06	53120 18068	NE	NE polished stone or flint axe.	114037 114039	
46	Kennington Rd	–	53125 17860	PA	Two Levallois flint flakes.	090054	
47	99–101 Waterloo Rd	LOO90	53126 17995	NE/BA	A N–S ditch sealed by an accumulation of horizontal timbers with two flint flakes, roots and branches, flood deposits and a peat horizon.	091329	‡ Filer 1991 Bird et al 1991–2
48	4–10 Lower Marsh 126–156 Westminster Bridge Rd	L10779	53130 17940	NE	Residual struck flints. The flint assemblage (c 220 pieces) included one ripple-flaked asymmetrically barbed arrowhead of Later NE form and several convex scrapers.	090210 090601 091064	‡ Richardson 1980
49	10–11A Theed St	THD89	53130 18020	PU	Prehistoric peat.	091298	‡ Heathcote 1990
50	Roupell St and Hatfields	LAM16277	53149 18012	PU	Prehistoric peat.	090201	‡ Hinton 1988
51	Joan St, Southwark	JOA91	53160 18010	NE/BA	Prehistoric peat.	091430–3	Sidell et al 2000
52	245 Blackfriars Rd	245BR87	53168 18042	IA	IA burnt flint and pottery.	091149	‡ Girardon and Heathcote 1988 Bird et al 1989
53	206 Union St	UNS91	53178 18001	NE/BA	Prehistoric peat.	091459–64	Heathcote 1990 Sidell et al 2000
54	47–67 Hopton St	HNT94	53182 18045	ME/NE/BA	A sand eyot with prehistoric settlement activity, principally small pits and post/stakeholes, together with traces of ard marks. The flint assemblage (c 300 pieces) comprised elements of ME–BA date, and included a Later ME microlith, four NE arrowheads (one leaf and three transverse forms), knives, convex scrapers, cores and a hammerstone. The pottery is principally of Beaker type and includes a complete bowl buried in a small pit with a flint core and blade.	092245 092246 092247	Ridgeway 1999
55	Southwark Leisure Centre, Elephant and Castle	SLC76	53190 17890	BA	BA peat.	091950	‡ Tyers 1988
56	31–43 Borough Rd	BOR91	53190 17955	PU	Residual flints. The flintwork could not be located for examination.	091437	
57	Risborough St	–	53190 17990	PU	Possible prehistoric tree-throw hollow.		Howe et al 2000
58	Copperfield St	CSSS75	53193 17998	PU	Two flint blades.	090350	‡

GAZ no.	Address	Site code	NGR (TQ)	Period	Description	GLSMR no.	Bibliographical references
59	Bankside CEGB Depot, Bankside Power Station	–	53200 18037	ME	A red deer antler mattock was found at a depth of 15ft (4.6m) below the surface.	090192	Lacaille 1966
60	London Bridge St, Area 2 Vent Shaft	LBB95	53200 17900	BA	Cylindrical loomweight, (fragmentary but largely intact), possibly LBA.	092393	
61	Alexander Fleming House, Odeon Cinema, Elephant and Castle	AFH91	53200 17910	PU	Peat deposits with fire-cracked flint and the bases of three . wooden stakes	091713–4	Filer 1991
62	Thames foreshore	FSW11	53208 18057	PU	Sand eyot and trees.	092625 092626 092633	Webber 1999
63	1–3 Pilgrim Hill off Auckland Hill	PIH00	53215 17200	PU	Struck and burnt flint.		Maloney and Holroyd 2001
64	Emerson Place	–	53215 18040	ME	ME flints.	091235	
65	Skinmarket Place, Bankside	SIP88	53217 18048	NE	NE pottery and flints. The flintwork could not be located for examination, but records indicate a fragment of ground NE axe and scrapers.	091289 091290	‡ Heathcote 1990 Bird et al 1990
66	Thames foreshore, New Globe Walk	FSW11	53217 18056	NE/IA	NE alluvial deposits, with evidence of an alder stand, NE and IA erosion channels and a possible large palaeochannel.		Webber 1999 Sloane 1998
67	Bankside Pontoon	–	53220 18055	NE/BA	NE and BA peats and clays.		
68	Benbow House, Bear Gardens, Bankside	BEN95	53223 18051	BA	Peat.		
69	2–10 Southwark Bridge Rd, Southbridge House	SBH88	53228 18043	BA	Peat.	091266	‡
70	Park St	–	53230 18040	NE	Ground flint axe.	090193	
71	Southwark Business Village, Southwark Bridge Rd	SUB00	53232 18023	PU	Fire-cracked flint.		Maloney and Holroyd 2001
72	Brockham St	BKM97	53234 17941	PU/BA	A small sub-circular pit (undated) and a LBA perforated clay slab (residual); and sherds from LBA jars.	092750–7	Thompson 1998.
73	289–298 Borough High St	289BHS90	53234 17959	NE/BA	NE or BA arrowhead. The flintwork could not be located for examination.	091358	‡ Heathcote 1990 Bird et al 1991–2
74	Anchor Terrace car park, Park St	ACT89	53235 18035	BA	Peat deposits with probable prehistoric timbers.	091271	‡
75	5–15 Bankside	BS81 and BKS81	53236 18045	PU/BA	Large prehistoric channel and a peat deposit, probably BA in date.	090855 09085501	‡
76	6–8 Marshalsea Rd	6MSRD88	53238 179242	PU	Late prehistoric channel.	091907	‡
77	Dickens Square, Harper Rd	DIC89	53238 17935	PU	Deep peats containing undated flint flakes filling glacial scour holes.	091249–51	‡ Heathcote 1990 Bird et al 1990
78	Former Southwark Sorting Office, Swan St	SWN98	53240 17960	PU	Probable pre-Roman agricultural ditches and post-built structures.		Howe et al 2000
79	Union St Borough High St Great Suffolk St	–	53240 18000	IA	Celtic bronze coin.	09060201	
80	Thames foreshore, Anchor Public House, Bankside	–	53240 18050	IA	Late IA copper alloy strap-union in figure-of-eight form.		Cotton and Merriman 1991
81	Courage's Brewery bottling plant, Park St	CO87, CO88, COSE84, CO89, CSW85, 38SBR79	53241 18020	ME/NE/BA	NE features, flint tools and pottery. The features include an E–W boundary ditch, a possible structure and hearths. A BA roundhouse with internal postholes, a pit and flint tools together with peat deposits were also recorded. The flint assemblage (181 pieces) incorporated a number of diagnostic ME–BA items including: an adze-sharpening flake; a ground axe fragment; a transverse arrowhead; a broken flake knife; a plano-convex knife; several cores and six scrapers. The pottery could not be located for examination.	091375 091376 091159 091193 091194 091195 091196 091301	‡ Cowan in prep Merriman 1992 Girardon and Heathcote 1988 Bird et al 1989 Willcox 1975

GAZ no.	Address	Site code	NGR (TQ)	Period	Description	GLSMR no.	Bibliographical references
82	Harper Rd Ralph St Dickens Square	HR77	53245 17930	ME/NE	Three blades and a flake.	090716	‡
83	170–194 Borough High St	170BHS79	53247 17982	PU	Water channel.	09052201	‡
84	213 Borough High St	213BHS77	53250 17981	ME/NE	One struck flint and a possible channel. A small group of abraded sherds, some flint; residual? The flintwork could not be located for examination.	090723 09051401	‡
85	116–126 Borough High St	BGG01	53250 17994	PU	Struck and fire-cracked flint.		
86	124–126 Borough High St	124BHS77	53250 17993	BA/IA	BA hearth and struck flint, an inhumation of possible IA date (sealed by a Roman road) with postholes and a bone wrist guard. The small flint assemblage (82 pieces) did not include any diagnostic finds. The bone wrist guard is recorded as from 120BHS. Late IA/ Early Romano-British pottery was recovered from below the road.	090846 090847 09084801	‡ Richardson 1978 Bird et al 1980 Hinton 1988
87	154 Swan St/Great Dover St	SS73 17958	53251	ME/NE	Flint blade.	090718	‡
88	201–211 Borough High St	207BHS72, 201BHS75 and 201BHS	53251 17983	ME/NE	One core and 25 struck flints. A single highly abraded sherd was found in a sand layer, probably prehistoric; with pitted fabric. Other pottery included large fragments of a jar dated to the 1st century BC–AD from ?pre-Conquest fills of main channel (BII–1); a round-shouldered jar with incised decoration and notched rim decoration in a hard sandy fabric, for which no parallels have been found.	090840	‡ Bird et al 1978
89	120–124 Borough High St	120BHS89	53251 17994	PU/?IA	Evidence of early occupation included a possible Late IA/Early Roman hearth and debitage from flint working. The small flint assemblage (27 pieces) included a discoidal core and a convex end scraper.	091277	‡ Heathcote 1990 Bird et al 1990
90	106–114 Borough High St	106BHS73	53252 17996	BA/IA	A flint assemblage (30 pieces) contained a core, two serrates and an awl. Pottery is predominantly flint-tempered, probably Mid–LBA/ Early IA. One decorated sherd, possibly from an EBA Beaker.	090841	‡ Bird et al 1978 Willcox 1975
91	15–23 Southwark St	15SKS80 (also known as CB80)	53252 18011	ME/NE/ BA/IA	A series of stakeholes, small linear and semi-circular gullies were excavated, probably from timber structures. Finds included an assemblage of struck flint, Beaker pottery of EBA date and IA pottery from some of the features. The flint assemblage (360 pieces) included a range of ME–BA finds comprising three Later ME microliths, an adze-sharpening flake and an Earlier NE leaf-shaped arrowhead, together with scrapers and cores. A small Beaker flint assemblage included three diminutive scrapers and a flake knife.	090827 09082701	‡ Cowan 1992 Hinton 1988
92	Silvester Buildings, Silvester St	SB76	53253 17970	ME/NE	A blade, flake and a core.	091065	‡ Richardson 1977 Bird et al 1980
93	199 Borough High St	199BHS74	53253 17986	ME/NE/BA	Two cores and 21 struck flints (two blades and 19 flakes). The pottery included flint-tempered fabrics and elements dated to the LBA. Published examples all appear to be residual.	090722	‡ Hinton 1988
94	175–177 Borough High St	175BHS76	53253 17990	ME/NE	Flint blade.	090721	‡
95	84–86 Borough High St	84BHS75	53254 18002	ME/NE	Two blades and six flakes.	090392	‡ Hinton 1988
96	Arcadia Buildings, Silvester St	AB78	53255 17967	NE/IA	A N–S aligned ditch of possible Late IA/Early Roman date and residual flints. The small flint assemblage (36 pieces) included one petit tranchet derivative arrowhead of Later NE type.	090851 090854	‡
97	179–191 Borough High St	179BHS79	53256 17987	PU/?NE	A prehistoric sand horizon (possible ground surface), a pit containing one sherd of prehistoric pottery, flint flakes and an arrowhead. The flintwork could not be located for examination.	091243	‡
98	Thames foreshore	FSW12	53256 18042	ME	A flint core and a ME pick.	092438 092448	Webber 1999
99	Thames foreshore	FSW12	53257 18044	PU	Prehistoric trees.	092443	Webber 1999
100	199 Borough High St Tennis St	199BHS74	53259 17982	PU	65 residual struck flints from a Roman context and 33 residual cortical flakes from post-Roman horizons.	091031 091043	‡ Hinton 1988

GAZ no.	Address	Site code	NGR (TQ)	Period	Description	GLSMR no.	Bibliographical references
101	107 Borough High St	107BHS81	53259 18005	ME/NE	Several sherds of prehistoric pottery and a flint flake. The material could not be located for examination.	090862	‡
102	Mermaid St	–	53260 17990	IA	Possible Late IA/Early Roman finds.	090798	
103	Old Marshalsea Prison, Borough High St	–	53260 17993	NE	NE flints.	090916	
104	97–99 Borough High St	BOH93	53260 18008	PU	Prehistoric silts.	091733	
105	Stoney St, Borough Market	–	53260 18022	IA	IA dagger with anthropoid hilt.	09037802	
106	Thames foreshore	FSW12	53260 18043	PU	Organic clay and a possible reed bed.	092467	Webber 1999
107	Former York clinic, 117 Borough High St and the Nags Head yard workshop	BHB00	53261 18000	PU	Flint scatter on sand eyot.		Maloney and Holroyd 2001
108	St Mary Overy Dock, Cathedral St	–	53263 18039	ME	ME flint tranchet adze.	090710	
109	Thames foreshore, St Mary Overy Dock	–	53264 18042	ME	ME flint tranchet adze.		Cotton and Merriman 1991
110	Chaucer House, Tabard St	CH75	53266 17962	BA	BA peat.	090327 090424–5	‡ Hinton 1988 Bloise 1976 Bird et al 1980
111	Southwark St 1A Bedale St	2SSBS85	53268 18013	ME/NE	Struck flint and a possible prehistoric feature. The flintwork could not be located for examination.	090724	‡
112	Northern Line Ticket Hall, Borough High St	BGH95	53269 18020	PU	Peat deposit.	092378	Drummond-Murray 2002
113	21–27 St Thomas St	STS88	53270 18010	PU	Residual finds.		‡
114	Thames foreshore	FSW12	53270 18040	PU	Timber roundwood structure.	092459	Webber 1999
115	King's Head Yard, Borough High St	–	532715 180120	PU/?IA	Barbed and tanged flint arrowhead, flints and possible IA rim sherd. The pottery could not be located for examination.	090297	
116	King's Head Yard, Borough High St	–	53272 18013	IA	IA pottery.	090616	
117	1–7 St Thomas St	1STS74	53274 18019	ME/NE	Two blades, three flakes and a core.	090725	‡ Bird et al 1978.
118	Hibernia Wharf, Montague Close	HIB79	53274 18040	BA	BA peat.	090584 090876–82	‡ Tyers 1988 Richardson 1980
119	Falmouth Rd Harper Rd	FLT95	53275 17945	IA	Pleistocene gravels sealed by peat containing one sherd of IA pottery.	092386	
120	Hunts House, Guy's Hospital	HHO97	53275 17995	ME/NE/BA	Possible ard marks, cut features, palaeosol, 203 struck flints, much fire-cracked flint		Jackson et al 1999
121	Guy's Hospital, St Thomas St	GHR82	53275 18010	PU	Flints and residual flint-tempered sherds. The small flint assemblage (ten pieces) included a small crested blade.	090888	‡ Richardson 1984 Bird et al 1984
122	4–26 St Thomas St	4STS82	53275 18015	?IA	Pits, flint tools and some residual flint-tempered sherds. The flintwork could not be located for examination.	090883	‡
123	127 Long Lane	LNL98	53280 17960	PU	Pre-Roman timber and brushwood trackway.		Howe et al 2000
124	1 Waterloo Rd, Cornwall House	WTR97	53280 17992	BA	BA peat.	092647	Jackson et al 1999
125	11–19 St Thomas St	11STS77	53280 18017	NE/BA	NE to LBA pottery.	090999 091000 091001	‡ Richardson 1978 Bird et al 1980
126	London Bridge	–	53280 18030	BA	EBA flint dagger.	090709	
127	River Thames, London Bridge	–	53280 18030	NE	Polished stone axe.	090712	

GAZ no.	Address	Site code	NGR (TQ)	Period	Description	GLSMR no.	Bibliographical references
128	River Thames, London Bridge	–	53280 18030	NE	Three flint flakes.	090713	
129	River Thames, London Bridge, Bermondsey side	FSW13	53280 18050	BA/IA	Copper alloy socketed axe and leaf-shaped spearhead, IA *Potin* coin, gold coin, Cunobelin coin and an uninscribed copper alloy coin.	114021 114028 114032 114034 114035 114033	Webber 1999
130	Fennings Wharf, Tooley St	FW83, FW84	53281 18037	BA/IA	A BA ring ditch and a number of pits and gullies with cremated bone from the fill of the ring ditch including identifiable remains of at least one adult and ?seven children. The flint assemblage (125 pieces) included an adze-sharpening flake, a core and two convex scrapers. LBA/Early IA transition ceramics.	090686 09068601	‡ Watson et al 2001 Richardson 1978 Bird et al 1986
131	London Bridge Station, MEPC Car park	LBE95	53286 18021	PU	Several residual artefacts.	092403	
132	Toppings Wharf, Tooley St	TW70	53286 18035	PU	Worked flints and abraded pottery.	090872	‡ Sheldon 1974 Willcox 1975
133	Bartholomew St, St Saviours and St Olaves School	SSB93	53287 17907	NE/BA	Pottery, worked flints, burnt daub and a loomweight of late NE/EBA were found in the bottom fill of a Roman ditch.	091630 091631 091632	
134	Joiner St, 'JLE East Escape Shaft'	LBD95	53287 180185	BA	BA pits with a small flint assemblage (seven pieces) contained no diagnostic finds.	092232 092234	
135	Tooley St, District Heating Scheme	DHS75	53290 18030	ME/NE	One blade and four flakes.	090719	‡ Hinton 1988 Bloise 1975
136	St Olaf House, Tooley St	SOH84	53290 18035	PU	Line of undated timbers.	090696–7 090428	‡ Richardson 1986 Bird et al 1987
137	Chamberlains Wharf, Tooley St	–	53294 18034	IA	Iron socketed spearhead.	090800	
138	Rephidim St	RS77	53295 17918	PU	One sherd of flint-tempered possibly prehistoric pot.	090505	‡
139	180–196 Long Lane	180LL79	53298 17952	ME/NE	Two blades and a flake.	090717	‡
140	74–90 Weston St	WET89	53298 17980	BA/PU	Two possible pits, one containing a flint tool sealed by mid BA peat. Three struck flints, two flakes and a small bladelet.	091965 091966	‡
141	Cotton's Wharf, Tooley St	CW83 and CWO84	53303 18013	PU	Several pits and a prehistoric soil horizon overlain by waterlain clays. Flint-tempered sherds, residual.	090892	‡
142	1 Tower Bridge Rd	SKT91 and TER96	53309 17902	PU	Two postholes containing burnt flint, one flint flake, residual prehistoric pottery and flint from later features. The flintwork could not be located for examination.	091503	
143	Leroy St, rear of 63–71 Old Kent Rd	ROY91	53310 17895	PU	Burnt flint and some struck flakes. One residual flint tool was recorded from a Roman context. Surviving flintwork comprised a single blade.	091397	
144	12 Tower Bridge Rd	TBR91	53310 17910	PU	Silts and organic clays possibly a watercourse or lake to the south of Bermondsey.	091513	Heathcote 1990
145	St Olaves Dock	–	53310 18030	NE	A flint flake.	090714	
146	9 Leathermarket St	NSL94	53311 17962	PU	Two possible water channels cutting prehistoric peat deposits.	091662 091663 091664	
147	6–14 Leroy St, Bermondsey Mews	LER91	533130 178930	PU	Possible prehistoric ground surface and several flint flakes. The flint assemblage (23 pieces) comprised a range of small undiagnostic flakes and blades.	091419	
148	Wilson's Wharf	WW78	53314 18023	BA	Peat.		Tyers 1988
149	London Bridge City, Battle Bridge Lane	BAB95	53315 18025	PU	Flood deposit.	091973	
150	6–8 Morocco St	MRC90	53316 17965	PU	Prehistoric peat.	091343–5	‡ Heathcote 1990 Bird et al 1991–2

GAZ no.	Address	Site code	NGR (TQ)	Period	Description	GLSMR no.	Bibliographical references
151	Morgans Lane	MOR86	53324 18020	PU	Prehistoric peat.	090812	‡ Richardson 1987 Bird et al 1990
152	Shand St (off Tooley St)	–	53328 18000	BA	'The lowest bed seen in section was a brownish sandy loam with a few pieces of burnt flints...and a small fragment of hand made pottery, perhaps BA.'		Kennard and Warren 1903
153	Caledonian Market, Bermondsey Square	BYQ98	53330 17930	IA	IA pottery in a ploughsoil.		Howe et al 2000
154	12–16 Whites Grounds/ 4–42 Brunswick Court	BRC93	53335 17975	PU	Fluvial and peat deposits.	091582 091583	
155	Whites Grounds, Southwark	WG87	53335 17980	ME/NE	Struck and fire-cracked flint and NE pottery from sand island deposits. The flint assemblage (139 pieces) included a single rod microlith of Later ME type, two-platform cores, blades, a polished flint axe fragment and a bifacially worked oval flint knife of NE type. Two flint-tempered undiagnostic pottery sherds were also recovered.	091168	‡ Girardon and Heathcote 1988 Bird et al 1989
156	36–40 Tanner St and 159–161 Tower Bridge Rd	TWE98	53338 17960	NE/BA	NE and BA peat.		Howe et al 2000 Elsden 2001
157	Mandela Way, Old Kent Rd	MDW88	53340 17870	PU	An undated, but potentially early, linear feature.	091175 091942	‡ Girardon and Heathcote 1989 Bird et al 1990
158	Willow Walk, Pages Walk, Mandela Way	WWK87	53340 17880	PU	Peat deposits.	091971	‡
159	Bermondsey Abbey, Long Walk, Abbey St	BA84	53340 17933	ME/NE/ BA/IA	Large amounts of residual IA pottery, struck flints and some small finds. The flint assemblage (277 pieces) included a number of diagnostic ME–BA finds including: a single bi-truncated microlith; an adze-sharpening flake; three arrowheads of leaf, transverse and barbed and tanged form; four cores; five scrapers of end and end/ side form; three blade knives, and five serrates. Residual pottery ranged in date from Mid BA to Late IA/Early Romano-British. The finds included a complete loomweight and a perforated red deer antler tine with multiple ring-and-dot decoration.	090572–3 090572–3 091202–4	‡ Steele in prep Richardson 1985
160	Vinegar Yard, 33 Tanner St		53340 17960	BA	Cooking pit with BA material cut by a channel.	092792	Jackson et al 1999
161	Brunswick Court	BNK97	53340 17970	PU	Struck and burnt flints together with pottery from waterlain sand at the southern edge of Horselydown eyot.		Jackson et al 1999
162	Vine Lane	VIN86	53340 18015	PU	Prehistoric peat.	090815	‡ Girardon and Heathcote 1989 Bird et al 1990
163	Vinegar Yard	VIY97	533410 179670	BA	Peat and a small cooking pit.		Jackson et al 1999
164	Long Walk Tower Bridge Rd Grange Walk, Bermondsey	LWK92	53343 17982	PU	Residual flints not located for examination.	092132–5	Filer 1991
165	167 Tower Bridge Rd	TWD99	533441 179654	PU	Peat with fire-cracked flints.	093215–21	Maloney and Holroyd 2000
166	169 Tower Bridge Rd	TWG00	53345 17975	NE/BA	Struck and fire-cracked flint.		Maloney and Holroyd 2001
167	168 Tower Bridge Rd, SE1	TBO00	53346 17962	PU	One flint tool.		Maloney and Holroyd 2001
168	45–49 Tanner St	TAT99	53353 17965	NE	Posthole and a ditch. Struck, fire-cracked flint and bone found within a peat overlying the ditch.		Maloney and Holroyd 2000
169	Mark Browns Wharf, Tooley St, Tower Bridge Rd	MBW73	53353 18013	BA	BA peat.	091052	‡ Hinton 1988 Tyers 1988 Bloise 1974 Willcox 1975
170	Former Alaska Works, Grange Rd	AW89	53355 17905	BA	Residual finds of LBA pottery and burnt flint. Late IA–Early Romano-British component; two of the sherds were flint-tempered, possibly LBA.	091287	‡ Heathcote 1990 Bird et al 1990
171	14–38 Albany Rd	ARB90	53358 17825	?IA	Waterlogged prehistoric to Roman landscape and a possibly IA drainage gully.	091270 091490 091492	

GAZ no.	Address	Site code	NGR (TQ)	Period	Description	GLSMR no.	Bibliographical references
172	Tooley St	–	53360 17985	BA	Copper alloy mount with 'embossed scrolls'.	090195	
173	River Thames, Tower Bridge	FSW14	53360 18020	ME/NE	Flint flake and axe.	081089 081088	Webber 1999
174	281–345 Old Kent Rd, Humphrey St	HUM90	53363 17835	NE/BA	Flints, pottery (several small flint-tempered sherds), daub, animal bone, a hearth and a gully. The flint assemblage (156 pieces) included a single burnt scraper, a multi-platform core reused as a hammerstone, a flake knife and a range of flakes and blades.	091332	‡ Filer 1991 Bird et al 1991–2
175	241–247 Tooley St	TLS95	53363 17984	ME/NE	Flints, including a blade (ME or NE) and burnt flint. The flintwork could not be located for examination.	092181	
176	1–2 Three Oaks Lane	TKL99	53365 17984	BA	Field boundary ditch and stake line and a broken fragment of ard.		Proctor 2000
177	Old Kent Rd/Dunton Rd/Humphrey St, Mandela Way	TCO93	53367 17844	PU	Numerous features cutting into natural sands and gravels. An ancient water channel, possibly associated with an assemblage of residual struck flints. A small flint assemblage (12 pieces) included an endscraper.	091739 091742 091743	
178	281–345 Old Kent Rd, Humphrey St	HUM91	53370 17830	NE/BA	Flints, pottery (several small flint-tempered sherds), daub, animal bone, a hearth and a gully. The flint assemblage (156 pieces) included a single burnt scraper, a multi-platform core reused as a hammerstone, a flake knife and a range of flakes and blades.	091332	
179	10–16 Lafone St	LAF96	53365 17986	NE/BA	A boundary ditch cutting a possible buried soil horizon; the soil contained a high proportion of worked flint and occasional prehistoric pottery. To the south of the ditch were a number of ard marks cutting sand. Most of the small flint assemblage (40 pieces) was recovered from the buried soil or from the sequence of peats sealing it. Diagnostic pieces included the butt of an adze, an adze-sharpening flake, a possible leaf-shaped arrowhead roughout, a flake knife together with a number of flakes and blades. Pottery included one sherd with fingernail decoration, possibly of NE/BA date.	092289	Jackson et al 1999 Bates and Minkin 1999
180	255 Tooley St, Three Oaks Lane	TYS00	53370 17980	IA?	Ditch, pits and stakeholes.		Maloney and Holroyd 2001
181	54 Gainsforth St	GFS93	53370 17990	PU	Two prehistoric flood events separated by a layer of peat.	092157 092158 091645	Maloney and Holroyd 2000
182	London Bridge City, Tooley St	TYT98	53370 18010	NE	Struck flint flakes and pottery with watercourse blocked with stakes.		
183	Tower Bridge	–	53370 18040	ME	Worked flake and blade.	080739	
184	Humphrey St/Row Cross Rd	HPS93	53375 17830	ME/NE	Struck flint dating to the ME or NE and an undated peat deposit. The small flint assemblage (ten pieces) included a single multi-platform core and three or four blades.	091623 091624	
185	Abbey St Grange Walk Maltby St Neckinger St	ABY91	53375 17936	IA	A large water channel, thought to be the former River Neckinger contained finds dating from the IA. Shallow pits and ditches were also found.	091465 091467	
186	271–281 Tooley St	TOY94	53375 17977	PU/IA	A Holocene channel with two pits containing Late IA/Early Romano-British pottery and a penannular copper alloy brooch.	092166	
187	283 Tooley St	TOS93	53375 17977	ME/IA	Part of the Horselydown eyot, ME struck flint and IA pits and postholes.	091552 091553 091555	
188	Queen Elizabeth St South	QESS88	53376 17985	NE	NE flint scatter and pottery. The small flint assemblage (46 pieces) included a retouched composite borer/knife and a single pebble core, together with flakes and blades. A number of pieces are not certainly prehistoric and may represent debitage resulting from the dressing of flint nodules for building purposes.	091132	‡ Girardon and Heathcote 1989 Bird et al 1990
189	Phoenix Wharf, 4 Jamaica Rd	PHW88	53379 17965	BA	EBA cooking pit and associated burnt mound and windbreak/revetment. An E–W channel may have provided a water source for the cooking pit. Mid–LBA features and agricultural activity in the form of ard and possible spade marks. The small flint assemblage (82 pieces) was mainly recovered from the BA ploughsoils (69 pieces). Diagnostic pieces comprised a plano-convex knife of Early/MBA form, an awl and four scrapers. The pottery was in very poor condition, mainly flint-tempered, some MBA. The illustrated sherds could not be located for examination.	091129–2 091130	‡ Merriman 1992 Bowsher 1991 Girardon and Heathcote 1989 Bird et al 1990

GAZ no.	Address	Site code	NGR (TQ)	Period	Description	GLSMR no.	Bibliographical references
190	285–291 Tooley St	TLT00	53379 17974	ME/NE/IA	An IA gully with pottery, daub, struck and fire-cracked flint and a pot placed in a pit cutting a deposit containing ME/NE flint.		Maloney and Holroyd 2001
191	Bricklayers Arms Railway yard, Rolls Rd	BLA87	53380 17850	NE/BA	A wooden 'platform', possibly BA in date, one complete chipped flint axe and one fragmentary ground flint axe, both NE, from alluvial silts, together with nine flint flakes and peat deposits.	091172 091173 091174	‡ Merriman 1992 Girardon and Heathcote 1988; 1989 Bird et al 1990
192	Alscot Rd	ARD93	53380 17910	IA	Two N–S aligned boundary ditches and associated cultivation.	091537 091538 091539	
193	River Thames, Butlers Wharf	–	53380 17980	PU	Worked red deer antler/bone tool.	090198	
194	Cayenne Court	BTW98	53380 17980	PU	Fire-cracked flint.		Ridgeway and Meddens 2001
195	Grinders and Operators site, Butler's Wharf Estate	GFD97	53380 17985	BA	Peat.		Ridgeway and Meddens 2001
196	West Courtyard, Butler's Wharf Estate	WCW96	53380 17990	ME/BA	Fire-cracked flint and two cut features with struck flint and pottery. Microlith, piercer or point and possible tranchet axe sharpening flake.		Jackson et al 1999 Ridgeway and Meddens 2001
197	Thames foreshore, Dockhead, St Saviour's Wharf	–	53390 17980	BA	MBA socketed side-looped copper alloy spearhead.		Cotton and Merriman 1991
198	Old Kent Rd	–	53393 17813	BA	LBA copper alloy socketed axe with double mouth moulding and side loop.	090194	
199	Wolseley St	WOY94	53397 17975	NE/BA	Prehistoric ard marks associated with flints and pottery dating to the Late NE/EBA. The flint assemblage (74 pieces) included two small opposed platform cores and a small convex scraper together with a number of flakes and blades.	091694–6	Drummond-Murray et al 1995 Greenwood and Maloney 1995
200	The Five Estates, land south of Lisford St	LFS96	53400 17680	PU	Three struck flints.		Jackson et al 1999
201	Jacob's Island, Bermondsey	JAC96	53408 17976	PU	Prehistoric peat deposits.		Maloney and Gostick 1998
202	Eagle Wharf, Peckham Hill St	–	53410 17690	NE/BA	One struck flint.		Howe et al 2000
203	Ossory Rd	OSS95	53410 17800	ME/NE	Possible ditched enclosure and other features including a channel. Finds included Late ME/Early NE flint flakes and blades.	092415 092416 092417	
204	283 Marlborough Grove	MAG93	53420 17810	PU/ME	A scatter of worked flints dating to the ME and possibly NE. The flint assemblage (255 pieces) included diagnostic Earlier ME pieces including: an adze-sharpening flake; four microliths (including three obliquely backed points) and two scrapers.	091587 091602	
205	Safeway Stores extension, Aylesham Centre, Hanover Park	–	53430 17660	NE/BA/IA	Pottery and residual flints indicating activity from Late NE to Early IA.		Jackson et al 1999
206	Thames foreshore, Bermondsey	BMF93	53430 17980	PU	Prehistoric peats and silts containing animal and human bone, flints and other artefacts.	092263 092264	
207	Thames foreshore, Chambers Wharf, Bermondsey	–	53438 17980	ME/BA	A large, pyramidal core, a naturally holed flint macehead, several sherds of NE pottery and part of a LBA copper alloy tongue-shaped sword chape. Prehistoric peats and clays.		Cotton and Wood 1996 Woodbridge 1998
208	Old Kent Rd/Bowles Rd	BAQ90 (and sites OKG91 and OKR90)	53440 17780	ME/NE	Two major in situ flint scatters. Later features include a hearth, two ditches, a gully and postholes. The larger of the two flint scatters appeared to focus on two hearths defined by concentrations of burnt flint. Diagnostic finds included a series of 18 microliths of Earlier ME form (principally obliquely backed points), together with micro-burins, cores of one-, two- and multi-platform type, scrapers, adze-sharpening flakes and hammerstones. It has proved possible to refit a number of flakes/blades back onto cores. Analysis of use-wear has identified traces of dry-hide scraping and antler-working. The smaller of the flint scatters included a single intrusive, leaf-shaped arrowhead of Earlier NE type.	091321	‡ Rogers 1990 Filer 1991 Bird et al 1991–2
209	River Thames, Jamaica Rd, Bermondsey	FSW01	53440 17980	BA	EBA copper alloy dagger, two timber structures, a raised bed of gravel with tufa and iron and a tree root.	114023 092495 092496 092497 092502 092513	Gerloff 1975 Webber 1999

GAZ no.	Address	Site code	NGR (TQ)	Period	Description	GLSMR no.	Bibliographical references
210	Southwark College, Surrey Docks Centre Playground, Storks Rd	–	53450 17920	PU	Struck and burnt flints together with pottery from waterlain deposit above natural clay.		Jackson et al 1999
211	Cherry Garden Pier, Bermondsey	CG87	53450 17968	IA	IA pottery and flint flakes from several pits and deposits. The flintwork comprised a single snapped blade. The pottery could not be located for examination.	091153	‡ Girardon and Heathcote 1988 Bird et al 1989
212	Platform Wharf, Paradise St	PW89, 90 and 91	53480 17970	ME/NE/ BA/IA	BA/IA ditch, aligned ESE–WNW and fence line, a ME flint blade, NE flint axe, a residual flint knife of NE/EBA date and IA pottery. The flint assemblage (111 pieces) included two convex scrapers, a small pebble core and a flake knife with shallow invasive ventral retouch.	091238 091371 091370 091369 091478 091479	‡ Heathcote 1990 Bird et al 1991–2
213	St Olave's Hospital, Rotherhithe	SOR91	53510 17933	PU	Flint flakes which could not be located for examination.	091495	
214	Culling Rd	CUG93	53510 17947	NE	Small quantities of NE flint blades and pottery. The pottery could not be located for examination.	091746–2	Sidell et al 2000
215	Bramcote Grove, Bermondsey	BEG92	53515 17805	BA	Two phases of a BA trackway. The first phase consisted of parallel planks or logs pegged down with cross-bracing pieces and the second of oak logs, laid on bark, pegged down by stakes.	092123	Filer 1991 Thomas and Rackham 1996 Rackham 1994
216	Rupack St, Rotherhithe	RUP88	53517 17967	PU	Trial work recovered a flint scraper, blade and flint-tempered pottery sealed by waterlain clays. There were traces of features and postholes. The pottery comprised a dozen or so flint-tempered sherds.	091157	‡ Girardon and Heathcote 1988 Bird et al 1989
217	Dundas Rd	DSR99	53523 17637	PU	Palaeochannel cutting natural clays.		Maloney and Holroyd 2000
218	Sharrat St Allderton Rd Rollins St	SHT94	53527 17781	ME/NE	Redeposited flint flakes. The flintwork could not be located for examination.	091709	
219	Southwark Park	–	53530 17900	BA	A basal-looped copper alloy spearhead of MBA type.	090906	
220	Silverlock, Rotherhithe	–	53534 17860	NE	NE peat.		Tyers 1988
221	Canada Water, Surrey Quays Rd	CAW91	53550 17950	BA	BA peat deposits that contained a large split tree (possibly worked timbers) and red deer antlers.	091455	Sidell et al 2000
222	River Thames, Rotherhithe	–	53560 17930	PA	Mousterian flint artefact.	114044	
223	River Thames, Bellamy's Wharf	–	53565 18030	NE	NE flint axehead.	114042	
224	Canada Dock, Rotherhithe	–	53570 17920	PA	Remains of deer, sheep, pig and dog were found in waterlain deposits in 1875.	090763	
225	Surrey Quays Rd	SUQ96	53571 17944	BA	Early to MBA organic silty clays and peat.	092288	
226	305–319 Lower Rd	LR88	53598 17864	PU	Several flints in a weathered sand horizon. The flintwork has not been located.	091127	‡ Girardon and Heathcote 1989 Bird et al 1990
227	Rotherhithe	–	53600 17900	PA	Two flint artefacts.	091092	
228	Surrey Docks, Rotherhithe	–	53600 17950	NE	An oval flint knife of Later NE discoidal type was found at c 10'6'' below OD 'in gravel overlaid with peat varying up to 6' in thickness'.	090918	
229	71–97 Plough Way	PWA96	53610 17890	PU	Residual flint from a peat deposit.		Maloney and Gostick 1998
230	Bryan Rd Salter Rd Rotherhithe St	BRY93	53653 17994	PU	Clay silts and peat; the latter dating to c 3800 BC.	092191	Sidell et al 1995
231	Deptford Strand foreshore	–	53684 17864	NE	Greenstone ground axe.		

6

Specialist appendices

6.1 The lithics

Jonathan Cotton

Information derived from the lithic data recovered from the study area has already been incorporated where appropriate in the above text. This chapter provides a basic introduction to and overview of the lithic material itself. Limitations of time and space have necessitated a degree of selectivity and this report will seek to draw attention to (rather than exhaustively explore) some of the potential avenues of enquiry. Following an introductory section incorporating comment on matters such as sample bias, context types, method of analysis, raw material, condition and distribution, this report will focus primarily on three subsets of the lithic dataset, as follows.

1) The in situ assemblages from the B&Q site and Marlborough Grove, incorporating the results of the microwear analysis undertaken by Randolph Donahue.
2) The Neolithic and Bronze Age arrowheads from the study area.
3) The material recovered from the early soil horizons at Phoenix Wharf, Wolseley Street and Lafone Street.

A concluding section provides a necessarily brief chronological overview of the lithic material from the study area, and attempts to place it within its regional setting. All finds and site records are stored by site code in the London Archaeological Archive and Research Centre at Eagle Wharf Road, London N1 7ED, and may be consulted there by appointment.

Introduction

Given the generally non-targeted and often small-scale nature of the fieldwork undertaken within the study area, a surprisingly large amount of struck flint has been collected from some 64 separate sites over the last 20 years or so (Table 4). A majority of this material has been recovered by MoLAS and its predecessor bodies, though recently several significant assemblages have been excavated by other organisations (eg Pre-Construct Archaeology (Gary Brown and Frank Meddens, pers comm)). Arrowheads apart, these are not considered here. A few small groups of lithics have been published previously as part of larger site reports (eg Cresswell 1974, 31–3; 1978, 197–8; 1988, 385–7; Cotton 1992, 62–7) and a series of 'impressionistic' distribution maps assembled (Merriman 1987), but no synthesis of the overall dataset has been attempted.

Sample bias/context types/method of analysis

On very few occasions has the recovery of struck flint been one of the primary objectives of the work undertaken, and on a number of sites it is clear that only the more obviously worked and/or retouched pieces were recognised and retained. The B&Q site and Marlborough Grove apart, none of the material was three-dimensionally recorded and on no site was any systematic sieving programme carried out. As such the quantities and distribution of the struck flint from the study area are, with a few notable exceptions, inevitably biased in favour of the larger pieces and should therefore be regarded as broadly illustrative of prehistoric activity only.

With the exception of the sites considered in more detail below (eg the B&Q site, Marlborough Grove, Phoenix Wharf, Wolseley Street and Lafone Street), the lithic material in the archive has been simply and swiftly scanned for diagnostic pieces without regard to contextual data. It is likely, however, that much of it was recovered from one or other of three main context types: from isolated features cut into the natural sands; from horizontal layers of 'weathered natural' usually underlying the earliest Roman levels; or from Roman and later contexts. At Southwark Street, for example, these three context types produced 27%, 34% and 39% of the flint assemblage, respectively (Cotton 1992, 62–3), although the unusually large number of early features is likely to have inflated the first figure compared to many of the other sites in the study area. (Across the river on Thorney Island, Westminster, these same three context types produced 11%, 63% and nearly 20% of the total lithic assemblage, for example.)

Raw material/condition

With very few exceptions the raw material comprised nodular flint from one of two main sources: river terrace gravels and the Chalk. A few quartzite cobbles were also utilised, usually as hammerstones or rubbers, though no 'foreign' stone in the form of groundstone axes or fragments. The vast majority of the nodular flint (estimated at >95%) was obtained from the local terrace gravels. It is of variable, usually poor, quality with water-worn, pitted cortex and frequent thermally fractured surfaces. A minor but recurrent component is the presence of Bullhead Bed flint, with distinctive greenish black cortex and orange sub-cortical banding. This better quality flint appears to occur naturally in the terrace gravels, usually sourced to the base of the Thanet Sand over Chalk. It could have been brought directly from there by human groups, or have been incorporated in local gravel deposits by river action. The small percentage of Chalk flint is more problematical and, while it is conceivable that it could have been transported from further afield, it too may have been collected locally from derived sources. Less likely to be local are the few fragments of ground flint axes; these were presumably brought in as complete artefacts from elsewhere and, once broken, were recycled as minor but useful sources of 'quality assured' flint.

The bulk of the assemblage was in good condition, though the number of broken flakes and blades indicated that it had been reworked by a range of cultural and post-depositional processes, including presumably trampling by people and animals. In this it is consistent with other inner London assemblages on Thorney Island, Westminster (Thomas et al in prep). The amount of recortication varied from site to site, but cannot usually be taken as an indicator of date. At certain sites

such as Whites Grounds, however, it was noticeable that the assemblage could be divided into patinated blades and non-patinated flakes. Even notionally contemporary assemblages provided considerable variation: less than 5% of the large B&Q site assemblage had been patinated, compared with some 50% of the Marlborough Grove assemblage (Lewis 1994b, 10), for instance. A few burnt pieces were present on most sites, and included both worked and unworked flint, though the latter was not always retained for analysis.

Table 4 provides a summary of the material recovered. From this the numerical importance of the B&Q site is readily apparent. Only seven other sites have produced more than 200 flints (to which number can be added Hopton Street, excavated by Pre-Construct Archaeology (Bishop 1996; Ridgeway 1999) while only a further six have produced more than 100.

These factors notwithstanding, certain broad trends can be identified. Firstly, there are some notable concentrations of sites producing struck flint. These tended to cluster in the areas adjacent to the Bermondsey Lake, on certain higher points of the north Southwark sand islands including Horselydown and around Waterloo Station in north Lambeth further west. Secondly, closer inspection of the lithic material itself indicated that debitage was numerically dominant, followed by retouched tools and tool waste. A majority of the debitage was composed of complete and fragmentary flakes, with fewer blades. Cores included a large number of opportunistically tested nodules, though the expected one-, two- and multi-platform types were also present. Core preparation flakes were not recorded for the majority of the sites, but they were certainly present and encompassed both core tablets and various types of rejuvenation flakes. Crested pieces were few, but examples were recorded from Guy's Hospital (GAZ 121), the B&Q site and Marlborough Grove.

As might be expected, scrapers dominated the retouched pieces, followed by microliths and arrowheads. The B&Q site aside, microburins (waste by-products from the manufacture of microliths) were hardly represented (a single example from Waterloo, WSB90). Core tools, in the form of adzes and axes, were also few and represented mainly by sharpening and other flakes, though a single complete chipped flint axe was recovered from the lacustrine silts at Bricklayers Arms. Other tool types were restricted in range and quantity but included a series of flake knives and serrates, with smaller numbers of notched pieces, hammerstones, plano-convex knives and a single fabricator. Post-prehistoric flint working is represented by a handful of gunflints and by several groups of large fresh flakes resulting from the dressing of flint for building purposes.

The *in situ* assemblages from the B&Q site (GAZ 208) and Marlborough Grove (GAZ 204)

Introduction

This section of the report summarises the lithic assemblages recovered from the excavations carried out at the B&Q site (Rogers 1990) and Marlborough Grove (Bruce 1994) 200m to

Table 4 Lithics summary

Type / Site	GAZ no.	Cores	Micro-liths	Micro-burins	Adze-sharpening flakes	Adze frags	Chipped axe	Pol axe flakes	Scrapers	Arrow-heads	Flake/blade knives	Plano-convex knives
King's Head Yard	115	–	–	–	–	–	–	–	1	1	1	–
Toppings & Sun Wharves	132	–	–	–	–	–	–	–	1	–	–	–
180–196 Long Lane	139	–	–	–	–	–	–	–	–	–	–	–
4–10 Lower Marsh Rd	48	–	–	–	–	–	–	–	2	1	–	–
Lambeth Palace kitchen gardens	27	1	–	–	–	–	–	–	4	–	–	–
Lambeth Palace North gardens	28	2	–	–	–	1	–	2	3	3	1	–
5 South Lambeth Rd	15	–	–	–	–	–	–	–	1	–	1	–
Lower Marsh, Lambeth	39	1	–	–	–	–	–	–	–	1	–	–
170–176 Grange Rd	–	–	–	–	–	–	–	–	2	–	–	–
Coronation Buildings	9	1	–	–	1	–	–	–	1	–	–	–
36–48 Albert Embankment	11	–	–	–	–	–	–	–	–	–	–	–
99–101 Waterloo Rd	47	–	–	–	–	–	–	–	1	–	–	–
Norfolk House	25	–	–	–	–	–	–	–	1?	–	–	–
29 Addington St, Lambeth	34	4	1	1	–	–	–	–	3	–	1	–
Addington St, Lambeth	33	7	8	–	–	–	–	–	4	1	1	–
Upper Marsh St, Lambeth	35	–	–	–	–	–	–	–	–	–	–	–
41–45 Grange Walk	–	–	–	–	–	–	–	–	–	–	–	–
Swan St	78	–	–	–	–	–	–	–	–	–	–	–
Chaucer House	110	–	–	–	–	–	–	–	2	–	–	–
15–23 Southwark St	91	6	3	–	1	–	–	–	21	1	5	–
Copperfield St	58	–	–	–	–	–	–	–	–	–	–	–
Courage's Brewery (COSE84)	81	–	–	–	–	–	–	–	1	–	–	–
Courage's Brewery (CSW85)	81	–	–	–	–	–	–	–	–	–	–	–
Courage's Brewery (CO87)	81	1	–	–	–	–	–	1	2	–	1	1
Courage's Brewery (CO88)	81	1	–	–	1	–	–	–	3	1	2	–
Courage's Brewery (CO89)	81	–	–	–	–	–	–	–	–	1	–	–
84 Borough High St	95	–	–	–	–	–	–	–	–	–	–	–
106 Borough High St	90	1	–	–	–	–	–	–	–	–	–	–
120 Borough High St	89	1	–	–	–	–	–	–	1	–	–	–
124 Borough High St	89	–	–	–	–	–	–	–	–	–	–	–
175 Borough High St	94	–	–	–	–	–	–	–	–	–	–	–
179 Borough High St	97	–	–	–	–	–	–	–	–	1	–	–
199 Borough High St	93	2	–	–	–	–	–	–	–	–	–	–
201–211 Borough High St	88	1	–	–	–	–	–	–	–	–	–	–
289 Borough High St	73	–	–	–	–	–	–	–	–	1?	–	–
London Bridge Station	131	–	–	–	–	–	–	–	–	–	–	–
Arcadia Buildings	96	–	–	–	–	–	–	–	–	1	–	–
Harper Rd	77	–	–	–	–	–	–	–	–	–	–	–
Silvester Buildings	92	1	–	–	–	–	–	–	–	–	–	–
Tooley St, District Heating Scheme	135	–	–	–	–	–	–	–	–	–	–	–
Guy's Hospital	120	–	–	–	–	–	–	–	–	–	–	–
1–7 St Thomas St	117	1	–	–	–	–	–	–	–	–	–	–
Fennings Wharf	130	1	–	–	1	–	–	–	2	–	–	–
Bermondsey Abbey	159	4	1	–	1	–	–	–	5	3	2	–
Bricklayers Arms	191	–	–	–	–	–	1	1	–	–	–	–
Cherry Garden Pier	211	–	–	–	–	–	–	–	–	–	–	–
Whites Grounds	155	4	1	–	–	–	–	1	–	–	1	–
Queen Elizabeth St South	188	1	–	–	–	–	–	–	–	–	–	–
Rupack St	216	–	–	–	–	–	–	–	–	–	–	–
Skinmarket Place	65	–	–	–	–	–	–	1	–	–	–	–
Phoenix Wharf	189	17	–	–	–	–	–	–	4	–	1	1
Wolseley St	199	4	–	–	–	–	–	–	1	–	–	–
Lafone St	179	–	–	–	1	1	–	–	–	1?	1	–
Phoenix Wharf	189	1	–	–	–	–	–	–	2	–	1	–
74–90 Weston St	140	–	–	–	–	–	–	–	–	–	–	–
B&Q	208	60	18	16	3	–	–	–	24	1	1	–
281–345 Old Kent Rd	174	3	–	–	–	–	–	–	1	–	1	–
6–14 Leroy St	147	–	–	–	–	–	–	–	–	–	–	–
Leroy St/rear of Old Kent Rd	143	–	–	–	–	–	–	–	–	–	–	–
Culling Rd	214	–	–	–	–	–	–	–	–	–	–	–
Humphrey St	184	1	–	–	–	–	–	–	–	–	–	–
Marlborough Grove	204	8	4	–	1	1	–	–	2	–	–	–
Bartholomew St	133	–	–	–	–	–	–	–	–	–	–	–
Old Kent Rd/Dunton Way	177	–	–	–	–	–	–	–	–	1	–	–
Totals		135	36	17	10	3	1	6	96	18	21	2

Burins/spalls	Serrates	Awls	Fabricator	Composite tool	Notched piece	Utilised flakes/blades	Hammerstone/rubber	Gunflints	Other	Debitage	Total	Type
												Site
–	–	1	–	–	–	–	–	–	–	–	4	King's Head Yard
–	–	–	–	–	1	–	–	–	–	25	27	Toppings & Sun Wharves
–	–	–	–	–	–	–	–	–	–	3	3	180–196 Long Lane
–	–	–	–	–	–	–	–	–	–	217	220	4–10 Lower Marsh Rd
–	–	–	–	–	1	–	–	–	–	63	69	Lambeth Palace kitchen gardens
–	–	–	–	–	2	–	1	–	–	222	237	Lambeth Palace North gardens
–	–	–	–	–	–	–	–	–	–	10	12	5 South Lambeth Rd
–	–	–	–	–	–	–	–	–	–	34	36	Lower Marsh, Lambeth
–	–	–	–	–	–	–	–	–	–	3	5	170–176 Grange Rd
–	–	–	–	–	–	–	–	–	–	45	48	Coronation Buildings
–	–	–	–	–	–	–	–	–	–	15	15	36–48 Albert Embankment
–	–	–	–	–	–	–	–	–	–	2	3	99–101 Waterloo Rd
–	–	–	–	–	–	–	–	–	–	13	14	Norfolk House
–	–	–	–	–	–	–	–	–	–	272	282	29 Addington St, Lambeth
1	–	–	–	–	–	–	–	–	–	417	439	Addington St, Lambeth
–	–	–	–	–	–	–	–	–	–	40	40	Upper Marsh St, Lambeth
–	–	–	–	–	–	–	–	–	–	1	1	41–45 Grange Walk
–	–	–	–	–	–	–	–	–	–	1	1	Swan St
–	–	1?	–	–	–	–	–	–	–	16	19	Chaucer House
–	–	1	–	–	–	5	–	–	–	317	360	15–23 Southwark St
–	–	–	–	–	–	–	–	–	–	2	2	Copperfield St
–	–	–	–	–	–	–	–	–	–	9	10	Courage's Brewery (COSE84)
–	–	–	–	–	–	–	–	–	–	21	21	Courage's Brewery (CSW85)
–	–	–	1	–	–	–	–	–	–	48	56	Courage's Brewery (CO87)
–	–	–	–	–	1	–	–	–	–	177	186	Courage's Brewery (CO88)
–	–	–	–	–	–	–	–	1	–	20	22	Courage's Brewery (CO89)
–	–	–	–	–	–	–	–	–	–	8	8	84 Borough High St
–	–	1	–	–	–	–	–	–	–	28	30	106 Borough High St
–	–	–	–	–	–	–	–	–	–	25	27	120 Borough High St
–	–	–	–	–	–	–	–	–	–	82	82	124 Borough High St
–	–	–	–	–	–	–	–	–	–	1	1	175 Borough High St
–	–	–	–	–	–	–	–	–	–	–	1	179 Borough High St
–	–	–	–	–	–	–	–	–	–	21	23	199 Borough High St
–	–	–	–	–	–	–	–	–	–	25	26	201–211 Borough High St
–	–	–	–	–	–	–	–	–	–	–	1	289 Borough High St
–	–	–	–	–	–	–	–	–	–	7	7	London Bridge Station
1?	–	–	–	–	–	–	–	–	–	34	36	Arcadia Buildings
–	–	–	–	–	–	–	–	–	–	4	4	Harper Rd
–	–	–	–	–	–	–	–	–	–	2	3	Silvester Buildings
–	–	–	–	–	–	–	–	–	–	5	5	Tooley St, District Heating Scheme
–	–	–	–	–	–	–	–	–	1	9	10	Guy's Hospital
–	–	–	–	–	–	–	–	–	–	5	6	1–7 St Thomas St
–	–	–	–	–	–	–	–	–	–	123	127	Fennings Wharf
–	5	–	–	–	–	1	–	1	–	254	277	Bermondsey Abbey
–	–	–	–	–	–	–	–	–	–	9	11	Bricklayers Arms
–	–	–	–	–	–	–	–	–	–	1	1	Cherry Garden Pier
–	–	–	–	–	–	–	–	–	–	132	139	Whites Grounds
–	–	–	–	1	–	–	–	–	–	45	46	Queen Elizabeth St South
–	–	–	–	–	–	–	–	–	–	1	1	Rupack St
–	–	–	–	–	–	–	–	–	–	–	1	Skinmarket Place
–	–	1	–	–	–	–	–	–	–	58	82	Phoenix Wharf
–	–	–	–	–	–	–	–	–	–	70	75	Wolseley St
–	–	–	–	–	–	–	–	–	–	36	40	Lafone St
–	–	–	–	–	–	–	–	–	–	107	111	Phoenix Wharf
–	–	–	–	–	–	–	–	–	–	3	3	74–90 Weston St
22	1	6	–	–	1	4	4	–	4	1684	1849	B&Q
–	–	–	–	–	–	–	–	–	–	151	156	281–345 Old Kent Rd
–	–	–	–	–	–	–	–	–	–	23	23	6–14 Leroy St
–	–	–	–	–	–	–	–	–	–	1	1	Leroy St/rear of Old Kent Rd
–	–	–	–	–	–	–	–	–	–	30	30	Culling Rd
–	–	–	–	–	–	–	–	–	–	10	10	Humphrey St
–	2	–	–	–	–	12	1	–	2	222	255	Marlborough Grove
–	–	–	–	–	–	–	–	–	–	11	11	Bartholomew St
–	–	–	–	–	–	–	–	1	–	11	12	Old Kent Rd/Dunton Way
24	**8**	**11**	**1**	**1**	**6**	**22**	**6**	**3**	**7**	**5234**	**5663**	**Totals**

the north. The Marlborough Grove flint assemblage was recorded by John Lewis (1994b) and the B&Q site flint assemblages by the present writer.

The material from B&Q was recovered during a five-month campaign of fieldwork conducted between March and August 1990. This involved an initial six-week evaluation of five trenches (A–E), followed by a 14-week excavation centred on two lithic scatters located some 40m apart in trenches B and C. In all, 98m^2 were excavated in trench B and 56m^2 in trench C. Flint densities per m^2 varied between 1 and 102 in trench B (average 22.6) and 1 and 25 in trench C (average 5).

The material from Marlborough Grove was recovered during a five-day evaluation conducted in late November and early December 1993 with a subsequent two-week excavation in late January and early February 1994. Only 11m^2 were excavated: 8m^2 in trench C and 1m^2 in each of trenches D, E and F. Flint densities per m^2 varied between 14 and 32 in trench B (average 23). The same on-site recording procedures as at the B&Q site were followed, the latter having been based on those developed for use at Three Ways Wharf, Uxbridge (Lewis 1991 and in prep).

Methodology

Each piece of struck flint from the three assemblages was examined and classified according to the system devised by Andrew David for work at Seamer Carr in the Vale of Pickering, Yorkshire, and adopted and modified by John Lewis for use on the Three Ways Wharf, Uxbridge, assemblages (Lewis 1991 and in prep). Artefacts were classified by type (eg long scraper, short scraper), with each type forming part of a group of similar types (eg scrapers). The length, breadth and thickness of each piece was measured and stored in an Oracle file lodged with the site archive. Other fields were used to record qualitative variables such as: raw material, colour, patination, extent of dorsal cortex, completeness, hammer stroke, and butt type.

The flint assemblage

In total there were 1849 artefacts assemblage from the B&Q site: 18 from trench A; 1588 from trench B; 242 from trench C and 1 from trench D. That from Marlborough Grove comprised 255 artefacts. In addition, a number of unworked nodules and pebbles were recovered from the B&Q site trench C and from Marlborough Grove. Table 5 sets out the quantities of artefacts recovered from the B&Q site trenches B and C and Marlborough Grove by groups of types, and provides the basis for the necessarily brief discussion that follows. The approach adopted is that originally advocated by Lewis (1994b, 8–21) in his consideration of the Marlborough Grove assemblage, which was itself based on the earlier work he had conducted at Three Ways Wharf, Uxbridge. It focuses on the similarities and differences between the three individual assemblages rather than on details of typology and highlights the refitting and microwear studies carried out on the B&Q material.

The report is based on two main assumptions, neither of which is beyond challenge. Firstly, it is assumed that a majority of the pieces within the three spatially discrete assemblages from the B&Q site trenches B and C and Marlborough Grove are at least broadly contemporary and predominantly of earlier Mesolithic type (but see below), the presence of a single Neolithic leaf arrowhead from B&Q trench C notwithstanding. This assumption has been based on a comparison of overall 'feel' and assemblage composition, on a close examination of the small (but admittedly largely broken) microlith population and on the application of statistical analyses such as the Kolmogrov-Smirnov 2 Sample test (method as quoted in Shennan 1997, 57–61; Peter Rauxloh pers comm). Variations are here taken to reflect differences of function/activity rather than chronology.

Secondly, examination of the distributions of burnt worked and burnt unworked flint within the B&Q site trench B has suggested the former presence of two hearth areas, referred to below as the 'northern' and 'southern' hearths. These were some 6m or 7m apart and appear to have acted as twin foci for a wide range of activities conducted around them. Unfortunately it has not proved possible to say whether or not these hearths were in contemporary or successive use; the suspicion remains that they may represent seasonal reoccupations of the same favoured place in the local landscape. In crude numerical terms, a majority of the struck flint within trench B was centred on the northern hearth, with a more diffuse scatter around the southern. No attempt has been made to reflect these subtle distinctions in Table 5.

Artefact distribution

Excavation of 0.05m spits within 1m squares allowed good control to be maintained over the three-dimensional recording of the assemblages (Fig 48). In all three cases a majority of the flints occurred close to the top of the sediments overlying the terrace gravels. There was relatively little vertical dispersal down the profile, although the evidence from the microwear and the refitting exercise indicates that some such movement had indeed taken place. However, it is suggested here that the artefacts are largely *in situ* and that the top of the artefact bearing layer may represent a weathered Early Holocene palaeo-landsurface (as Lewis 1994b, 18).

The horizontal distribution of the artefacts at Marlborough Grove and, to a lesser extent, the B&Q site trench C is difficult to interpret, as neither produced large numbers of finds. Both could lie on the fringes of higher density scatters or simply represent a relatively low level of activity within the contemporary Early Holocene landscape. (The presence on both sites of numbers of unworked and partially worked flint nodules is returned to later.) The situation in the B&Q site trench B, 40m or so to the south of trench C, is very different, however. Here relatively large numbers of flints were recorded, apparently focused on two hearth areas (see above) situated towards the western edge of the excavation. This density allowed the distribution of individual artefact types to be

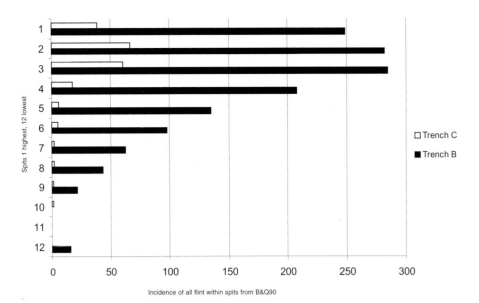

Spits 1 highest, 12 lowest

Incidence of all flint within spits from B&Q90

Fig 48 Vertical distribution of flints by spit

☐ Trench C

■ Trench B

plotted and discussed in the various sections below with a reasonable degree of confidence. Furthermore, preferential use of different coloured flint was also noted, with grey-brown material (and possibly also the few pieces of Chalk-derived flint) focused on the northern hearth, and yellow-brown flint more widely dispersed. However, space has precluded discussion of the full implications of this matter here.

Debitage (groups 8–17)

The figures for the total unmodified component of the assemblages were in excess of 90% in all cases, rising to over 96% for the B&Q site trench B (the largest of the three). The bulk of the debitage was made up of complete and fragmentary flakes followed, in descending order of magnitude, by blades and blade fragments, core preparation flakes, spalls, cores and core fragments, with smaller percentages (ie <1%) of tool debitage such as microburins, burin spalls and axe/adze sharpening flakes. The one notable exception here was the relatively large number of unworked and partially worked nodules recorded from the B&Q site trench C (41 and 9 respectively) and Marlborough Grove (97 and 19), and the few such pieces recorded from the B&Q site trench B (0 and 14), a point returned to below.

Flakes and blades (groups 9 and 10)

All three assemblages contained a high proportion of broken and edge-damaged flakes and blades, attributable both to knapping failures and/or deliberate breakages, and to post-depositional processes. This was particularly marked in the blade category, where broken pieces comprised close on 70% of all three populations. Broken flakes were less common in the B&Q site trench C (32% of all flakes, as opposed to 50% from trench B and Marlborough Grove). It is just possible that the presence of Roman Watling Street shielded this assemblage from later disturbance, though the percentage of broken blades

was consistent with the other two assemblages. A clear majority of the complete flakes in all three assemblages were of tertiary form, with fewer secondary flakes and only the occasional primary flake. A number of different flake/blade butt types were recorded, although plain and punctiform types dominated. Hard and soft hammer techniques were used, with soft hammer preferred for blade production.

Table 5 Quantification of struck flint from the B&Q site (trenches B and C) and Marlborough Grove

Group		B&Q trench B	% of total	B&Q trench C	% of total	Marlbo-rough Grove	% of total
0	Unassigned	5	0.3	–	–	–	–
1	Microliths	15	0.9	3	1.23	4	1.5
2	Scrapers	23	1.4	1	0.4	2	0.75
3	Serrates	1	0.06	–	–	2	0.75
4	Burins	10	0.6	–	–	–	–
6	Multiple tools/awls	3	0.18	3	1.23	1	0.5
7	Retouched pieces	1	0.06	2	0.8	12	4.5
83	Leaf arrowhead	–	–	1	0.4	–	–
Subtotal		**58**	**3.34**	**10**	**4.13**	**21**	**8**
8	Utilised pieces	–	–	1	0.4	2	0.75
9	Flakes/frags	731	46	152	62.8	121	47.5
10	Blades/frags	548	34.5	40	16.5	75	29.5
11	Core prep flakes blades & tablets	89	5.6	10	4.1	7	2.75
12	Cores & fragments	53	3.3	6	2.47	8	3
13	Microburins	15	0.9	1	0.4	–	–
14	Burin spalls	10	0.6	2	0.8	–	–
15	Partially worked nodules	14	0.88	9	3.7	19	7.5
16	Spalls	63	3.9	11	4.5	–	–
17	Axe/adze sharp/thin flakes	3	0.18	–	–	2	1
Subtotal		**1526**	**96.1**	**232**	**95.8**	**234**	**91.4**
18	Hammerstones & rubbers	4	0.25	–	–	1	0.5
Total assemblage		**1588**	**100**	**242**	**100**	**256**	**100**

Cores, core-preparation flakes and unworked and partially worked nodules (groups 11, 12, 15)

Core maintenance and reduction was most clearly represented in the large assemblage from the B&Q site trench B. Here there was a marked preference for single-platform cores, with 22 of the 31 complete examples of this type. The remainder comprised two- and multi-platform types. Core preparation and maintenance flakes formed over 5% of the total assemblage from trench B, and were made up of 68 edge and edge/platform rejuvenators, 17 tablets and 4 crested pieces. However, unworked and tested/partially worked nodules appeared to be proportionately fewer here than in both of the other assemblages, where 'caching' and initial quartering of suitable raw material may have been undertaken.

Tool debitage (groups 13, 14, 17)

This apparent dichotomy between the B&Q site trench B and the smaller assemblages from the B&Q site trench C and Marlborough Grove is manifested in other ways too, most notably in the presence within the former of a higher number of tool categories, complete and broken tools and debitage relating to tool manufacture.

Tool debitage comprises microburins, burin spalls and adze-sharpening/thinning flakes. No microburins or burin spalls were recorded at Marlborough Grove, and few from the B&Q site trench C. Of the 15 microburins from the B&Q site trench B, 12 were complete, with 3 mis-hits. None of the microburins could be joined with any of the microliths, despite overlapping distributions centring on the northern hearth area. An adze-sharpening flake and a possible thinning flake were recovered from Marlborough Grove; two of the three adze-sharpeners from the B&Q site trench B lay immediately to the east of the southern hearth area (the third was unlocated within the same trench).

Hammerstones/rubbers (group 18)

In all, five hammerstones or rubbers were recorded, four of which were composed of cobbles of quartzite or micaceous sandstone. All four of the examples from the B&Q site trench B (three of quartzite and one of flint) were centred on the southern hearth area, with the three quartzite pieces lying on its west or south-west side.

Retouched pieces (groups 1–7 and type 83)

The figures for retouched pieces varied between 8% for Marlborough Grove and just over 3% for the B&Q site trenches B and C. The high percentage figure for the former may be explained by the small size of the sample (Lewis 1994b, 13), and by the number of miscellaneously retouched pieces. Subtraction of the latter brings the percentage figure wholly into line with the others. As might be expected, scrapers make up the bulk of the retouched tool category, followed by microliths and burins.

Scrapers (group 2)

The largest number of scrapers were recovered from B&Q site trench B (Fig 49). Here 12 of the 23 pieces were endscrapers worked on short flakes; 7 were worked on blades, and there were 3 fragmentary pieces with one atypical form. The scrapers were distributed around the northern and north-eastern sides of the hearth areas, and microwear analysis clearly indicates that the majority were being used on dry hides (see Donahue, this volume). Only two scrapers were recovered from Marlborough Grove, of which one was complete. Both comprised endscrapers on short flakes.

Microliths (group 1)

A total of 22 microliths were recovered from the three assemblages: 15 from the B&Q site trench B; 3 from B&Q trench C; and 4 from Marlborough Grove. Of these, only 5 can be considered complete: 3 from B&Q trench B and one each from B&Q trench C and Marlborough Grove. However, 13 of the other 17 pieces are complete enough to be broadly classified according to the scheme proposed by Clark (1934), since modified by Jacobi (1976) and others. The available data are presented in Table 6.

From Table 6 it can be shown that 13 of the points are likely to belong to Clark's type A (obliquely blunted points) (1934, 54); 3 to his type B (microliths); and 2 to his type D (geometric points). Although not conclusive, the preponderance of type A points is suggestive of an earlier Mesolithic date. Furthermore, the narrowness of many of the pieces suggest that the bulk of the microlith population conforms with Reynier's so-called 'Deepcar' type, currently thought to post-date c 8500–7700 cal BC (Reynier 1998, 174–5) The presence of several D types is more problematical. One of these <8403> comprises a fine isosceles point with inverse retouch at its distal tip that would not be out of place in an Early Mesolithic assemblage. The other <12>, however, is either a diminutive narrow rhomboid or scalene point and therefore clearly a Late Mesolithic form. As such it points to a Late Mesolithic presence in the locality, though what proportion (if any) of the remainder of the assemblage(s) are of this date cannot be readily determined.

Microwear analysis carried out on a number of the B&Q pieces (including the Late Mesolithic point just discussed) identified distal impact fractures, which tends to confirm the traditional assumption that these pieces functioned as armatures for arrows. Furthermore, three or four of the points had been burnt, possibly during the cooking of carcasses in which they had lodged.

Burins (group 4)

The few burins were confined to B&Q trench B, and were mostly represented by fragments. There was one dihedral burin, with others manufactured on breaks or truncations. Microwear analysis demonstrated that one of the latter

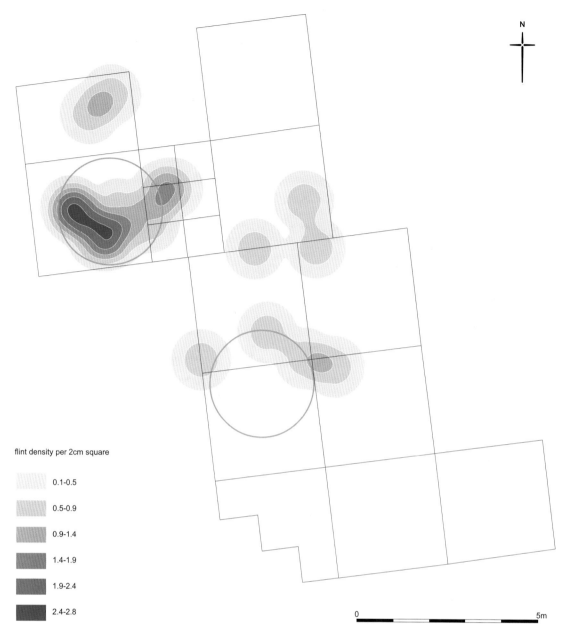

flint density per 2cm square

0.1-0.5

0.5-0.9

0.9-1.4

1.4-1.9

1.9-2.4

2.4-2.8

0   5m

Fig 49 Scraper density plot (scale 1:100)

retained use traces consistent with antler graving and working (see Donahue, below) and that another had been used on hide.

Serrates (group 3)

Three blades display minute notches along their lateral edges and may be classed as microdenticulates or serrates. Of these, two were from Marlborough Grove, and the third from B&Q trench B. This latter piece is of particular interest, in that microwear analysis has identified traces of its having been used to cut silica-rich herbaceous plant fibre. Although there is every reason to suppose that plant gathering and processing formed an integral part of the activities likely to have been undertaken, this piece was recovered early in the excavation (context 6) and its stratigraphic integrity is therefore open to question.

Leaf arrowhead

A single bifacially worked leaf arrowhead was recovered from B&Q trench C, spit 6. In the absence of any other obviously earlier Neolithic material in the assemblage, its position deep within the sediments sealed beneath Roman Watling Street is currently difficult to explain, but it is here assumed to be intrusive. The presence of at least one Late Mesolithic microlith from the same area (see above) bears testimony to the importance that the Bermondsey/Bramcote lake margin presumably continued to exert. Microwear analysis indicated that the arrowhead had sustained an impact fracture.

Refitting work at the B&Q site

A modest refitting exercise was undertaken at the B&Q site focusing on the two areas in trench B in which the notional

Table 6 Microliths from the B&Q site trenches B and C and Marlborough Grove (* denotes microwear impact fracture)

Site	Accession no.	Spit no.	Context	Complete?	Burnt?	Clark form	Jacobi form	Length (mm)	Breadth (mm)	Thickness (mm)
B&Q B	<4126>	3	[275]	proximal tip	y	A1?	1a?	18	12	2.5
B&Q B	<1728>	2	[283]	?proximal tip	y	A2?	1a?	23	7	3
B&Q B	<4245>	–	[275]	proximal tip	y	A1?	1a?	18	8	1.5
B&Q B	<1907>	1	[283]	y*	n	B	5a/12a	19	4.5	2.5
B&Q B	<4500>	6	–	segment	n	–	–	9	4	3
B&Q B	<4271>	–	[275]	proximal tip	n	A2?	1bc	17	5	1.5
B&Q B	<4459>	8	[275]	distal tip	n	A2?	1ac	21.5	12	3
B&Q B	<4836>	6	[275]	segment*	n	B?	5a/12a	20	7	1.5
B&Q B	<6251>	1	[283]	proximal tip	n	A1?	1a?	19	7	2
B&Q B	<7305>	2	[276]	segment	n	–	–	19	7	2
B&Q B	<8227>	5	[275]	proximal tip	n	B	5a/12a	29	7	3
B&Q B	<4926>	–	[275]	proximal tip	n	A1?	1a?	21	7	2
B&Q B	<8403>	1	[275]	y	n	Da	2a	35	10	4
B&Q B	<7559>	2	[276]	proximal tip*	n	A1?	1a?	25	6	2
B&Q B	<4650>	–	[275]	y*	n	A2	1ac	31	8	2.5
B&Q C	<35>	–	[25]	distal tip	y?	A?	1a?	26	12	3
B&Q C	<12>	–	[23]	y?*	n	D7?	7a2?	19	4	1
MAG	<395>	–	–	y	n	A1	1a	30	7	2
MAG	<138>	–	–	n	n	A	1	–	–	–
MAG	<218>	–	–	n	n	A	1	–	–	–
MAG	–	–	–	tip	n	–	–	–	–	–

hearths were sited (squares 4000 and 1000). A further but more limited search in trench C (squares 1000, 2000 and 4000) located several further straight conjoins and potential nodule linkages but this work is not reported on here. In Barton's words, refitting 'allows a strong relationship to be established between the manufacturing process and the pattern of artefact discard' (Barton 1992, 21). It also allows some comment to be made on the nature and extent of post-depositional movement of individual flints within the sediment body. Initial results from the northern hearth area in trench B (square 4000) were not promising, with one straight conjoining blade from the same 1m square (spit 9), together with several possible nodule linkages (but no actual refits).

The single refit identified in trench B, square 4000 is as follows:

<408>, spit 9→<0411>, spit 9

The nodule linkages from trench B, square 4000 are as follows:

<4287>, spit 5 ?→<4396>, spit 8
<4335>, spit 4 ?→<4317>

Work on the flint from the southern hearth area in trench B (square 1000) was more successful, in that it was possible to focus on a series of large secondary flakes and cores of visually similar mottled orange-brown flint with smooth off-white/buff cortex. A number of straight conjoins and dorsal-ventral refits were quickly established, including a small refitting group of four pieces comprising a core with three flakes, and it is clear that further concentrated work would locate others.

The refits from trench B, square 1000 can be summarised as follows:

<7959>, spit 2
<1416>, spit 5

<1204>, spit 1→<7155>, spit 1
<1220>, spit 3→<1865>, spit 5
<1404>, spit 4→<1507>, spit 2
<1928>, spit 3→<2705>, spit 1
<1910>, spit 2→<5610>, spit 1
<7805>, spit 2→<7809>, spit 3 (burnt)
<1520>, spit 3→<0106>

The data summarised above support the picture of a generally in situ lithic assemblage in the B&Q site trench B. However, the linkages established across various spits confirm that some post-depositional movement has taken place within the sediments, which in turn corroborates the results obtained from the microwear study (see Donahue, below). The refits from the southern hearth area also furnish several far-flung linkages, one in excess of 7m and a second in excess of 5m. These are much more likely to be of cultural origin as opposed to post-depositional movement.

Discussion

The excavations conducted around the edge of the Bermondsey Lake have revealed the best evidence for hunter-gatherer activity within central London as a whole. Detailed study of the flint assemblages suggests that they can be compared with the other, larger, early assemblages recovered from West Heath, Hampstead (Collins and Lorimer 1989), and Three Ways Wharf, Uxbridge, Scatter C west (Lewis 1991 and in prep). On the basis of their microlith populations, all of these sites appear to conform with Reynier's 'Deepcar' type river valley assemblages thought to have developed after c 8500 cal BC (Reynier 1998, 174–5).

A preliminary comparison of blade lengths/breadths from B&Q trenches B and C, Marlborough Grove and Three Ways Wharf Scatter C was carried out using the Kolmogrov-Smirnov 2 Sample test. The aim of this exercise was to determine the contemporaneity or otherwise of the four assemblages. In the event the results were inconclusive. They indicated that the assemblages from the B&Q site trench C and Marlborough Grove were similar in terms of blade length and, to a slightly lesser extent, in terms of blade breadth. By the same token, the blades from B&Q trench B and Marlborough Grove appeared to be much more dissimilar in both length and breadth. B&Q trenches B and C appeared similar in terms of blade length but were dissimilar in terms of breadth. Furthermore, comparison of B&Q trench B and Three Ways Wharf Scatter C showed that the two assemblages could not reasonably be expected to have come from the same population, ie they were certainly different. In retrospect, this latter observation was entirely predictable, in that the eastern area of Three Ways Wharf Scatter C is now known to belong within the currency of 'long-blade' assemblages, which pre-date the true Early Mesolithic (John Lewis, pers comm). Less predictable was the separation of the B&Q site trench B from B&Q trench C/Marlborough Grove. It may be that this is a reflection of differences in blade population size, though equally it could point to differences in date and/or function. Given the presence of small numbers of Early Mesolithic type A microliths in all three assemblages, the latter possibility is preferred here. Nevertheless, the presence of a Late Mesolithic microlith (and of a Neolithic leaf arrowhead) from the B&Q site trench C should be noted, as this strongly suggests successive later reuse of this particular spot.

Study of the assemblage composition from the B&Q site trench B and the identification of two notional hearth settings strongly suggests the presence of a site whose users had adopted a subsistence strategy geared to the hunting and processing of animal game. Processing of plant resources was, typically, less well represented. Furthermore the microwear analysis (see Donahue, below) has usefully enlarged our understanding of the ways in which the various retouched tools were used, and of the long vanished materials (particularly dry hide) on which they had been deployed.

Neolithic and Early Bronze Age arrowheads from Southwark and Lambeth

Seventeen Neolithic and Bronze Age arrowheads of various forms have been recovered during excavations conducted across the study area by MoLAS and its predecessor bodies. To this total may be added the single barbed and tanged example recovered from King's Head Yard by Kathleen Kenyon (1959, fig 37) and four others, one leaf and three transverse forms, recovered from Hopton Street during excavations conducted by Pre-Construct Archaeology (Bishop 1996; 1998; Ridgeway 1999, 72). Table 7 incorporates data on all 21 arrowheads known to the writer.

Discussion

The arrowheads span the known range of Neolithic and Bronze Age types, although meaningful associations are absent. Most appear to have been recovered from the sandy silts over natural, from 'flood clays' or from later contexts. There is

Table 7 Flint arrowheads from Southwark and Lambeth

Site	GAZ no.	Arrowhead type	Context type	Context no./ Accession no.	Condition
Bermondsey Abbey	159	leaf	?residual	–	complete
15–23 Southwark St	91	leaf	residual in Roman context	[26] <2938>	broken, bifacially worked
179 Borough High St	97	leaf	?	?	no details available
B&Q	208	leaf	sands beneath Roman Watling Street	[224] <5701>	complete, bifacially worked (impact fracture)
Hopton St	54	leaf	charcoal-flecked silty sand over natural	[1807] <2120>	broken, bifacially worked
Courage's Brewery (CO88)	81	leaf	flood clay	[6343] <1216>	broken bifacially worked mid section
Lafone St	179	?leaf roughout	Bronze Age 'ploughsoil'	[252]	complete, blade with invasive bifacial retouch
Lambeth Palace North Garden	28	transverse	?'waterlain sand'	[11]	complete, on a flake
Lambeth Palace North Garden	28	?transverse	?'waterlain sand'	[15]	no details available
Arcadia Buildings	96	transverse (Petit Tranchet derivative)	?	?	no details available
Bermondsey Abbey	159	transverse	?residual	[4046]	complete
Hopton St	54	transverse (chisel)	charcoal-flecked silty sand over natural	[1431] <750>	complete, on a flake segment
Hopton St	54	transverse (chisel)	charcoal-flecked silty sand over natural	[1351] <621>	complete, on a flake
Hopton St	54	transverse (oblique)	charcoal-flecked silty sand over natural	[1477] <1088>	complete, on a blade segment
4–10 Lower Marsh	48	single barbed oblique	'waterlain sand'	[50] <2057>	complete, ripple flaked
Lower Marsh	39	triangular	?'waterlain sand'	[3049]	complete, bifacially worked with a natural hole
Addington St, Waterloo	32	triangular		[190]	broken butt, bifacially worked
Courage's Brewery (CO89)	81	?transverse/ triangular		[738]	complete, on flake
Bermondsey Abbey	159	barbed and tanged	?residual	[536]	complete
Lambeth Palace North Garden	28	barbed and tanged	?'waterlain sand'	[11]	complete
King's Head Yard	115	barbed and tanged	'levels immediately overlying the natural sand'		broken tang/barb
289 Borough High St	73	'arrowhead'			no details available

virtually no earlier Neolithic pottery to set alongside the leaf arrowheads, save for a single sherd recovered from the Thames foreshore in front of Chambers Wharf, Bermondsey (Cotton and Wood 1996, 10–12 and fig 7 no. 16) and some dubious scraps from Hopton Street (Gibson 1997). The series of transverse, barbed and tanged and triangular arrowheads is better served, however, with sherds of Peterborough Ware, Beaker and Collared Urn recorded from a number of sites (see Rayner, 6.2). Though not directly associated, the transverse pieces from Hopton Street can be set alongside the small Beaker pottery assemblage recovered from that site. Furthermore, the triangular arrowheads from Lower Marsh and Waterloo C are likely to be broadly contemporary with the sherds of Collared Urn recovered from several other sites in this same area of north Lambeth (see Green 1980, 142–3).

Struck flint from Phoenix Wharf (GAZ 189), Wolseley Street (GAZ 199) and Lafone Street (GAZ 179)

This summary report on the three assemblages has drawn on the original flint assessment reports prepared by Nick Merriman (Phoenix Wharf; Merriman nd a), John Lewis (Wolseley Street; Lewis 1994a) and the present writer (Lafone Street; Cotton 1997). It has not been possible to re-examine the material from Phoenix Wharf. All three sites produced small lithic assemblages, of which those pieces from the soil horizons overlying traces of cross ploughing etched into the natural sands are the most numerous. The total assemblages from the three sites are summarised in Table 8, and detailed breakdowns of the material recovered from the soil horizons are presented in Table 9.

Discussion

The combined size of the three assemblages is clearly still small, yet the bulk of the material (nearly 84%) was recovered from a series of soil horizons sealed by humified peats and alluvium (Table 9). A large proportion of this subset was made up of unretouched flakes and a few blades, nearly 40% of which were broken or had suffered edge damage. This observation is consistent with the interpretation of these horizons as cultivated soils.

Diagnostic finds from these soil horizons were few. The 'plano-convex knife' from Phoenix Wharf is likely to belong within the Late Neolithic/Early Bronze Age, so too the single small scraper from Wolseley Street. Other pieces, for example the leaf arrowhead roughout from Lambeth, could be earlier. On the other hand, the numbers of broad, thick flakes and the high incidence of opportunistic nodule testing at Phoenix Wharf were there interpreted as evidence of Bronze Age activity, perhaps linked to the use of the adjacent cooking pit and burnt mound (Merriman nd a).

Taken together, it is likely that the material recovered from the soil horizons represents earlier episodic use of a locality subsequently disturbed by a series of Bronze Age cultivation phases. As such, it is hardly surprising that a range of artefacts became incorporated in the soils created. The occurrence of an adze butt and an adze-sharpening flake in the humified peats sealing these soils at Lafone Street can also be noted. The presence of these artefacts, usually regarded as Early Holocene, serves to underline the amount of disturbance to which this low-lying area was later subjected and the ease with which notionally earlier finds came to be redistributed across it.

Chronological overview

It remains to provide a brief summary of the lithic evidence, and to place it within its local and regional setting. In so doing it should be pointed out that, despite the casual recovery of the occasional Palaeolithic artefact within the study area in the past (eg Wymer 1968, 278–9; GAZ 3, 10, 44, 46, 222, 224, 227), nothing of this early date was recognised during the work reported on here.

Mesolithic

The earliest material dates to the Mesolithic, and comprises several demonstrably in situ flint assemblages (the B&Q site and Marlborough Grove), together with a scatter of diagnostic pieces such as microliths and adze-sharpening flakes (eg Fig 50). The dating of the in situ scatters relies on a consideration of the retouched microlithic elements yet,

Table 8 *Struck flint from Phoenix Wharf, Wolseley Street and Lafone Street*

Context type	Phoenix Wharf	Wolseley St	Lafone St	Totals
Uncertain/unstratified	3	–	3	6
Channel fills	8	–	–	8
Alluvium	–	–	3	3
Humified peats	2	–	10	12
Soil horizons	69	72	24	165
Fill of ard marks	–	1	–	1
'Contaminated natural'	–	2	–	2
Totals	82	75	40	197

Table 9 *Struck flint from the early soil horizons*

Artefact type	Phoenix Wharf	Wolseley St	Lafone St	Totals
Flakes/spalls	22	25	13	60
Blades	2	4	3	9
Flake/blade fragments	17	35	5	57
Cores/tested nodules	17	4	–	21
Irregular waste	1	–	1	2
Scrapers	4	1	–	5
Flake knives	1	–	1	2
?Plano-convex knife	1	–	–	1
?Leaf arrowhead	–	–	1	1
Awl/borer	1	–	–	1
Utilised/retouched pieces	3	3	–	6
Totals	69	72	24	165

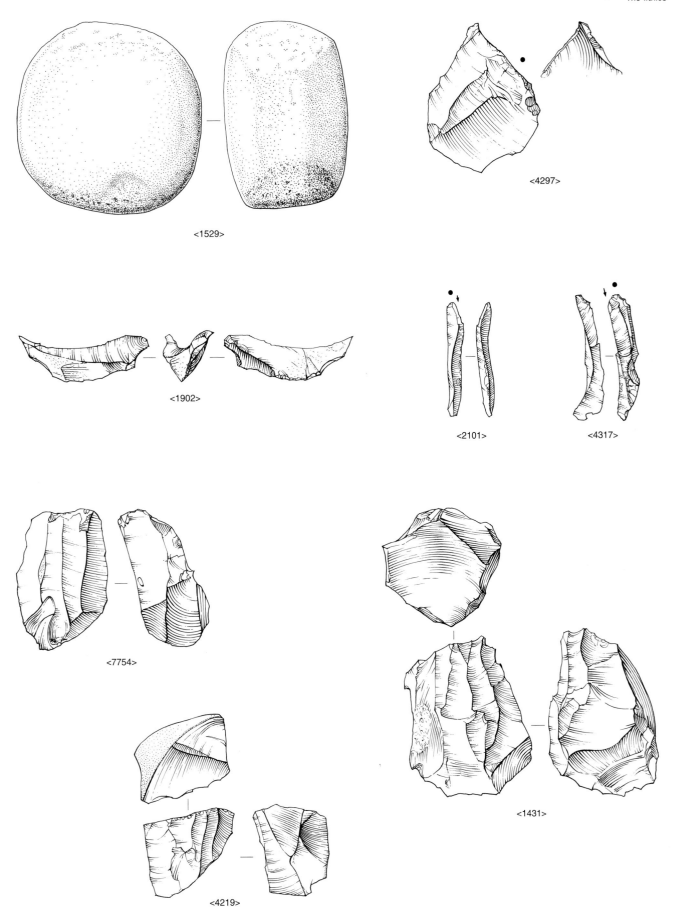

<1529>

<4297>

<1902>

<2101>   <4317>

<7754>

<1431>

<4219>

Fig 50 *Additional flints from B&Q90: hammerstone, adze-sharpening flake, burin spalls and platform cores (scale 2:3)*

as we have seen, the lack of complete pieces makes this difficult to assess. On the slender basis of 13 or so fragmentary points of obliquely backed form, Clark's type A (1934, 54), with 'Deepcar' type affinities, we might suggest an early rather than a late date for the B&Q site and Marlborough Grove assemblages. However, there was clearly a Late Mesolithic presence on the former site as a diminutive point of scalene or possibly rhomboid form, cf Clark's types D1b/D7 (1934, 57–8), demonstrates. Assuming that all three assemblages were broadly contemporary, the presence of unworked and tested/partially worked nodules at B&Q trench C and Marlborough Grove suggests that initial caching and sorting of raw material was taking place away from the notional hearth areas identified in B&Q trench B further south. Microwear analysis has also shown that a number of the points from B&Q had sustained impact damage, presumably through successful use. Moreover, 12 of the 24 scrapers from the site bore traces of dry hide or hide working, while there were single occurrences of meat cutting (blade), hide piercing (truncated blade) antler/bone working (burin) and plant fibre cutting (serrate) (see Donahue, below).

Although relatively small, the Early Mesolithic flint assemblages from the edge of the Bermondsey Lake find several ready parallels within the London region. These include those recovered from sites located high on the sand-capped London Clay at West Heath, Hampstead (Collins and Lorimer 1989), and deep within the valley of the River Colne at Three Ways Wharf, Uxbridge, further west (Lewis 1991, Scatter C (west) and in prep). Taken together, all suggest that foraging strategies geared to the hunting and processing of large animal game had been adopted. Furthermore the presence of numbers of microliths of slender obliquely backed and partially backed form from these sites is of note and suggests that they too conform to the so-called 'Deepcar' type assemblages, currently dated to between c 8500–7700 cal BC (Reynier 1998, 174–5).

Single obliquely backed and bi-truncated Early Mesolithic points from Waterloo (GAZ 34) and Bermondsey Abbey apart (Clark 1934, types A and C1), the remainder of the microliths recovered from the study area hint at episodic Late Mesolithic activity. These comprised a single straight backed bladelet or 'rod' type from Whites Grounds (Jacobi 1976, 16, fig 6 classes 5a, 5b and 6) three points of rod, crescentic and scalene form from Southwark Street (Cotton 1992, 63–5 and fig 17, nos 2–4) together with an important collection of eight small points from Waterloo (GAZ 33). These included four rods, and single points of obliquely backed, scalene, crescentic and asymmetric hollow-based form. The latter piece is of particular interest as it is one of the few so-called 'Horsham' points (Clark 1934, type F) recorded from the London region hitherto. Other finds from Waterloo (GAZ 33) included cores and core-preparation flakes, scrapers and a single burin spall, though not all of these need be of Mesolithic date. Neolithic activity is certainly attested by part of a triangular arrowhead and pottery.

Compared to the early period, the Late Mesolithic is historically poorly represented in the region. However, more recently flint assemblages, including narrow blade geometric microliths, have been recovered from the edge of the terrace gravels at Brookway Allotments, Rainham (Gilman 1993, 205; Pamela Greenwood, pers comm), and within the Thames floodplain at Erith (Taylor 1996). The latter site also produced numbers of adze-sharpening and adze-thinning flakes.

Adze fragments and adze-sharpening flakes are widely scattered across the study area too, though they are not in themselves susceptible to close dating. The sharpening flakes from the B&Q site and Marlborough Grove may belong within the Early Holocene; a majority of the others were recovered from disturbed or demonstrably later contexts (as at Lafone Street). Either way such finds can be compared with the complete adzes recovered from the modern Thames and its foreshore (eg Cotton and Merriman 1991, 38–9 and fig 6 no. 7), many of which have been resharpened by the removal of the characteristic transverse flake.

Earlier Neolithic

Diagnostic Early Neolithic material is limited, and confined to a small series of mostly fragmentary leaf arrowheads, none of which were securely stratified. Doubt surrounds the integrity of the complete example from B&Q trench C, as this may have been an intrusive hunting loss which became incorporated within an early flint scatter (microwear indicates that it had sustained an impact fracture). A handful of flakes from ground flint axes were neither closely datable nor, with one exception, well stratified; they could as easily be assigned to the later Neolithic/Bronze Age as the earlier Neolithic. The exception comprised the blade portion of an axe of unusual mottled grey-green flint reused as a core which was recovered from a sequence of freshwater lake sediments at Bricklayers Arms (GAZ 191) (Merriman nd b; Jones 1991). Ten metres away and within the same deposits was a second complete chipped flint axe of poor quality cherty flint, 168mm in length, weighing 347g. The latter comprised the only complete axe recorded during the work. It can be compared with other complete axes recovered from adjacent stretches of the modern Thames (eg Adkins and Jackson 1978, 67).

Later Neolithic/Bronze Age

Diagnostically Late Neolithic and Bronze Age flint was both more common and better stratified. It includes a series of arrowheads of transverse, barbed and tanged and triangular forms, together with small groups of material recovered from discrete features and early soil horizons. The arrowheads have been considered above. Although not in direct association, the three transverse arrowheads from Hopton Street were found on the same site as a small, predominantly Beaker pottery assemblage (Bishop 1996; Gibson 1997; Ridgeway 1999,

72–4). Several of the triangular arrowheads were recovered from or close to sites in north Lambeth that produced sherds of Collared Urn. Large numbers of transverse arrowheads of various forms have been recovered from other sites within the region, particularly on the higher gravel terraces of west London. Here direct ceramic associations encompass Peterborough and Grooved Ware, but not Beaker or Collared Urn.

Though likely to fall within the Early Bronze Age, the barbed and tanged arrowheads from King's Head Yard, Bermondsey Abbey and Lambeth Palace need not have been the sole prerogative of Beaker users they are often taken to be, as grave associations confirm (eg Needham 1987, 101). However, several small Beaker flint assemblages were present within the study area, including two possible 'placed deposits'. These comprised a flint core and blade buried in a small pit with a complete beaker bowl at Hopton Street (Ridgeway 1999, 73), and a group of sherds and flints including three thumbnail scrapers and a small flake knife from a pit or posthole at Southwark Street (Cotton 1992, 65). Cremated bones apart, no 'placed deposits' were recognised during the excavation of the small ring ditch at Fennings Wharf, and no diagnostic struck flint was recovered from the ditch fills. Finds from other contexts on the site included several scrapers, a core and a large adze-sharpening flake.

Unretouched flakes with wide striking platforms and terminal hinge fractures typical of Bronze Age flint knapping dominate the material recovered from the early soil horizons at Phoenix Wharf, Wolseley Street and Lafone Street. Up to 40% of the assemblage had been broken or suffered edge damage. Tool types were restricted to a single plano-convex knife, five end and end/side scrapers and a borer with an elongated tip, all of which would fit comfortably into a later Neolithic/Bronze Age context. Broad confirmation was provided by two radiocarbon dates: a *terminus post quem* of 1690–1510 cal BC (BM-2766; 3310±40 BP) from an earlier cooking pit at Phoenix Wharf, and a date of 1520–1220 cal BC (Beta-107981; 3100±60 BP) from the soil horizon itself at Lafone Street (Bates and Minkin 1999, 327). The associated ceramics from Phoenix Wharf and Wolseley Street incorporate flint-filled Neolithic and Bronze Age fabric types but are not otherwise diagnostic (see Rayner 6.2; Drummond-Murray 1994, 15); a single grog/sand-filled sherd from Lafone Street may be of Grooved Ware/Collared Urn type.

Post-prehistoric

In addition to the prehistoric use of flint discussed above, several sites produced evidence for its later exploitation. This came in two forms: debitage produced by the dressing of building flint with hard (possibly metal) hammers, and musket- and pistol-sized gunflints.

Dressed building flint was noted at Bermondsey Abbey, Queen Elizabeth Street south, Phoenix Wharf and Norfolk House, and on three of the four sites was probably associated with the construction and maintenance of a series of high status buildings. Single gunflints were recovered from Bermondsey Abbey, Coronation Buildings and the Old Kent Road/Dunton Road and serve to underline the volatile nature of life in the post-medieval borough and its environs. Judged purely on their size, those from Bermondsey Abbey and Old Kent Road/Dunton Road belonged to pistols and that from Coronation Buildings to a musket.

Microwear analysis

Randolph Donahue

Introduction

Lithic microwear analysis is becoming a more frequently used technique in the study of Stone Age sites. While the principal aim of the technique remains the study of stone tool use, it is becoming increasingly apparent that the microscopic study of surface modifications of stone artefacts is providing a far greater range of possible applications, many of which have little to do with tool use (Donahue 1994; 1998; 1999). Lithic microwear analysis of the B&Q site assemblage provides the opportunity to investigate a variety of questions regarding both the prehistoric occupants and the processes that later modified the site.

Lithic microwear analysis is the microscopic examination of surface wear and fracture scars that form along the edges of fine-grain siliceous stone such as flint and chert. Experimental studies demonstrate that microscopic wear and fracture scar characteristics result from tool use and vary systematically according to the worked material (eg, hide, wood, meat, bone) and to the applied forces and motions (eg, cutting, scraping, wedging). The development of principles regarding these relationships permits microwear analysts to infer the past use or uses of lithic artefacts with a greater degree of precision and accuracy than through reliance on either macroscopic attribute analysis or ethnographic analogues of tool form. Natural processes also produce systematic microwear features which can often make inferences about tool use more difficult (Keeley 1980; Levi-Sala 1986a; 1986b), but can aid in the understanding of site formation processes (Donahue 1994; 1998; 1999).

Method

A sample of 94 lithic artefacts was selected for microwear analysis (see Table 10). The sample is biased strongly towards formal tool forms showing little development of white patina. As a result, this is not representative of the entire site assemblage as recovered by the archaeological excavations, but maximises the potential identification of use related wear that has survived the sandy sediments of the site locality. If it can be assumed that the selected tools are representative of the tool types at the site, then one can infer back to the assemblage

Table 10 Artefacts examined for microwear

Accession no.	Spit no.	Type	Edge	Material	Action	Ridge microns	Comments
<8609>	2	microlith		undetermined	undetermined	21	mild post-depositional modification
<5711>	1	blade	lateral	hard	impact	71	mild patina
<8603>	3	endscraper	front	dry hide	scraping	28	mild post-depositional modification
<4538>	3	endscraper	front	dry hide	scraping	28	mild post-depositional modification
<1907>		microlith	tip(s)	undetermined	impact		probably a projectile point
<222>		crest blade		undetermined	undetermined	35	
<4589>	5	side scraper	left	dry hide	scraping		
<448>	8	endscraper	front	undetermined	scraping		minimal use-wear
<4816>	3	backed blade		undetermined	undetermined	57	manufacture damage evident
<1421>	6	burin		undetermined	undetermined	35	much post-depositional damage
<5713>	1	crest blade		undetermined	undetermined	35	many fresh fracture scars
<7771>	4	endscraper	front & opposite	dry hide	scraping	14	unretouched edge is thin and sharp
<3579>	6	endscraper	front	dry hide	scraping	21	lateral edges are undetermined
<6261>	3	endscraper/truncate		undetermined	undetermined	21	much post-depositional modification
<4650>		microlith	tip (distal)	undetermined	impact	21	probably a projectile point
<42/>	6	microburin		unused	unused	7	
<6653>		piercer	projection	soft	undetermined	14	may be hide, but may be post-depositional
<4379>		endscraper		undetermined	undetermined		little wear except post-depositional
<7373>	4	flake		unused	unused	14	retouched edge is fresh
<4576>	5	burin		undetermined	undetermined	21	observed wear is likely post-depositional
<7901>	6	decorticated flake		unused	unused	7	ridge measured from an edge
<4924>		side scraper	left	undetermined	undetermined	14	much plastic deformation
<81>		microburin	distal	hard	impact	35	uncertain if results from use as a projectile point
<1604>	1	burin		undetermined	undetermined	71	much post-depositional wear
<150>		backed blade	distal left	hard	undetermined	28	edge was likely used prior to backing
<6251>		microlith		undetermined	undetermined	57	no evidence of use
<4459>	8	microlith		undetermined	undetermined	28	proximal break is fresh much post-depositional wear
<4297>	6	flake		undetermined	undetermined	21	much post–depositional wear
<8403>	1	microlith		undetermined	undetermined	7	no impact damage much fresh post-depositional modification
<8227>	5	microlith		undetermined	undetermined	7	patina and thermal fracturing
<7559>	2	microlith	tip	undetermined	impact	21	lateral edges may have been used
<4583>	5	blade mid section		undetermined	undetermined	28	used, but much post-depositional modification; proximal snap is fresh
<4271>		microlith		undetermined	undetermined	28	some damage to tip
<4126>	3	microlith		undetermined	undetermined	21	thermal fracturing and spalling
<4704>	3	microburin		undetermined	undetermined	21	post-depositional modification; unused?
<4290>	5	endscraper		undetermined	undetermined	14	much recent post-depositional modification
<58>		abrupt	right	hide	working	14	some plastic deformation
<4648>		endscraper	front	hide	working		much post-depositional modification but some hide characteristics
<4615>		endscraper	front	dry hide	scraping		
<1903>		truncate	distal corners	dry hide	piercing	21	uncertain; wear extends to centre of face
<4836>	6	microlith fragment	tip proximal	undetermined	impact	71	probably a projectile point
<4230>		endscraper	front	dry hide	scraping	50	much post-depositional modification
<4142>	5	flake		undetermined	undetermined	35	much post-depositional modification
<4588>	5	endscraper	front	dry hide	scraping	43	some post-depositional wear
<1844>		burin/core		undetermined	undetermined	14	much post-depositional modification
<1902>		refresher flake		undetermined	undetermined	106	material is unsuitable for study
<7160>	2	endscraper		undetermined	undetermined	78	much post-depositional wear
<8627>	3	endscraper	front	hide	scraping	21	much of front retouched after last use
<132>		serrated blade	right	plant	sickling	21	much post-depositional modification
<12.1>		microlith	tip (distal)	undetermined	impact	142	may be hafted end other end is fresh
<12.2>		flake		undetermined	undetermined	28	thermal fractures and heavily patinated
<214>		flake		undetermined	undetermined	64	heavily patinated
<4698>		burin		undetermined	undetermined	14	moderate post–depositional modification; possibly unused
<4673>		endscraper		unused	unused	35	no evidence of use
<428>	6	microlith		unused	unused	14	no evidence of use
<1706>	3	blade		undetermined	undetermined	58	heavily patinated
<7358>	2	endscraper	front	hide	scraping	43	moderate post-depositional wear
<1728>	2	microlith		unused	unused	78	thermal fracturing; heavily patinated; varnish
<4245>		microlith		undetermined	undetermined		thermal fracturing and patinated
<7352>	1	blade or burin spall		undetermined	undetermined	28	proximal end damaged by platform prep
<6661>		blade or burin spall		unused	unused	35	no use-wear evident

(*Table 10 cont*)

Accession no.	Spit no.	Type	Edge	Material	Action	Ridge microns	Comments
<4826>		microlith		undetermined	undetermined	14	backed and truncated ?blade; knife or ?armature
<7779>	6	flake/burin	bit	undetermined	undetermined	35	fracture scars are fresh
<4248>		microburin		undetermined	undetermined	14	thermal fracturing
<5801>		burin on crest	bit	soft	scraping	21	hide-like wear may be post-depositional modification
<2730>	3	endscraper	front	dry hide	scraping	50	lateral edge has fresh fractures
<4632>		blade		undetermined	undetermined	2.4	thermal fractures and heavily patinated
<4101>	1	blade		undetermined	undetermined	35	heavy post-depositional modification
<4317>		burin on crest		undetermined	undetermined	14	much wear on 'bit', but uncertain cause
<4526>	3	blade (overshot)	lateral	soft	whittling	14	fractures indicate soft wood
<153>		core		undetermined	undetermined	57	heavy post-depositional modification
<6664>		endscraper	front	dry hide	scraping	28	thermal fracturing
<146>		blade	distal left	hide/meat	cutting	35	wear is 5mm in length along edge
<4703>	3	blade fragment		unused	unused	7	fresh fracture damage; no use indicated
<4752>	9	burin	bit	hard	graving	14	possibly results from post-depositional modification
<3572>	5	burin spall fragment		unused	unused	14	mild post-depositional modification
<5701>	6	arrowhead	tip	undetermined	impact	7	some fresh fractures
<4131>	3	burin spall		undetermined	undetermined	14	thermal fracturing; much post-depositional modification?
<4683>		core		unused	unused	7	no usable edges
<429>	6	burin spall fragment		unused	unused	14	platform (proximal end) is missing
<4573>	5	burin spall fragment		unused	unused	7	fracture scars are fresh
<7869>	6	microburin		unused	unused	7	virtually no post-depositional modification
<37>		blade		undetermined	undetermined	7	no wear on 'bit'
<256>		blade		undetermined	undetermined	43	much post-depositional modification
<3574>	5	microburin		undetermined	undetermined	28	much post-depositional modification
<88>		burin	bit & lateral	antler	working	71	perhaps post-depositional modification
<4558>	4	blade		undetermined	undetermined	57	much post-depositional modification; many fresh fracture scars
<5202>		flake		undetermined	undetermined	113	transverse retouch is fresh
<211>		backed & truncated blade		undetermined	undetermined	78	much patina; much fresh edge damage
<7957>	2	microburin		unused	unused	21	no evidence of use
<4568>	4	flake		undetermined	undetermined	7	retouch and scarring (right edge) are fresh
<118>		burin		unused	unused	85	some fractures are fresh
<1917>		microburin?		unused	unused	7	no evidence of use
<35>		microlith		undetermined	undetermined	14	heavily patinated; much fracture scarring
<3538>		missing					

populations of tool types to estimate the proportion of activities represented (see Donahue 1988). As will be discussed, because of the degree of post-depositional modification to the surfaces of the flints, this probably would not reflect accurately the proportion of categories of tool use at the site.

The sampled artefacts were bathed for 10 minutes in a 10% solution of hydrochloric acid and thoroughly rinsed and bathed in water for 20 minutes. The artefacts were viewed with an Olympus KL-BHM metallurgical microscope principally at 200× magnification. Microwear characteristics were recorded, categorised following Donahue (1994), and interpreted.

Results

Of the 94 artefacts examined, 31 have microscopic wear on their edges that can be attributed to some category of use and 16 artefacts are interpreted as unused (at least since the last episode of retouch. The microwear analysis did not provide adequate information to infer use on any of the remaining 47 artefacts as a result of one or more confounding factors.

ARTEFACT USE-WEAR

The working of hide is the most common form of tool use evident at the site with 16 artefacts (51.6% of identified uses) displaying some or all of the characteristic wear patterns for hide (see Keeley 1980). Most of these artefacts were used for scraping dry hides, but piercing by using the distal corners of a truncated blade <1903>, and possibly cutting of hide are also evident. Although not excluded as a possible activity at the site, no fresh hide working was identified. The high proportion of hide working tools is probably the result of sample bias in favour of endscrapers over other tool forms, resulting in the preferential survival of microwear evidence of scraping hides.

Where survival of wear characteristics is very good on lithic artefacts from hunter-gatherer assemblages, one will generally see a large proportion of tools used for cutting meat (eg, Donahue 1988). Where post-depositional processes mildly affect the surfaces of flints evidence for meat cutting is virtually nil as observed in Dumont's (1989) study of the Star Carr assemblage. This indicates the extreme sensitivity of wear produced by cutting meat. At the B&Q site only one tool, a blade <146>, showed evidence of possible meat cutting (the evidence slightly favours fresh hide) and none was clearly identified as used for meat cutting or butchering. This poor showing of meat cutting results from post-depositional processes at the site and does not reflect the likely importance of, or numbers of tools used on, meat.

This is more apparent with the observation that the second most common tool use appears to be those that undergo impact. In six cases <1907>, <4650>, <12.1>, <7559>, <4836>, and the arrowhead <5701> the tools are carefully modified and display damage that is likely to result from use as projectile points (see Fischer 1989; Fischer et al 1984; Odell and Cowan 1986). The other artefacts, a microburin <81> and a blade <5711>, have numerous large invasive fracture scars on opposing edges which are suggestive of wedging (or attempts to splinter the flake through bipolar knapping). It was not possible to identify what material was being worked.

One artefact <132>, a serrated blade, shows evidence of having been used on a soft material associated with many fine abrasive particles. The slightly concave lateral edge displays the remnants of an extensively modified surface, heavily smoothed, but covered with long fine striations orientated slightly oblique to the cutting edge. Associated with some striations are comet-shaped pits. Both faces display wear, although it is more evident on the ventral surface. The edge is extremely rounded, and would have been quite 'non-functional' for most kinds of applications by the time the tool was discarded. The tool was likely used with a stroking motion to cut silica-rich herbaceous plant fibre; that is, used in a way consistent with Neolithic sickle blades for cutting cereals. The lack of surface polishing, typical of cutting grasses and originally thought to be the result of post-depositional processes (eg, Donahue 1994, fig 1), may possibly result from a larger size of abrasive particle (either phytoliths or contaminants), from local conditions (eg, much moisture), or from working different material.

The only other use identified beyond a soft/hard dichotomy is antler working which was found on a multiple burin <88>. Traces of wear occur on one burinated edge as well as on two burin bits. The wear is bright, undulating, and relatively smooth. It is not as extensive as wood, but much more so than bone, indicating that the antler was either fresh or soaked.

There is a limited variety of materials identified as having been worked at the site. In addition to the already mentioned problem with evidence of meat cutting there is concern about evidence for the manufacture of tools and ornaments

that involve the working of hard materials such as antler, bone, and wood. While evidence of bone is unlikely to be observed given the common occurrence of silica wear, woodworking is more likely to survive these post-depositional processes. Given that burins are not rare at the site, it is probably fair to argue that the working of bone and antler, and possibly wood, occurred on site more often than the microwear evidence indicates. If the evidence for working any hard materials is considered, then five of 33 artefacts or 13.7% of the identified used tools were probably involved in tool and ornament manufacture, and this compares well with other hunter-gatherer sites (Donahue 1988; Donahue et al 1992).

Discussion

THE RELATIONSHIP BETWEEN ARTEFACT USE AND TYPE

Sample sizes tend to be relatively small owing to the expense of microwear analysis. For this reason, it becomes a very valuable exercise to determine if there are any specific relationships between tool types and use. Such associations can then be used to generalise more widely about economic activities at the site. Some artefact types do appear to be associated with certain kinds of use, but the low number of interpreted artefacts and the non-random selection procedures mean that one must be cautious about drawing conclusions. Among tool forms that do conform to previously hypothesised uses are endscrapers and microliths, to some extent burins, the serrated blade, and microburins.

Eighteen endscrapers were examined (Table 11). Of these, 12 display wear characteristics of hide scraping while the remaining endscrapers were undetermined as to use or thought unused since their last retouch episode. There was no case where the endscraper fronts indicated any kind of use other than scraping hide. This pattern is not surprising. Research on European stone age assemblages by microwear analysts consistently show Upper Palaeolithic and Mesolithic endscrapers to be used almost solely on hide. Even Neolithic endscrapers appear to be used predominantly on hide. The one Mesolithic exception to note is Star Carr, where Dumont (1989) identified bone scraping on some endscrapers. His interpretation is probably correct, but experimental evidence shows that just a small addition of abrasives in the hide will cause a tool used for scraping hide to develop a brightly polished edge similar to that generated by use on bone or wood. Many of the endscrapers from the B&Q site displayed some silica polishing on their fronts, as well as on ridges and other edges. Such bright, smooth wear could easily be mistaken for use on bone or other hard material.

Five of the 16 microlith forms examined display use indicative of projectile points. Most studies on Mesolithic points tend to indicate this is a common, if not their principal, use, with the exception of Grace (1992) who identified many for piercing or drilling soft and medium materials. Previous research indicates that such forms are

Table 11 Association between tool type and tool use

Use	Antler	Hard	Hide	Impact	Plant	Soft	Undetermined	Unused	Total
Tool type									
Abrupt	0	0	1	0	0	0	0	0	1
Arrowhead	0	0	0	1	0	0	0	0	1
Backed tool	0	1	0	5	0	0	12	2	20
Blade	0	0	1	1	0	1	10	2	15
Burin	1	1	0	0	0	1	6	1	10
Burin spall	0	0	0	0	0	0	1	3	4
Core	0	0	0	0	0	0	1	1	2
Flake	0	0	0	0	0	0	8	2	10
Microburin	0	0	0	1	0	0	3	4	8
Piercer	0	0	0	0	0	1	0	0	1
Scraper	0	0	13	0	0	0	6	1	20
Serrated blade	0	0	0	0	1	0	0	0	1
Truncate	0	0	1	0	0	0	0	0	1
Total	1	2	16	8	1	3	47	16	94

designed to be used as armatures or as knives principally for the cutting of meat. At the sites of Paglicci Cave, Italy, and Lismore Fields, Derbyshire, there were measurable differences in the sizes of tools used as projectile points and those used for meat knives (Donahue 1988; 1990 and nd). Because of the problems of post-depositional modification of the artefacts at the B&Q site, it cannot be ascertained if such tools were also being used as knives. There certainly were examples with edge fracture scars typical of meat cutting, but that alone was considered an inadequate basis to make such an inference. Interestingly, all backed tool forms that displayed impact fractures on their tips were less than 30mm in length, albeit some were fragments.

Six burins (and possibly another two) were included in the analysis. Most proved to have undetermined uses, but three were interpreted as having been used on their bits: on antler, hide, and an unknown hard material. In addition, one burin did not appear to have been used since manufacture. The results are inadequate to confirm these tools were used as chisels or gravers as is generally believed, but neither is there evidence to reject this proposition.

Although only a single serrated blade was recovered, thus making a generalisation regarding use on site inappropriate, other research investigating the use of serrated flakes and blades recovered from Neolithic features and contexts and as isolated finds (May et al 1996) indicates that serrated blades characterised by numerous fine U- or V-shape notches of 8 to 20 per 10.0mm along one or both lateral edges are recognised as an early Neolithic tool form. Yet they also occur in Mesolithic deposits elsewhere in Britain (see Rankine and Rankine 1960; Wymer 1962). The microwear on this particular specimen is not equivalent to other British specimens examined by the author. However, it is very similar to that observed on some Danish microdenticulates examined by Juel Jensen (1994). She claims, quite adamantly, that the Danish microdenticulates were not used as sickle blades and that the microwear is formed from some

other use. She remains uncertain as to how or on what the tools were used, although she still favours some form of herbaceous plant fibre.

The final artefact form that appears to have a consistent use is the microburin. Of the eight microburins examined, only one displayed use (wedging); the rest were either unused or no use could be determined. This conforms to microwear analysis of microburins at other sites (Donahue 1988; 1990; Donahue et al 1992) where they consistently support studies of lithic technologists indicating that they are debris from the manufacture of microliths. This permits us to indicate that not only were projectile points being discarded at the site, but that they were being manufactured there as well.

THE ASSOCIATION BETWEEN CONTEXTS AND ARTEFACT USE
The sample size taken from each context and the low percentage of interpretable tools limits the investigation of the spatial organisation or contextual associations of activities at the site. The relationship with contexts is examined in Table 12 and it shows that there is no association that cannot be explained as resulting from chance. Also to be noted is that no patterning is evident regarding tool use and vertical distribution (Table 13). This may result from inadequate spit information, but the low number of interpreted artefacts seriously influences it.

ARTEFACT DEPTH AND POST-DEPOSITIONAL PROCESSES
As previously mentioned, the microscopically examined artefacts display wear and fracture scars identified as having resulted from various post-depositional processes. Further study of these post-depositional modifications, particularly their intensity, interaction, sequence of formation, and context can provide valuable additional information regarding site formation processes. One of the most important aspects to examine is the spatial distribution of variations in the intensity of wear and fracturing. How to measure in part, the intensity of natural wear processes by

Table 12 The relationship between tool use and spatial contexts

Use	Context	Antler	Hard	Hide	Impact	Plant	Soft	Undetermined	Unused	Total
Locale										
B	[6]	1	0	0	0	1	0	0	1	3
	[22]	0	0	1	0	0	0	0	0	1
	[23]	0	0	0	1	0	0	1	0	2
	[60]	0	1	1	1	0	0	1	0	4
	[224]	0	0	0	0	0	0	1	0	1
	[275]	0	1	8	2	0	1	25	4	41
	[276]	0	0	1	1	0	0	2	3	7
	[281]	0	0	0	0	0	1	0	0	1
	[283]	0	0	4	2	0	1	9	4	20
	[285]	0	0	1	0	0	0	1	0	2
	[428]	0	0	0	0	0	0	0	1	1
	[429]	0	0	0	0	0	0	0	1	1
	[4500]	0	0	0	0	0	0	0	1	1
B subtotal		1	2	16	7	1	3	40	15	85
C	[31]	0	0	0	0	0	0	1	0	1
	[67]	0	0	0	0	0	0	1	0	1
	[206]	0	0	0	0	0	0	1	0	1
	[224]	0	0	0	1	0	0	2	1	4
C subtotal		0	0	0	1	0	0	5	1	7
X	[25]	0	0	0	0	0	0	2	0	2
X subtotal		0	0	0	0	0	0	2	0	2
Total		1	2	16	8	1	3	47	16	94

Table 13 The vertical distribution of tool uses at the B&Q site (spit 1=highest)

Use	Antler	Hard	Hide	Impact	Plant	Soft	Undetermined	Unused	Total
Spit no.									
1	0	0	0	1	0	0	5	0	6
2	0	0	1	1	0	0	2	2	6
3	0	0	4	0	0	1	6	1	12
4	0	0	1	0	0	0	2	1	4
5	0	0	2	0	0	0	6	2	10
6	0	0	1	2	0	0	3	5	11
8	0	0	0	0	0	0	2	0	2
9	0	1	0	0	0	0	0	0	1
(blank)	1	1	7	4	1	2	21	5	42
Total	1	2	16	8	1	3	47	16	94

viewing dorsal ridge rounding has already been discussed. While there appears to be little association between the amount of ridge rounding with spatial contexts, there is a distinct pattern with depth in sediment as indicated by spit levels (Table 13 and Table 14). The more deeply buried specimens tend to have less, not more, rounding than those near the top of the deposit. This suggests that the amount of wear is not related to the distance artefacts may have drifted down in the deposit. This relationship between wear and depth also leads us to reject the hypothesis that there may be multiple deposits across an extended time period, since one would expect the older and deeper material to undergo more surface modification than the material more recently incorporated into the deposit. This suggests that the impact is occurring from forces more

common near the surface than further down, and that it is affecting the site principally after the relative stabilisation of artefact positions in the deposit. This would suggest that dynamic forces on the surface, pedological processes related to changing humidity or temperatures, or bioturbation are likely forces producing the natural wear on ridges and edges. And we should not rule out the possible effects of Neolithic agriculture that may have been practised in this locality.

MICROWEAR AND ARTEFACT HISTORIES
Microwear on the surfaces of the artefacts permits reconstruction of 'life histories' of the artefacts, which, when integrated, can provide data for the construction of a model of site formation processes. Following tool use and discard there

Table 14 Relationship between ridge rounding and depth (spit 1=highest)

Ridge rounding (microns)	7	14	21	28	35	42	50	57	64	71	78	85	106	114	142	170	Mean
Spit no.																	
1	1	0	0	1	2	0	0	0	0	2	0	0	0	0	0	0	41.1
2	0	0	3	0	0	1	0	0	0	0	2	0	0	0	0	0	44
3	1	2	4	2	0	0	1	2	0	0	0	0	0	0	0	0	28
4	1	2	0	0	0	0	0	1	0	0	0	0	0	0	0	0	23.4
5	2	2	1	2	1	1	0	0	0	0	0	0	0	0	0	0	22
6	4	2	2	0	2	0	0	0	0	1	0	0	0	0	0	0	22
8	0	0	0	1	0	0	0	0	0	0	0	0	0	0	0	0	28
9	0	1	0	0	0	0	0	0	0	0	0	0	0	0	0	0	14
(blank)	3	9	4	4	5	1	1	2	1	1	1	1	1	1	1	1	46
Total	12	18	14	10	10	3	2	5	1	4	3	1	1	1	1	1	34

appears to be a period of time in which some artefacts are undergoing quite severe treatment. Ancient fracture scars not related to use are evident on many artefacts. Such edge damage is highly variable; it will occur extensively on some artefacts, and yet not be observed at all on others. Although influenced by edge angle, this damage may be the result of trampling or perhaps some other processes prior to artefact burial in sediment.

Perhaps during the period of time while being scuffed around on the surface, but more likely over a fairly lengthy time period while in the buried environment, the artefacts begin attaining silica polishing and ridge rounding that results from rubbing with fine grain sediments such as sand. The reason why it is thought that this polishing is a later process is because we observe a strong correlation between the amount of ridge rounding and surface polishing with depth in the sediment; the deeper in the sediment, the less rounding is evident (see Table 14). This suggests that most of the wear results from a time after artefacts have attained their relatively stable positions within the deposit. There may be multiple causes for this wear, including animal bioturbation, later human activity (eg, agriculture), or even soil formation processes.

Silica polishing of artefact surfaces, suspected of being long term, precedes a second episode of fracture scarring of the lithic material. This damage is often haphazard and ragged, but it can also be shockingly systematic. Although this fracture scarring could be thousands of years old, it is most likely very recent since no silica polishing appears on these freshly fractured edges. In some cases the edge fracture scars are almost certainly the result of archaeological excavation, but for some artefacts, the fracture scarring is so intense that some fairly severe impact on the site context must have occurred. I suspect that this may relate to local construction, demolition, or excavation by heavy machinery.

Sometimes associated with some smaller scarring along edges are metal residues that almost certainly result from hand-tool excavation procedures. This is one reason it is believed that some of the fresh fracture scars result from the archaeological excavation. Other patches of metal residue, associated with much less or no edge fracture scarring, may result from post-excavation processing and measuring of the artefacts.

SITE FUNCTION

Microwear analysis has been used previously to examine the site function of prehistoric hunter-gatherer sites (Donahue 1988; Keeley 1988). The basis for resolving site function, however, is not easy, as it is possible for the activities performed at a site to have little relationship to the function of the site (Binford 1978). As a result it is necessary to have archaeological signatures for site functions that lithic microwear analysis can measure or resolve. Such archaeological signatures, as they currently exist, must be viewed as provisional. Relevant archaeological signatures here include Keeley's (1988) observation that dry hide scraping predominates over fresh hide scraping at residential bases, but may represent less than a third of the hide scraping tools at hunting camps. Binford (1980) has noted that, in general, there is a predominance of maintenance activities at residential bases and a prevalence of resource procurement activities at logistical sites. Donahue (nd) has compared a variety of hunter-gatherer sites and noted that variations in certain activities can primarily relate to seasonal variations in activities. If the high proportion of dry hide scraping is valid for the site as a whole, then it would suggest that the site was a residential base. This is not contradicted by the frequency of projectile points, since the microburins indicate that they are also manufacturing new points. Instead, if the high percentages of armatures and hide working are valid, then one would expect this to be an autumn or winter occupation site. Much further analysis would be required to test these propositions more fully.

Conclusion

The lithic microwear analysis of the B&Q site has led to a number of observations regarding tool use, the activities occurring on site, the role of the site within a subsistence-settlement system, and the formation processes and the sequencing of the processes that have modified the site and its artefacts. There is evidence for material processing and tool maintenance activities occurring here, primarily that of dry hide scraping, which supports the hypothesis that this is a residential base for hunter-gatherers. Evidently, meat is being procured, given the damaged points and, with the variety of other activities, plus the manufacture of new projectile points as indicated by the discard of microburins, it is possible to argue that this is not simply a resource procurement location. Post-depositional processes that have come close to obliterating all use-wear evidence have substantially affected the site. Some of these processes appear to be ancient, some long-term processes related to the gentle shifting of the matrix primarily near the surface, and some from recent and fairly severe forces that may relate to episodes of site preparation and excavation. The results of this analysis hopefully contribute to our understanding of the Early Mesolithic in the region.

6.2 The ceramics

Louise Rayner

Introduction

In the past, misconceptions and low expectations hampered the study of prehistory in central London. These are outlined in Merriman's article on prehistory in central London and do not require reiteration here; what is important are the implications these had for the study of prehistoric pottery (Merriman 1987, 318–19). The lack of awareness, expectation and non-standardised approach to recording often resulted in prehistoric pottery being misidentified or languishing in the archive unrecorded and unpublished. The conception of this project and the opportunity to examine assemblages from backlog sites was an important step towards addressing this problem. The assessment of these assemblages marked the introduction of a standardised approach to recording within the MoLAS database.

During the period of assessment a number of ceramic assemblages were examined in order to confirm the presence of prehistoric pottery, as well as record and assess the potential. Despite archive problems and difficulties in locating material, prehistoric pottery was recorded from a total of 14 sites (see Table 15). The most important assemblages were then selected for further work and are presented on a site by site basis below. The most diagnostic sherds have also been presented in the main thematic chapters. After assessment, it was decided that the assemblages from Alaska Works (AW89), 170–176 Grange Road and 41–45 Grange Walk (GRW91) should be published within the Roman Southwark publication (Cowan and Wheeler in prep) as these produced stratified Late Iron Age–early Romano-British pottery, of more relevance to the origins of Roman London. The presence of pottery from these sites is noted in the Gazetteer.

Table 15 List of sites for which prehistoric pottery is recorded

Site name	LAARC site code	GAZ no.
Bermondsey Abbey	BA84	159
Coronation Buildings	COR89	9
Fennings Wharf	FW84	130
Humphrey Street	HUM90	174
Lambeth Palace Kitchen Gardens	L52585	27
Lambeth Palace North Garden	L58286	28
Phoenix Wharf	PHW88	189
Queen Elizabeth Street South	QUESS88	188
Lower Marsh	WBR88	39
Whites Grounds	WG87	155
Waterloo	WSB90	34
Waterloo	WSC90	33
4 St Thomas Street	4STS88	122
11 St Thomas Street	11STS77	125

Methodology

The prehistoric pottery has been recorded using standard Museum of London Specialist Services (MoLSS) codes on pro-forma sheets and entered into an ORACLE database. The recording system was established in accordance with the guidelines outlined by the Prehistoric Ceramics Research Group (PCRG 1995; revised 1997). The sherds have been examined with a ×20 binocular microscope and recorded by fabric, form, decoration and condition. Further details on finish, surface treatment, and manufacture have been noted in the comment field. For the larger Bermondsey Abbey assemblages the dominant fabric groups were subdivided and allocated a four-character code; these codes are site specific. The first two characters indicate the main inclusion type (Table 16), the third and fourth characters relate to the frequency and size of inclusions (Table 17). In all other cases each assemblage is presented using the common name

Table 16 Fabric codes used in fabric descriptions and expansions

Fabric code	Expansion
Bermondsey Abbey only	
FL	Flint
QU	Quartz/sand
SH	Shell
All sites, common name fabric codes	
CALC	Calcareous other than shell
CLAYP	Clay pellets (not grog)
FLIN	Flint
GLAUC	Glauconite
GROG	Grog
IRON	Iron oxides
MIX	Mixed grits
OXID	Oxidised wares
QUTZ	Quartz sand
SAND	Miscellaneous sandy wares
SHEL	Shell
VOID	Indeterminate voids

Table 17 *Summary of frequency and modal size classes of inclusions (Bermondsey Abbey only)*

Modal size	Very fine/fine <0.25mm	Medium >0.25–1mm	Coarse >1–3mm	Very coarse >3mm
Quantity				
Rare <3 %	RF	RM	RC	RV
Sparse 3–10%	SF	SM	SC	SV
Moderate 11–25%	MF	MM	MC	MV
Common 26–40%	CF	CM	CC	CV
Abundant >40%	AF	AM	AC	AV

Table 18 *Bermondsey Abbey ceramics; quantities by main fabric groupings*

Fabric	Count	% count	Weight	% weight	EVEs	% EVEs
FLIN	83	21	1060	17	0.21	12
GLAUC	1	<1%	10	<1%		
QUTZ	101	26	1961	31	0.48	27
SHEL	179	46	2934	46	1.1	62
GROG	25	6	415	6		
OXID	3	1	32	<1%		
Total	392		6412		1.79	

fabric codes in Table 16. Quantification of each assemblage is by sherd count, weight and equivalent number of vessels (EVEs). All diagnostic sherds and other fired clay objects have been illustrated where possible.

Site assemblage summaries

Bermondsey Abbey (GAZ 159)

The prehistoric assemblage from Bermondsey Abbey produced a total of 392 sherds (6412g/1.79 EVEs). The assemblage ranges in date from the Mid Bronze Age (Deverel-Rimbury type) to the Late Iron Age–early Roman period. The assemblage was recovered from 60 contexts and, although in some cases this is the only datable material present, is considered residual, with the exception of one feature. One pit (subgroup 566) pre-dating the medieval activity produced a Late Iron Age–early Roman assemblage without any other later material. The site also produced a substantial Roman assemblage, which is again predominantly residual, but ranges in date from the mid 1st to the mid 4th centuries. A small number of features and deposits have been interpreted as evidence for Roman activity but these produced a relatively small amount of stratified Roman pottery.

The quantities of both prehistoric and Roman pottery recovered are indicative of activity in these periods of a greater intensity than the excavated features would suggest, and the amount of redeposited pottery in later features implies extensive truncation by the medieval and later settlement. Despite the residual nature of the assemblage, the sherds are in relatively good condition. Although there is some surface abrasion, many of the sherds are medium to large in size and the average sherd weight is just over 16g. One vessel <P28> was recovered almost complete and 32 other rim sherds were identified. Decorated sherds totalled 18, with a range of techniques including finger-tipping, fingernail impressions, impressed dimples and burnished and incised decoration.

FABRICS

The most common fabric groups recorded in this assemblage are flint (FL), sand (QU), shell (SH) and grog (GROG), although a glauconitic fabric is also represented by one sherd (GLAUC) (see Table 18). The dominant fabric types are clearly shell-, quartz-rich and flint-tempered. On the whole the fabrics are chronologically exclusive, but there is overlap with some of the quartz-rich fabrics. The Late Bronze Age–Early Iron Age material is predominantly flint-tempered, although there is one flint and shell variant (FLRC/SHSM); probable Early Iron Age rim sherds are in a quartz-rich fabric (QUSM). The Middle Iron Age pottery marks an increased use of quartz-rich fabrics and in general does not contain coarse, flint inclusions. Shell-tempered fabrics have also been tentatively dated to this period (SHSF) and the glauconite-rich body sherd may date from this period onwards. The later Iron Age–early Romano-British material continues with the use of shell-tempered and sandy fabrics and also marks the introduction of grog-tempered wares.

FABRIC DESCRIPTIONS BY PERIOD

The following section describes the fabrics by period and details associated forms. Not all fabrics could be assigned a date, particularly when diagnostic featured sherds are not present. All flint is white crushed, burnt flint unless stated and therefore likely to be added temper rather than naturally occurring in the clay body.

MIDDLE BRONZE AGE
FLMC Hard, oxidised fabric; moderate coarse flint; rare sub-rounded quartz. This fabric has the highest density of flint amongst the assemblage.
Count (Ct) 1; weight (wt) 20g
Forms: Deverel-Rimbury urn <P6>

LATE BRONZE AGE–EARLY IRON AGE
FLRM(1) Hard, reduced fabric, silty matrix; rare, fine to medium flint; rare quartz, sub-rounded.
Ct 2; wt 38g; EVEs 0.1.
Forms: Carinated fineware bowl <P13>; shoulder sherd with red iron-rich coating and decorated with impressed dimple <P12>
FLRC Very hard fabric in dense matrix; Patchy oxidised surfaces, reduced core; very rare sub-angular quartz; rare medium flint; few other inclusions visible resulting in smooth, soapy feel.

Ct 10; wt 162g; EVEs 0.05
Forms: Weakly carinated bowl with fingernail decoration <P21>
FLRC(2) Hard fabric in dense matrix, oxidised surfaces with reduced core; rare to sparse coarse flint; black elongated organic inclusions; rare to sparse, sub-rounded quartz. Some examples have larger voids and wipe marks on exterior surface.
Ct 44; wt 478g; EVEs 0.01
Forms: Flaring rim jar with fingernail decoration; sharply carinated bowl; shoulder sherds from shouldered jars with finger tip decoration. <P14>; <P22>; <P23>; <P19>; base with flint-gritted underside
FLRC/SHSM Hard, reduced fabric, dense matrix; rare, coarse flint; rare to sparse, medium to coarse shell (more visible as voids on surface); rare, sub-angular

89

quartz and black elongated organic inclusions. One example has more common finer shell.
Ct 8; wt 206g; EVEs 0.05
Forms: Shouldered jars with finger-tip impressions on rim and/or shoulder for example <P16> and <P18>; base sherd with wipe marks

QUCM/FLRM Hard reduced fabric; common medium quartz, moderately well-sorted, sub-rounded; rare medium flint; rare black organic inclusions.
Ct 2; wt 32g
Forms: Body sherd with applied cordon <P24>; decorated sherd <P20>

SHSC Hard, reduced fabric, dense matrix; sparse coarse shell, visible as voids on the surface; rare rounded quartz.
Ct 1; wt 13g; 0.06 EVEs
Forms: Tall flaring rim <P17>

SHMM Hard, reduced fabric, dense matrix; moderate medium shell; rare black elongated organic inclusions; flint visible on the surface but not in fresh break. (Similar to FLRC/SHSM but sparse finer flint.)
Ct 3; wt 54g
Form: Carinated jar <P15>

QUAF Hard, reduced fabric, granular matrix with abundant fine well-sorted quartz; rare coarse flint. Burnished surfaces.
Ct 2; wt 12g
Form: Jar <P27>

EARLY IRON AGE AND MIDDLE IRON AGE

QUSM Hard, fabric with sparse medium quartz, poorly sorted sub-rounded; very rare medium flint.
Ct 46; wt 559g; 0.24 EVEs.
Forms: Rim <P30>; rim <P29>; rim <P25> and rim <P26>

MIDDLE IRON AGE

QURM Hard, reduced fabric, very dense matrix; rare medium quartz and dark grog? inclusions.
Ct 24; wt 931g; 0.1 EVEs
Forms: Wide-mouthed jar <P28>

QUCM Hard, reduced fabric with silty matrix; common medium quartz with rare organic inclusions. Burnished ext surfaces
Ct 12 sherds; wt 135g

NO FEATURE SHERDS

QUSM/SHSM Hard, reduced fabric; sparse fine to medium shell; sparse, poorly sorted, medium quartz; rare fine flint.
Forms: 4016 (rim) <P31> MIA

SHCC hard, reduced fabric; common, fine to coarse shell predominately leached on the surface; rare, medium–coarse flint, rare sub-rounded quartz.
Ct 64 sherds; wt 673g; 0.05 EVEs
Forms: 1436 (rim) MIA?; 1535 (shoulder sherd) MIA?

MID/LATE IRON AGE

GLAUC Hard, reduced fabric; common, well-sorted, well-rounded black inclusions (probably glauconite). Burnished surface.
Ct 1; wt 10g
Forms: Only 1 body sherd identified

QUMM Hard, reduced fabric; moderate medium quartz, moderately well-sorted. Few other inclusions visible. Occasional sherds have rare medium flint and rare red iron-rich inclusions. Burnished surface.
Ct 8 sherds; wt 126g
Forms: 1184 (short pedestal bowl) M/LIA <P32>

LATE IRON AGE–EARLY ROMANO-BRITISH

GROG Grog-tempered fabrics not further defined.
Ct 24 sherds; wt 403g

GROG2 Hard, dark reduced fabric with hackly fracture; dark angular grog pellets; rare quartz sub-angular; smooth, soapy texture.
Ct 1; wt 12g
Forms: Jar or bowl with rippled shoulder <P38>

QUCF/SHSM Relatively soft (can be scratched with fingernail) fabric with silty matrix; common fine well-sorted quartz, with rare medium quartz; sparse medium shell; silver mica visible on surface.
Ct 1 sherd; wt 36g; 0.14 EVEs
Forms: 1693 (jar) <P36> LIA/ERB

QUCF Hard, oxidised fabric, silty matrix; common fine quartz, well sorted
Forms: 3456 (decorated body sherd) <P39> LIA/ERB

SHCC(2) Hard, reduced fabric, dense matrix; common to very common coarse shell, moderately well sorted; leached on interior surface; rare sub-angular quartz. Burnished ext surface.
Ct 9 sherds; wt 248g; 0.12 EVEs
Forms: 4200 (decorated jar) <P40> LIA; 4200 (jar) <P41>

SHSM/QUSM Hard fabric,

oxidised external surface; sparse medium to coarse shell; sparse quartz, poorly sorted, sub-angular. Horizontal wipe marks internally.
Ct 1 sherd; wt 10g
Forms: 4315 (decorated sherd) <P42>

SHSM Hard, reduced fabric, silty matrix; sparse medium shell.
Ct 4 sherds; wt 23g; 0.09 EVEs
Forms: 1723 (rim) <P37> LIA

SHMC Hard fabric; moderate coarse to very coarse shell; rare black organic inclusions; rare quartz sub-angular.
Ct 1 sherd; wt 107g
Forms: Large bead-rim storage jar <P43>

SHCC/QUCM Hard fabric, silty matrix; patchy oxidised ext surface, reduced core. Common, coarse shell; common medium quartz, sub-rounded moderately well sorted.

Ct 1 sherd; wt 48g; 0.10 EVEs
Forms: 4315 (jar) <P35> M/LIA
OXID Miscellaneous oxidised wares
Ct 3 sherds; wt 32g
SAND Miscellaneous sandy wares
Ct 6 sherds; wt 102g; 0.14 EVEs
SHEL Miscellaneous shelly wares
Ct 94 sherds; wt 1745g; 0.68 EVEs
Undated

FLSM Hard, reduced fabric, silty matrix; spare fine to medium flint spare fine quartz, sub-rounded. Ct 18; wt 156g
Forms: No feature sherds; some sherds with burnished surfaces. Early/Middle Iron Age?

QUMC/FLRV Hard, reduced fabric with moderate coarse quartz, poorly sorted sub-angular; rare, very coarse flint. Very pimply surface.
Ct 1 sherd; wt 64g
Forms: 1497 (thick-walled sherd, rough surfaces) date?

Coronation Buildings (GAZ 9)

Hedley Swain originally examined the assemblage and a full archive report was prepared. This summary is based on the archive report and only diagnostic sherds were re-examined. The original fabric classifications have been retained and are presented by weight, which was the sole method of quantification used in the original recording (Swain nd). The majority of the pottery is in poor condition, with small, fragmentary sherds. A total weight of 1010g of pottery was recovered from 19 contexts.

FABRIC AND FORM

Six rim sherds and eight base sherds are recorded. All rims are plain with square or round profiles and all of the bases are flat-bottomed, with the exception of two slight footrings. The sherds have predominantly quartz-rich fabrics, although a few sherds also have flint inclusions (see Table 19). There is one vessel with a glauconite-rich fabric. There are no decorated sherds, but many have smooth, burnished external surfaces.

Table 19 Coronation Buildings ceramics; quantities by main fabric groupings (taken from archive report)

Fabric	Weight	% weight
SAND	654	65
SAND & QUTZ	81	8
FLIN	58	6
VOID	163	16
MIX	54	5
Totals	1010	

DATING

The assemblage has been dated to the Middle Iron Age. However, not all of the pottery could be located for re-examination, including some of the Roman sherds noted in the archive text. There is clearly Middle Iron Age activity on this site and undoubtedly some of the features in group 3 date to this phase. Whether the small amount of Roman pottery is intrusive (which seems likely given the small quantity involved) is difficult to assess.

Fennings Wharf (GAZ 130)

An assemblage of 165 sherds, totalling 576g and 0.22 EVEs was recovered. The majority of the sherds are in poor condition, very friable with abraded surfaces. One fabric type in particular has suffered very badly from leaching, probably due to adverse soil conditions. The assemblage, although small, was recovered from the ring ditch and associated features and therefore is important for the dating of this activity. Pottery was recovered from nine contexts. Some material attributed to this site was found in the archive without context information. These sherds are described below, but cannot confidently be assigned to excavated contexts.

FABRICS

The sherds were divided into four main fabric types based on the dominant inclusions: flint, quartz, grog, and a vesicular fabric (see Table 20). The most abundant type represented is the vesicular fabric, although a large number of these consist of very small fragments, resulting in an average sherd weight of just over 2g. The sherds are lightweight and very friable with only voids remaining in the clay matrix. The shape of the voids suggests the predominant inclusion was fine shell. The flint temper is crushed calcined flint and ranges in density from rare to moderate. The size of the flint is more uniform, ranging from medium to coarse, but is poorly sorted. Only one sherd of grog-tempered pottery and two sherds of quartz-gritted fabric are recorded. The grog-tempered sherd is soft and very abraded with rare, pale grog inclusions and very rare fine flint. The quartz-gritted sherds have sparse to moderate quartz grains, sub-rounded and relatively well sorted with very rare fine flint; both have reduced dense matrices.

Table 20 Fennings Wharf ceramics; quantities by main fabric groupings

Fabric	Count	% count	Weight	% weight	EVEs
FLIN	54	33	323	56	0.1
QUTZ	2	1	13	2	
GROG	1	1	4	1	
VOID	108	65	236	41	0.12
Total	165		576		0.22

FORMS

With the exception of the vessels from the central oval feature [2078] very few forms could be identified because of the small and fragmentary nature of the assemblage. The rim sherds and bases with flint-gritted undersides probably derived from jars.

FIRED CLAY OBJECTS

Six fragments of perforated clay slab were recovered. Three of these fragments <S2> join and relate to one slab. The other fragments do not join and there are enough differences to suggest they derive from at least two, if not three, individual slabs (Fig 43, <S1> and <S3>). All fragments are reddish-brown in colour with a flint-tempered fabric. Traces of perforation are visible on all examples but there are no complete perforations surviving.

DATING

The dating of this assemblage relies heavily on a limited number of traits and characteristics identified. The two identifiable vessels from the central oval feature are suggested as Late Bronze Age–Early Iron Age in date based on the presence of the cup <P7>. This dating is supported by the presence of bases with flint-gritted underside, which are recorded from other Late Bronze Age sites and the perforated clay slabs which are also characteristic of sites of this date (see Chapter 2.3 for more detailed discussion).

Lower Marsh, Lambeth (GAZ 39)

INTRODUCTION

The assemblage totalled 112 sherds of prehistoric date. There are few feature sherds or diagnostic features and most of the sherds are abraded.

FABRICS AND FORMS

The sherds are predominantly flint-tempered and, where datable, range from Mid to Late Bronze Age (see Table 21). Base sherds with flint-gritted undersides suggest a Late Bronze Age component, as do thin-walled sherds (including one slack carinated shoulder sherd) with highly burnished surfaces, probably from fineware jars. Some of the thicker walled sherds with coarse flint temper are possibly earlier, with one lower body sherd likely to derive from a Deverel-Rimbury type urn. There is also one sherd in a fabric with clay pellet inclusions. The body sherd has rows of twisted cord impressions and probably comes from the body of a Collared Urn.

Table 21 Lower Marsh ceramics; quantities by main fabric groupings

Fabric	Count	% count	Weight	% weight
CLAYP	2	2	28	4
FLIN	102	91	585	78
IRON	1	1	5	1
SAND	2	2	12	2
SHEL	2	2	110	15
VOID	3	3	13	2
Total	112		753	

Waterloo (WSD89-GAZ 32, WSC90-GAZ 33, WSB90-GAZ 34)

INTRODUCTION

These three sites are situated close to each other on the floodplain sands and gravels. The pottery assemblages recovered from each site are small in size, but some of the material is stratified. The presence of Late Bronze Age pottery is noted from WSD89. However, the assemblages from WSB and WSC are discussed below. The assemblage recovered from WSB totalled 50 sherds (168g), whilst that from WSC was smaller and totalled only 18 sherds (84g). The sherds are small and in poor condition; many are very fragmentary, abraded and have damaged surfaces. This is particularly the case for the material from the disturbed prehistoric horizon (WSB group 5) which is very fragmentary.

FABRICS AND FORMS

The fabrics are predominantly flint-tempered although there are two quartz fabrics, one without flint (see Table 22). Few forms could be identified due to the condition of the sherds; the WSC material is entirely composed of body sherds and decoration is confined to a single piece with fingernail impressions. The majority of the WSB assemblage was recovered from a series of pits (group 4). The most diagnostic material came from one pit (subgroup 3, context 114) and included rim fragments from two Neolithic Peterborough Ware bowls and one decorated sherd probably from a Collared Urn. Feature sherds are absent from the group 5 assemblage (disturbed prehistoric horizon); there is only one decorated body sherd, with short twisted cord impressions, which is probably of Neolithic date (not illustrated).

Table 22 Waterloo ceramics; quantities by main fabric groupings

Fabric	Count	% count	Weight	% weight
FLIN	58	85	213	83
GROG	6	9	0	0
QUTZ	4	6	43	17
Total	68		256	

DATING

The small assemblage size and poor condition of the pottery recovered hamper the dating of this activity. The decorated sherds from Peterborough Ware bowls are Neolithic in date (early–middle 3rd millennium), which also seems the most likely date for the single decorated sherd from the soil horizon. The decorated sherd <P3>, if derived from a Collared Urn, is definitely later than the Peterborough bowls.

11 St Thomas Street (GAZ 125)

INTRODUCTION

An assemblage of 63 sherds of prehistoric date was recovered from St Thomas Street, totalling 689g and 0.15 EVEs. The sherds are abraded, but relatively stable and consist mainly of undiagnostic body sherds. The sherds were recovered from five contexts, two of which are post-Roman. The remaining sherds were found on the natural gravels (Open Area 1) which appear to have been scoured by water action and then overlain by flood deposits (Open Area 2) that contained Roman pottery of 1st century date. No prehistoric features were identified, although shallow patches of discoloration in the natural gravels were noted but not investigated further.

FABRICS

The sherds were divided into four main fabric types based on the dominant inclusions: flint, clay pellets, quartz, grog and one sherd with voids (see Table 23). The flint-tempered sherds are all hard, predominantly oxidised and tempered with white, crushed burnt flint. The density of flint inclusions ranges from rare to moderate, and the size ranges from fine to very coarse. The one sherd with voids, is small and very abraded; the inclusions may have been shell, based on the shape of the remaining voids.

Table 23 St Thomas Street ceramics; quantities by main fabric groupings

Fabric	Count	% count	Weight	% weight	EVEs
FLIN	54	86	595	86	0.15
QUTZ	5	8	14	2	
VOID	1	2	2	<1%	
GROG	3	5	78	11	c 0.05
Total	63	100	689		

NATURAL GRAVELS

Group 1, 1001

[83] The earliest element in this context is a rim sherd from a Peterborough Neolithic (Mortlake Ware) bowl, in a grog-tempered fabric. Twenty-six flint-tempered sherds were also present in this context. The flint inclusions are coarse to very coarse. Some of the sherds, including base sherds, have a thick wall measuring between 9–15mm. One rim sherd is present with finger-tip impression on the upper edge. The sherd is slightly inturning and probably derives from a Deverel-Rimbury type bucket urn. The other sherds are possibly of a similar date and the thickness of the walls certainly suggests large heavy vessels, such as Deverel-Rimbury urns. In addition, there is a fragment of perforated clay slab from this context (not illustrated). Also from this context is one sherd of grog-tempered fabric and one sandy sherd. These are likely to be later in date, most probably Late Iron Age to early Romano-British, reflecting the mixed nature of these gravel surfaces.

[153] From this context there is a total of 16 flint-tempered sherds. Three joining rim sherds are from a plain hooked-rim jar. The remaining sherds are predominantly undiagnostic but do include some fragments of base with densely gritted undersides. Both the hooked rim jar and the gritted bases are elements characteristic of Late Bronze Age assemblages in the

lower Thames valley. However, some of the body sherds are more densely tempered with coarse flint and have thicker walls which, as with context 83, may derive from Deverel-Rimbury type vessels.

FLOOD DEPOSITS

Group 2, 1002

[152] A total of 12 flint-tempered sherds are present from this context but none of them are feature sherds or have diagnostic traits.

Phoenix Wharf assemblage (GAZ 189)

The Phoenix Wharf pottery had been previously examined and assigned to broad chronological groupings (see Table 24). During work for this publication the material was re-examined, with the exception of two diagnostic sherds that could not be located. The majority of the pottery is very fragmentary, very abraded and generally in very poor condition. All of the fragments appeared to be flint-tempered but, because of their small and fragile nature, it was not possible to identify the fabrics properly. The archive list assigned the pottery to the ?Neolithic, Early Bronze Age, Deverel-Rimbury type, Mid to Late Bronze Age and possibly the Iron Age. Re-examination of the fragments could not refine or confirm many of these identifications.

Most of the pottery was recovered from the ploughsoil layers [213] and [214] that overlay the burnt mound and cannot be associated with either the mound or boiling pit. Of the remaining material, two sherds were found on the underlying natural sand [217] and a handful of sherds were recovered from the fills of shallow depressions [243] and [274]; these contexts had been ploughed through and were considered part of the same stratigraphic horizon as the ploughsoil layers.

Table 24 Phoenix Wharf Pottery descriptions (taken from archive report)

Deposit	Context and accession no.	Description
Natural sand	[217] <199>	earlier than Deverel-Rimbury, probably Early Bronze Age, from a food vessel
	[217] <202>	–
Dark silt ploughsoil	[213] <185>	–
	[213] <186>	very worn, Late Neo/Early Bronze Age
	[213] <187>	possibly Deverel-Rimbury
	[213] <188>	possibly Deverel-Rimbury
	[213] <190>	Early Bronze Age/Deverel-Rimbury base?
	[213] <193>	–
	[213] <194>	–
	[213] <195>	Iron Age?
	[213] <196>	later prehistoric
	[213] <197>	?Neolithic
	[213] <198>	?Neolithic
	[214] <189>	probably Deverel-Rimbury
	[214] <191>	very worn Deverel-Rimbury
	[214] <192>	Early Bronze Age
Fills of depressions	[243] <200>	rim, Mid to Late Bronze Age
	[243] <201>	Deverel-Rimbury
	[274] <203>	–

Catalogue of pottery illustrations

<P1> WSB90 [114] pit (Fig 18) Peterborough Neolithic bowl (Mortlake type). Dense fabric with very rare, coarse flint and rare quartz. Oblique impressed decoration on upper rim edge and twisted cord 'maggot' impressions below rim. Wt 81g.

<P2> WSB90 [114] pit (Fig 18) Peterborough Neolithic bowl (Mortlake type). Flint-tempered fabric with rare, very coarse flint (up to 6mm). Impressed herringbone decoration on upper rim and first row of impressed herringbone? below rim. Wt 3g.

<P3> 11STS77 [83] Natural gravels (Fig 18) Peterborough Neolithic bowl (Mortlake ware). Dense, grog-tempered fabric. Impressed herringbone pattern on rim; impressed oblique lines under the rim and below the concave neck. Wt 43g.

<P4> WSB90 [114] pit (Fig 18) Sherd with stabbed and incised decoration of collared form. Fine, dense fabric with few visible inclusions. Possibly from small Collared Urn. Wt 16g.

<P5> 11STS88 [83] Natural gravels (Fig 42) Flint-tempered Deverel-Rimbury urn with finger-tip impressions on the upper edge. Wt 33g.

<P6> BA84 [4315] (Fig 42) Flint-tempered Deverel-Rimbury urn with fingernail decoration on the upper edge and the edges of two perforations below the rim. Wt 20g.

<P7> FW84 [2078] pit (Fig 22) Cup in finely flint-tempered fabric with lightly burnished surfaces; incised lines above the shoulder. Wt 13g.

<P8> FW84 [2078] pit (Fig 22) Rim from bowl. Soft, vesicular fabric. Wt 23g.

<P9> FW84 [1077] pit or hollow (Fig 38) Upright rim sherd. Wt 8g.

<P10> FW84 unstrat (Fig 38) Plain rim. Wt 5g.

<P11> 11STS77 [153] gravels (Fig 38) Flint-tempered hooked rim jar. Wt 62g.

<P12> BA84 [850] (Fig 38) Shoulder sherd with red iron-rich coating on exterior surface and single impressed dimple. (FLRM). Wt 9g.

<P13> BA84 [1330] (Fig 38) Carinated bowl with incised grooves on upper edge of carination and at base of neck. Fineware vessel with burnished surfaces both internally and externally. Very similar to an LBA/EIA vessel from Heathrow (Canham 1978, 27, fig 17 no. 59). (FLRM). Wt 29g.

<P14> BA84 [1497] (Fig 38) Flaring rim sherd with pinched fingernail decoration. (FLRC2). Wt 16g.

<P15> BA84 [2752] (Fig 38) Carinated shoulder sherd with finger-tip impressions. (SHMM). Wt 34g.

<P16> BA84 [3025] (Fig 38) Rim sherd from large, weakly shouldered jar with finger-tipping on outer edge of rim. (FLSH). Wt 94g.

<P17> BA84 [4044] (Fig 38) Flaring rim sherd with finger-tip impressions on the upper edge. (SHSC). Wt 13g.

<P18> BA84 [4046] (Fig 38) Rounded shoulder sherd with finger-tip impression. (FLRC/SHSM). Wt 17g.

<P19> BA84 [4044] (Fig 38) Carinated shoulder sherd with two finger-tip impressions. (FLRC2). Wt 15g.

<P20> BA84 [4044] (Fig 38) Small carinated shoulder sherd with fingernail impressions on ?top edge of shoulder. (QUCM/FLRM). Wt 4g.

<P21> BA84 [4315] (Fig 38) Upright rim of weakly carinated bowl with fingernail decoration on outer rim edge. (FLRC1). Wt 31g.

<P22> BA84 [3235] (Fig 38) Rim from sharply carinated bowl. (FLRC2). Wt 9g.

<P23> BA84 [1405] (Fig 38) Carinated shoulder sherd. (FLRC2). Wt 13g.

<P24> BA84 [1497] (Fig 38) Body sherd with plain applied cordon. (QUCM/FLRM). Wt 28g.

<P25> BA84 [4044] (Fig 38) Tall flaring rim. (QUSM). Wt 19g.

<P26> BA84 [4044] (Fig 38) Slightly everted rim. (QUSM). Wt 9g.

<P27> BA84 [2199] (Fig 38) Upright rim. (QUAF). Wt 20g.

<P28> BA84 [563] (Fig 39) Almost complete jar with slightly everted rim and gently curving body. The top end of the rim is flattened and decorated with fingernail impressions. The fabric is hard and reduced with a slightly lumpy appearance. The inclusions consist of rare, poorly sorted, sub-rounded quartz in a silty matrix with rare, coarse flint (not burnt or crushed and therefore likely to be naturally present in the clay body) and sparse, sub-angular grog. There are patches of sooting or burnt residue on the exterior rim. (QURM). Wt 805g.

<P29> BA84 [2950] (Fig 39) Rounded rim sherd, slightly everted. (QUSM). Wt 8g.

<P30> BA84 [1576] (Fig 39) Upright rim sherd probably from a jar. (QUSM). Wt 14g.

<P31> BA84 [4016] (Fig 39) Everted-rim sherd. (QUSM/SHSM). Wt 10g.

<P32> BA84 [1184] (Fig 39) Base from jar or bowl with footring, lightly burnished surface. (QUMM). Wt 64g.

<P33> COR89 [547] <116> (Fig 39) Bowl or wide-mouthed jar in glauconite-rich fabric. Wt 111g.

<P34> COR89 [578] <258> (Fig 39)

Rim sherd with short everted rim. Quartz-rich oxidised fabric, with reduced core. Lightly burnished surfaces. Wt 10g.

<P35> BA84 [4315] (Fig 39) Beaded-rim jar with bevelled internal edge. Vertical wipe marks internally. (SHCC/QUCM). Wt 47g.

<P36> BA84 [1693] (Fig 39) Bead-rimmed wide-mouthed jar or bowl with double cordon. Sparse shell inclusions. (SAND). Wt 36g.

<P37> BA84 [1723] (Fig 39) Tall rim with double cordon at base of neck and carinated shoulder. (SHSM). Wt 7g.

<P38> BA84 [3456] (Fig 39) Rippled neck sherd from bowl or jar. (GROG). Wt 12g.

<P39> BA84 [3456] (Fig 39) Decorated body sherd with four rows of incised decoration, wheel thrown. (SAND). Wt 6g.

<P40> BA84 [4200] (Fig 39) Globular-necked jar with a band of incised decoration on the shoulder. (SHCC2). Wt 180g.

<P41> BA84 [4200] (Fig 39) Lid-seated jar with diamond-shaped rim profile. (SHEL). Wt 68g.

<P42> BA84 [4315] (Fig 39) Decorated body sherd with incised lines and notches. (SHEL). Wt 15g.

<P43> BA84 [4315] (Fig 39) Large bead-rimmed jar with heavy internal thickening. (SHEL). Wt 148g.

Catalogue for fired clay objects

<S1> FW84 [1084] (Fig 43) Perforated clay slab fragments Reddish brown ill-sorted flint-tempered fabric. Traces of two perforations. Both fragments have one finished edge and one has the beginning of a corner.

<S2> FW84 [1077] (Fig 43) Perforated clay slab. Ill-sorted flint-tempered fabric; reddish-brown in colour. Denser fine flint grit on surfaces, traces of two perforations.

<S3> FW84 unstratified (Fig 43) Fragment of perforated clay slab. Flint-tempered reddish-brown fabric with fine, dense flint grit on the surface, trace of one perforation.

<S4> BA84 [4315] (Fig 41) Large fragments of triangular loomweight (now restored).

<S5> COR89 [575] <254> (Fig 41) Very abraded fragment of fired clay from triangular loomweight.

<S6> COR89 [578] <259> (Fig 41) Two joining fragments of fired clay – loomweight? Two finished edges remain but no trace of perforation.

6.3 Radiocarbon determinations

Jane Sidell

Table 25 lists all available prehistoric radiocarbon measurements that have been collected from the study area; no screening took place with the exception of one record from 1976 identifying only that the measurement came from 'Southwark'. The OD height has been inserted where it was available; however, it was deemed better to publish the dates without or only with a large altitudinal range rather than leave dates out.

Details of the dating methods used have already been described (see Chapter 1.8). The material dated column identifies (where known) exactly what the date was obtained on. Care has been taken with the most recent dates to ensure that heartwood was not dated; however, it cannot be stated with confidence that the earlier samples were as rigorously checked.

Table 25 Radiocarbon determinations from the study area

Laboratory code	Site	GAZ no.	OD height (where available)	Sample	Radiocarbon age (BP)	δ ¹³C (λ)	Calibrated date (95% confidence)
OxA-1198	between Vauxhall and Battersea Bridge	1		human skull	2950±60		1380–970 cal BC
Beta-122969	Nine Elms, Vauxhall	6		oak pile	3180±70	-25.0*	1620–1260 cal BC
Beta-122970	Nine Elms, Vauxhall	6		oak pile	3380±40	-25.0*	1750–1520 cal BC
GU-5723	Nine Elms, Vauxhall	6		wood: *Quercus* sp fairly young heartwood (R Gale)	2330±100	-25.0	770–170 cal BC
GU-5724	Nine Elms, Vauxhall	6		wood: *Alnus* sp worked tapered stem/round wood max diameter 45mm (R Gale)	2440±50	-28.6	790–390 cal BC
Beta-85222	Stamford St	43	c +0.15m OD	organic sediment	2770±60	-25.0*	1050–800 cal BC

(Table 25 cont)

Laboratory code	Site	GAZ no.	OD height (where available)	Sample	Radiocarbon age (BP)	δ ¹³C (λ)	Calibrated date (95% confidence)
Beta-85223	Stamford St	43	c 0.0m OD	organic sediment	3320±60	-25.0*	1750–1440 cal BC
Beta-119783	Joan St	51	-2.35 to -2.25m	organic sediment	4850±80	-25.0*	3790–3380 cal BC
Beta-119784	Joan St	51	-0.55 to -0.50m	organic sediment	2340±60	-25.0*	760–210 cal BC
Beta-119785	Joan St	51	-1.46 to -1.41m	wood	3420±70	-25.0*	1890–1520 cal BC
Beta-122928	Joan St	51	-2.32 to -2.27m	wood	3970±70	-25.0*	2840–2230 cal BC
Beta-119786	Union St	53	-0.60 to -0.55m	peat	2290±90	-25.0*	760–110 cal BC
Beta-199787	Union St	53	-2.32 to -2.27m	peat	4630±100	-25.0*	3650–3030 cal BC
Beta-199788	Union St	53	-1.60 to -1.55m	wood	3930±80	-25.0*	2620–2140 cal BC
HAR-2346	Southwark Leisure Centre	55	+0.37m	wood: probably Corylus. Alnus sp and Betula sp; c 50% identified (C A Keepax)	2910±70	-27.9	1370–900 cal BC
Beta-117088	Southwark foreshore	62		wood	4660±50	-25.0*	3630–3350 cal BC
Beta-107320	Bankside Pontoon	67		wood	4430±80	-25.0*	3370–2880 cal BC
Beta-107321	Bankside Pontoon	67		wood	4420±80	-25.0*	3360–2880 cal BC
Beta-110971	Bankside Pontoon	67		organic sediment	2410±70	-25.0*	790–380 cal BC
Beta-114003	Bankside Pontoon	67	-1.82m	wood	4370±70	-25.0*	3340–2880 cal BC
Beta-129555	Benbow House	68	between -0.5 and +0.7m	peat	2890±50	-25.0*	1260–920 cal BC
HAR-2506	Chaucer House	110	between -0.11m and +0.14m	wood Betula sp strips of bark, function unknown (C A Keepax)	2700±60	-28.7	1000–790 cal BC
HAR-3931	Hibernia Wharf	118		organic clay	2630±80	-28.6	970–540 cal BC
OxA-8763	Fennings Wharf	130	c 0.0m	charcoal: Quercus sp sapwood (R Gale)	3360±40	-22.7	1750–1520 cal BC
OxA-8764	Fennings Wharf	130	c 0.0m	charcoal: Quercus sp sapwood (R Gale)	3400±45	-22.6	1880–1530 cal BC
OxA-8765	Fennings Wharf	130	c 0.0m	charcoal: Quercus sp sapwood (R Gale)	3345±45	-22.6	1740–1520 cal BC
OxA-8766	Fennings Wharf	130	c 0.0m	charcoal: Quercus sp sapwood (R Gale)	3425±40	-22.9	1880–1620 cal BC
OxA-8767	Fennings Wharf	130	c 0.0m	charcoal: Quercus sp sapwood (R Gale)	3420±40	-22.7	1880–1620 cal BC
OxA-8678	Fennings Wharf	130	c 0.0m	charcoal: Quercus sp sapwood (R Gale)	3490±40	-22.5	1920–1690 cal BC
OxA-8769	Fennings Wharf	130	c 0.0m	charcoal: Quercus sp sapwood (R Gale)	3430±45	-22.7	1880–1620 cal BC
OxA-8770	Fennings Wharf	130	c 0.0m	charcoal: Quercus sp sapwood (R Gale)	3545±40	-22.8	2020–1740 cal BC
UB-4431	Fennings Wharf	130	c 0.0m	charcoal: Quercus sp sapwood (R Gale)	3407±33	-23.49±0.2	1860–1620 cal BC
HAR-3926	Wilson's Wharf	148	+0.18m	wood: root-like nodules, originally c 30mm in diameter (A J Clark)	2770±80	-30.8	1190–790 cal BC
HAR-3925	Wilson's Wharf	148	0.10m	peaty soil	3010±70	-31.1	1430–1010 cal BC
HAR-3927	Wilson's Wharf	148	+0.38m	peat	2570±80	-30.5	900–400 cal BC
Beta-120218	159–161 Tower Bridge Rd	156	-0.7m	organic sediment	3360±70	-25.0*	1880–1460 cal BC
Beta-120219	159–161 Tower Bridge Rd	156	-0.25m	organic sediment	3030±70	-25.0*	1440–1040 cal BC
Beta-133411	159–161 Tower Bridge Rd	156	-0.01m	organic sediment	2990±60	-25.0*	1400–1020 cal BC
Beta-118941	Vinegar Yard	163		peat	2450±50	-25.0*	790–400 cal BC
Beta-118942	Vinegar Yard	163		peat	2730±50	-25.0*	1000–800 cal BC
Beta-141037	167 Tower Bridge Rd	165		peat	2550±50	-28.6	820–410 cal BC
Beta-141038	167 Tower Bridge Rd	165		peat	3340±50	-28.9	1740–1510 cal BC
HAR-333	Mark Browns Wharf	169		peat	2810±80	-24.2	1260–800 cal BC
Beta-136117	Three Oaks Lane	176		timber stake	3270±50	-28.2	1690–1430 cal BC
Beta-136118	Three Oaks Lane	176	+0.16–0.26m	peat	2720±80	-29.4	1050–790 cal BC
Beta-107981	Lafone Street	179	+0.4m	organic sediment	3100±60	-25.0*	1520—1130 cal BC
Beta-107982	Lafone Street	179	+0.4m	organic sediment	3080±70	-25.0*	1520–1120 cal BC
BM-2766	Phoenix Wharf	189	+0.1–0.2m	charcoal: Salix/Populus sp	3310±40	-25.9	1690–1500 cal BC
GU-2900	Bricklayers Arms	191		alder wood	3260±60		1690–1410 cal BC
GU-2901	Bricklayers Arms	191		willow wood	3300±60		1740–1430 cal BC
Beta-108653	Grinders & Operators	195	c +0.22m	peat		-25.0*	1430–1045 cal BC
Beta-108654	Grinders & Operators	195	c +0.08m	peat		-25.0*	1404–1030 cal BC
GrN-22181	Bermondsey foreshore	207	c 2.8m	wood	5400±100		4460–3980 cal BC
Beta-70409	Bramcote	215	-3.13 to -3.07m	organic silt	11020±60	-25.0*	11230–10920 cal BC
Beta-70408	Bramcote	215	-2.36 to -2.31m	organic silt	8280±120	-25.0*	7580–7050 cal BC
Beta-68574	Bramcote	215	-2.22	wood	4110±70	-25.0*	2890–2460 cal BC
Beta-68575	Bramcote	215	-1.90 to -1.80m		4940±100	-25.0*	3970–3520 cal BC
Beta-70407	Bramcote	215	-2.17m to -2.12m	organic silt	6110±120	-25.0*	5320–4720 cal BC
Beta-68577	Bramcote	215			5040±80	-25.0*	3990–3650 cal BC

(*Table 25 cont*)

Laboratory code	Site	GAZ no.	OD height (where available)	Sample	Radiocarbon age (BP)	δ ¹³C (λ)	Calibrated date (95% confidence)
Beta-68573	Bramcote	215	-2.07 to -1.96m	organic silt	4330±70	-25.0*	3260–2760 cal BC
Beta-70406	Bramcote	215	-1.56 to -1.52m	peat	3630±80	-25.0*	2210–1740 cal BC
Beta-68572	Bramcote	215	-1.30 to -1.20m	organic clay	3570±60	-25.0*	2130–1740 cal BC
Beta-70410	Bramcote	215	-1.14 to -1.00m	wood, *Quercus* sp outer 25 sapwood rings	3350±60	-25.0*	1860–1510 cal BC
Beta-70411	Bramcote	215	-0.96m	wood, *Quercus* sp outer 25 sapwood rings	3410±70	-25.0*	1890–1520 cal BC
Beta-70412	Bramcote	215	-0.96m	wood, *Quercus* sp outer 25 sapwood rings	3370±60	-25.0*	1880–1510 cal BC
Beta-70413	Bramcote	215	-1.45m	wood *Quercus* sp outer rings	3500±80	-25.0*	2030–1620 cal BC
Beta-70405	Bramcote	215	-1.01 to -0.971m	peat	2970±60	-25.0*	1390–1000 cal BC
Beta-68571	Bramcote	215	-0.95 to -0.850m	peat	2980±60	-25.0*	1400–1000 cal BC
Beta-68576	Bramcote	215			4910±80	-25.0*	3940–3520 cal BC
SRR 435	Silverlock	220		peat	2947±50	-29.4	1320–100 cal BC
SRR 436	Silverlock	220		peat	3180±80	-29.2	1680–1650 cal BC
Beta-122968	Canada Water	221	-1.21 to -1.17m	peat	3650±100	-25.0*	2300–1740 cal BC
Beta-93691	Surrey Quays Rd	225		peat	2940±60	-25.0*	800–400 cal BC
Beta-93692	Surrey Quays Rd	225		peat	3640±70	-25.0*	2200–1770 cal BC
Beta-99295	71–97 Plough Way	229	between +0.35 and +0.8m	organic sediment	2890±70	-25.0*	1370–890 cal BC
Beta-99296	71–97 Plough Way	229	between +0.35 and +0.8m	organic sediment	2180±60	-25.0*	400–40 cal BC
Beta-68576	Bryan Rd	230	c -2.6m	peat	4910±80	-25.0*	3940–3510 cal BC
Beta-68577	Bryan Rd	230	c -2.6m	peat	5040±80	-25.0*	3970–3700 cal BC

* = estimated

FRENCH AND GERMAN SUMMARIES

Résumé

Dans ce volume, on trouvera une description des traits culturels qui indiquent une présence humaine dans la partie nord de Southwark et Lambeth à Londres pendant la période allant de 9500 cal BC à 50 après J.-C. On y trouvera également les indices des changements apportés à l'environnement et aux abords de la rivière pendant cette période et aussi la manière dont les communautés humaines furent la cause de ces changements et réagirent face à leurs effets. Dans un chapître d'introduction, on a souligné les éléments de base de cette étude qui fait partie du programme de publication pour le Grand Londres commissionné par English Heritage. Cette étude est le premier essai de synthèse de toute l'information préhistorique et topographique faite en utilisant les données obtenues par le service archéologique du Musée de Londres et par ses prédécesseurs. La plupart de ces données proviennent des résultats de fouilles non publiés des années 80 avec en plus autant d'information nouvelle que possible provenant des sites récents.

Dans ce volume, une structure chronologique n'a pas été adoptée car pendant l'analyse on a trouvé que les divisions habituelles du système des trois âges correspondant à un cadre chronologique rigide: chasseurs-cueilleurs, cultivateurs sédentaires fabricant des poteries puis ceux produisant des objets en métal ne pouvaient être appliquées dans ce cas. On a donc remplacé ce cadre chronologique par une approche thématique large comprenant d'abord les communités mobiles, suivi de l'aspect rituel des rivières et finalement des communautés sédentaires. Ces sections sont en fait descriptives. La première donne les résultats des données obtenues pour un site mésolithique situé près d'un lac de la période glacière tardive à Bermondsey; la deuxième section, ceux d'un monticule brulé et d'un fossé d'enceinte avec des crémations et la dernière décrit une série de traces de charrues préservées. Les éléments montrant les changements de l'environnment et du régime de la rivière sont incorporés aux discussions sur le paysage et l'impacte humain sur cet environnement.

Plusieurs courtes discussions font suite à la présentation des données; elles portent d'abord sur les étapes écologiques à travers les temps et l'influence humaine sur elles. Ensuite elles se concentrent sur la préhistoire de Southwark et Lambeth replacée dans un cadre régional large afin d'évaluer avec justesse le sens de cette nouvelle information dans le contexte élargi de la vallée de la Tamise. Les ressemblances et les différences entre les centres préhistoriques les mieux connus de Heathrow et de l'est de Londres ont été identifiés: par example l'agencement des champs anciens de Southwark et Heathrow. Le contraste entre le manque de données pour les villages de l'Age du Fer au centre de Londres et le nombre de villages et 'hillforts' plus à l'est est mis en évidence.

Il a été fait un registre de tous les emplacements des objets retrouvés datant de l'époque préhistorique qui donne les adresses de ces emplacements, une description brève de ces objets et des mentions publiées ainsi que leur enregistrement dans la carte archéologique du Grand Londres (GLSMR) si possible. Les numéros du registre se retrouvent dans le texte lorsqu'un site est mentionné et à l'en-tête du chapître là où un site est décrit en plus grands détails. Plusieurs articles techniques sont inclus à l'intention des lecteurs plus spécialisés. L'un d'eux donne les détails des outils en silex retrouvés dans le site et ses alentours ainsi que les résultats de l'analyse des traces faite sur l'important ensemble de silex du Mésolithique ancien du site B&Q (GAZ 208). Un autre article donne les détails de la quantification de la potterie et ceux des formes et des fabriques de tout le matériel décrit pour le site et ses environs. Un dernier rapport donne toutes les dates radiocarbones disponibles.

Zusammenfassung

Dieser Band berichtet über kulturelle Zeugnisse menschlicher Präsenz im Gebiet von Nord-Southwark und Lambeth, London, in der Zeit von ca. 9500 v. Chr. bis ca. 50 n. Chr. Es werden die Umwelt- und Flußveränderungen während dieser Periode dokumentiert und die Art und Weise untersucht, wie die menschlichen Gemeinschaften diese Veränderungen verursachten und wie sie wahrscheinlich auf sie reagiert haben. Das einleitende Kapitel beleuchtet den Hintergrund zu dieser Studie, wie sie als Teil des Publikationsprogramms von English Heritage für Groß-London entstand. Diese Studie ist der erste konzertierte Versuch, die vorhandenen prähistorischen und topographischen Informationen zu vereinen. Dabei werden Daten des Museums of London Archaeology Service und seiner Vorläufer verwendet. Dazu gehören auch unpublizierte Arbeiten aus den 1980er Jahren, die hier durch die Einbeziehung soviel wie möglich neuen Materials ergänzt werden.

Dieser Band hat keine zwingende chronologische Struktur, da es sich während der Analyse herausstellte, daß die konventionelle Einteilung eines Drei-Zeitaltersystems, wie es durch Jäger und Sammler, seßhafte Bauern mit Keramikproduktion, gefolgt von Metallverarbeitung definiert ist, einen zu starren Rahmen liefert und hier nicht paßt. Statt dessen wird das Material innerhalb weiter gefaßter Themen behandelt. Dies beginnt mit der 'mobilen Gesellschaft', gefolgt von der 'rituellen Flußszene' und schließt mit einer Untersuchung über Anzeichen für 'seßhafte Gemeinschaften'. Diese Abschnitte sind wirkungsvoll diskutiert in der Art wie

sie die Nachweise zusammenfassen, nämlich zu einem mesolithischen Lager an einem späteiszeitlichen See in Bermondsey im ersten Teil, zu einem brandgezeichneten Erdhügel mit Ringgraben in Verbindung mit einer Gruppe von Feuerbestattungen im zweiten Teil, und im abschließenden Teil zu einer Reihe erhaltener flacher Pflugspuren. Belege für Umwelt- und Flußveränderungen werden in den Text der Diskussionen über die Landschaft und die Wechselwirkung mit der menschlichen Bevölkerung eingeflochten.

Nach einem Abriß der verfügbaren Nachweise untersuchen mehrere Kurzartikel erstens die ökologische Aufeinanderfolge und die Rolle der Menschen darin, und zweitens die Vorgeschichte Southwarks und Lambeth im weiteren regionalen Zusammenhang, um genau herauszufinden, was diese neue Information im weiteren Kontext des Themsetals bedeutet. Es überrascht nicht, daß Ähnlichkeiten und Unterschiede zu den besser bekannten frühgeschichtlichen Zentren, wie Heathrow und Ost-London, herausgearbeitet werden, wie z. B. das Feldsystem in Southwark und Heathrow, und auch der Gegensatz zwischen dem Fehlen eisenzeitlicher Besiedlung in Zentral-London gegenüber den Hillforts/ Siedlungen, wie sie weiter im Osten gefunden wurden.

Ein alphabetisches Verzeichnis faßt alle Fundstellen der vorgeschichtlichen Materialien unter Angabe der örtlichen Anschriften zusammen mit einer kurzen Beschreibung der Funde, publizierten Quellenangaben, sowie Angaben des Greater London Site and Monument Record (GLSMR), soweit vorhanden. Die Numerierungen im Verzeichnis (GAZ#) enthalten Querverweise im Haupttext, wenn eine besondere Ausgrabung erwähnt wird und bei den Kapitelüberschriften, wo eine Ausgrabungsstätte in größeren Einzelheiten erörtert wird. Mehrere technische Abhandlungen wurden für die Spezialisten aufgenommen. Eine davon präsentiert Einzelheiten über bearbeiteten Flint, der im untersuchten Gebiet gefunden wurde, zusammen mit einer Mikroabnutzungsanalyse der bedeutenden frühmesolithischen Fundgruppe von der B&Q-Ausgrabung (GAZ 208). Eine zweite Abhandlung beschäftigt sich mit allen Einzelheiten der Töpferwaren-Mengenbestimmung, sowie mit Formen und Materialien für das gesamte, beschriebene Material aus der untersuchten Gegend. Der abschließende Bericht führt alle verfügbaren Radiokarbonbestimmungen auf.

BIBLIOGRAPHY

Adkins, R, and Jackson, R, 1978 *Neolithic stone and flint axes from the River Thames: an illustrated corpus*, Brit Mus Occas Pap 1, London

Adkins, L, and Needham, S, 1985 New research on a Late Bronze Age enclosure at Queen Mary's Hospital, Carshalton, *Surrey Archaeol Collect* 76, 11–50

Akerman, J W, 1855 Notes of antiquarian researches in the summer and autumn of 1854, *Archaeologia* 36, 175–86

Allen, T, and Welsh, K, 1996 Eton Rowing Lake, *Current Archaeol* 148, 124–7

Allen, T, Hey, G, and Miles, D, 1997 A line of time: approaches to archaeology in the upper and middle Thames valley, England, *World Archaeol* 29(1), 114–29

Andrews, D, and Merriman, N, 1986 A prehistoric timber structure at Richmond Terrace, Whitehall, *Trans London Middlesex Archaeol Soc* 37, 17–21

Andrews G, Barrett, J, and Lewis, J, 1998 Perry Oaks assessment, unpub archive report for British Airports Authority

Andrews, P, and Crockett, A, 1996 *Three excavations along the Thames and its tributaries, 1994*, Wessex Archaeol Monogr 10, Salisbury

Anon, 1937 Oval flint knife, *Antiq J* 17, 70

Ashmore, P, 1999 Radiocarbon dating: avoiding errors by avoiding mixed samples, *Antiquity* 73, 124–30

Barclay, A, Boyle, A, Bradley, P, and Roberts, M R, 1995 Excavations at the former Jewsons Yard, Uxbridge, Middlesex, *Trans London Middlesex Archaeol Soc* 46, 1–25

Barfield, L, and Hodder, M, 1980 The excavation of two burnt mounds in South Birmingham, *West Midlands Archaeol* 23, 15–26

Barrett, J, 1975 Types, affinities, chronology and significance, in Bradley, R, and Ellison, A, *Rams Hill: a Bronze Age defended enclosure and its landscape*, BAR Brit Ser 19, 101–18, Oxford

Barrett, J, 1978 The prehistoric pottery from 106–114 Borough High Street, in Bird et al 1978, 197–9

Barrett, J, 1980 The pottery of the later Bronze Age in lowland England, *Proc Prehist Soc* 46, 297–319

Barrett, J C, Lewis, J S C, and Welsh, K, 2000 Perry Oaks – a history of inhabitation, *London Archaeol* 9(7), 195–9

Barrett, J C, Lewis, J C S, and Welsh, K, 2001 Perry Oaks – a history of inhabitation, part 2, *London Archaeol* 9(8), 221–7

Barton, R N E, 1992 *Hengistbury Head Dorset: Vol 2, The Late Upper Palaeolithic and Early Mesolithic sites*, Oxford Univ Comm Archaeol Monogr 34, Oxford

Barton, R N E, Berridge, P J, Walker, M J C, and Bevins, R E, 1995 Persistent places in the Mesolithic landscape: an example from the Black Mountain uplands of South Wales, *Proc Prehist Soc* 61, 81–116

Bates, J, and Minkin, J, 1999 Lafone Street, Southwark: prehistoric farming and a medieval bridge, *London Archaeol* 8(9), 325–30

Bates, M, and Barham, A, 1995 Holocene alluvial stratigraphic architecture and archaeology in the Lower Thames area, in *The Quaternary of the lower Thames* (eds D R Bridgland, P Allen and A Haggart), Quat Res Ass, London

Bates, M R, and Bates, C R, 2000 Multidisciplinary approaches to the geoarchaeological evaluation of deeply stratified sedimentary sequences: examples from Pleistocene and Holocene deposits in southern England, United Kingdom, *J Archaeol Sci* 27, 845–58

Bayliss, A, 1999 On the taphonomy of charcoal samples for radiocarbon dating, in *Actes du 3ième Congrès International «Archéologie et* ¹⁴*C», Lyon, 6–10 Avril 1998* (eds J Evin, C Oberlin, J P Daugas, and J F Salles), *Revue d'Archéométrie* Suppl 1999 et Soc Préhist Fr Mémoire 26, 51–6, Lyon

Bell, M, 1992 Archaeology under alluvium: human agency and environmental process: some concluding thoughts, in *Alluvial archaeology in Britain* (eds S Needham and M Macklin), Oxbow Monogr 27, 271–6, Oxford

Bell, M, and Neumann, H, 1997 Prehistoric intertidal archaeology and environments in the Severn estuary, Wales, *World Archaeol* 29(1), 95–113

Bennell, M, 1998 *Under the road*, Bexley Borough Council, London

Binford, L R, 1978 Dimensional analysis of behavior and site structure: learning from an Eskimo hunting stand, *American Antiquity* 43, 330–61

Binford, L R, 1980 Willow smoke and dogs' tails: hunter-gatherer settlement systems and archaeological site formation, *American Antiquity* 45, 4–20

Bird, J, Graham, A H, Sheldon, H L, and Townend, P, 1978 *Southwark excavations 1972–4*, London Middlesex Archaeol Soc and Surrey Archaeol Soc Joint Pub 1, London

Bird, D G, Crocker, A G, Crocker, G, and McCracken, J S, 1980 Archaeology in Surrey 1976–8, *Surrey Archaeol Collect* 72, 231–53

Bird, D G, Crocker, G, and McCracken, J S, 1984 Archaeology in Surrey 1982, *Surrey Archaeol Collect* 75, 263–72

Bird, D G, Crocker, G, and McCracken, J S, 1986 Archaeology in Surrey 1984, *Surrey Archaeol Collect* 77, 213–26

Bird, D G, Crocker, G, and McCracken, J S, 1987 Archaeology in Surrey 1985–6, *Surrey Archaeol Collect* 78, 133–48

Bird, D G, Crocker, G, and McCracken, J S, 1989 Archaeology in Surrey 1987, *Surrey Archaeol Collect* 79, 179–89

Bird, D G, Crocker, G, and McCracken, J S, 1990 Archaeology in Surrey 1988–9, *Surrey Archaeol Collect* 80, 201–28

Bird, D G, Crocker, G, and McCracken, J S, 1991–2 Archaeology in Surrey 1990, *Surrey Archaeol Collect* 81, 147–68

Bishop, B J, 1996 Excavations at 47–67 Hopton Street London SE1: the lithic material, unpub MA dissertation, School of Archaeological Sciences, Univ Leicester

Bishop, B J, 1998 Lithic assessment, Hopton Street, unpub Pre-Construct Archaeology archive rep

Bloise, B, 1974, Excavation round-up 1973, *London Archaeol* 2(6), 133–5

Bloise, B, 1975, Excavation round-up 1974, *London Archaeol* 2(10), 256–9

Bloise, B, 1976, Excavation round-up 1975, *London Archaeol* 2(14), 370–5

Bonsall, C, and Smith, C, 1989 Late Palaeolithic and Mesolithic bone and antler artefacts from Britain: first reactions to accelerator dates, *Mesolithic Misc* 10(1), 33–8

Bowsher, J M C, 1991 A burnt mound from Phoenix Wharf, south-east London: a preliminary report, in *Burnt mounds and hot stone technology: papers from the 2nd international burnt mound conference, Sandwell, 12–14 October 1990* (eds M A Hodder and L H Barfield), Sandwell Metropolitan Borough Council

Bradley, R, 1990 *The passage of arms*, Cambridge

Bradley, R, and Gordon, K, 1988 Human skulls from the River Thames, their dating and significance, *Antiquity* 62, 503–9

Bronk Ramsey, C, 1995 Radiocarbon calibration and analysis of stratigraphy, *Radiocarbon* 36, 425–30

Bronk Ramsey, C, 2000 *OxCAL v3.5 radiocarbon calibration programme*, Res Lab Archaeol Hist Art, Oxford

Bronk Ramsey, C, in prep Development of the radiocarbon calibration program OxCal, *Radiocarbon*

Bronk Ramsey, C, and Hedges, R E M, 1997 Hybrid ion sources: radiocarbon measurements from microgram to milligram, *Nuclear Instruments and Methods in Physics Research B* 123, 539–45

Brown, N, and Cotton J F, 2000 The Bronze Age, in *The archaeology of Greater London* (ed MoLAS), 81–100, London

Bruce, P, 1994 21–35 Marlborough Grove, London SE1, London Borough of Southwark: an archaeological excavation, unpub MoLAS archive rep

Brück, J, 1995 A place for the dead: the role of human remains in Late Bronze Age Britain, *Proc Prehist Soc* 61, 245–77

Buck, C E, Cavanagh, W G, and Litton, C D, 1996 *Bayesian approach to interpreting archaeological data*, Chichester

Cameron, N G, 2000 Assessment of the diatoms from Tower Bridge Road, Southwark, unpub archive rep, ECRC, Univ College London

Canham, R, 1978 Excavations at London (Heathrow) Airport 1969, *Trans London Middlesex Archaeol Soc* 29, 1–44

Champion, T, 1980 Settlement and environment in later Bronze Age Kent, in *Settlement and society in the British later Bronze Age* (eds J Barrett and R Bradley), BAR Brit Ser 83, 223–46, Oxford

Clark, A, 1993 *Excavations at Mucking: Vol 1, The site atlas*, London

Clark, J G D, 1934 The classification of a microlithic culture: the Tardenoisian of Horsham, *Archaeol J* 90, 52–77

Clark, J G D, 1954 *Excavations at Star Carr: an Early Mesolithic site at Seamer near Scarborough, Yorkshire*, Cambridge

Coles, J M, 1962 European Bronze Age shields, *Proc Prehist Soc* 28, 156–90

Collins, D, and Lorimer, D H (eds), 1989 *Excavations at the Mesolithic site on West Heath, Hampstead 1976–81*, BAR Brit Ser 217, Oxford

Cotton, J F, 1992 The struck flint, in Cowan 1992, 62–7

Cotton, J F, 1997 Lafone Street, Bermondsey: finds assessment, unpub Museum of London archive rep

Cotton, J F, 1999 Ballast-heavers and battle-axes: the 'Golden Age' of Thames finds, in *Mark Dion: archaeology* (eds A Coles and M Dion), 58–71, London

Cotton, J F, 2000 Foragers and farmers: towards the development of a settled landscape in London, c 4000–1200 BC, in *The archaeology of London* (eds I Haynes, L Hannigan and H Sheldon), 9–34, Oxford

Cotton, J F, and Merriman, N, 1991 Some recent prehistoric finds from Greater London, *Trans London Middlesex Archaeol Soc* 42, 33–57

Cotton, J F, and Wood, B, 1996 Recent prehistoric finds from the Thames foreshore and beyond in Greater London, *Trans London Middlesex Archaeol Soc* 47, 1–33

Cowan, C, 1992 A possible *mansio* in Roman Southwark: excavations at 15–23 Southwark Street, 1980–6, *Trans London Middlesex Archaeol Soc* 43, 3–191

Cowan, C, in prep *Urban development in north-west Roman Southwark: excavations 1974–90*, MoLAS Monogr Ser, London

Cowan, C, Wheeler, L, and Westman, A, in prep, *Roman Southwark: origins, development and economy*, MoLAS Monogr Ser, London

Cresswell, J, 1974 Flints, in Sheldon 1974, 31–3

Cresswell, J, 1978 The flintwork, in Bird et al 1978, 197–8

Cresswell, J, 1988 Flint, in Hinton 1988, 385–7

Department of the Environment, 1990 *Planning policy guidance note 16; archaeology and planning*, London

Devoy, R J N, 1979 Flandrian sea-level changes and vegetational history of the lower Thames estuary, *Phil Trans Roy Soc London*, B 285, 355–410

Devoy, R J N, 1980 Postglacial environmental change and man in the Thames estuary: a synopsis, in *Archaeology and coastal change* (ed F H Thompson), Soc Antiq Spec Pap 1, 134–48, London

Dillon, J, Jackson, S, and Jones, H, 1991 Excavations at the Courage Brewery and Park Street 1984–90, *London Archaeol* 6, 229–31

Donahue, R E, nd [1997] Tool function and settlement in the Italian Epigravettian, unpub paper presented to the Lithic Stud Soc, Bradford, May 1997

Donahue, R E, 1988 Microwear analysis and site function: an Italian Upper Palaeolithic example, *World Archaeol* 19, 357–75

Donahue, R E, 1990 Microwear analysis of lithic artefacts from the Mesolithic and Neolithic site at Lismore Fields, Buxton, unpub manuscript prepared for Trent and Peak Archaeol Trust

Donahue, R E, 1994 The current state of lithic microwear research, in *Stories in stone* (eds N Ashton and A David), 156–68, Oxford

Donahue, R E, 1998 Lithic microwear analysis of artefacts from Barnham, in *Excavations at the Lower Palaeolithic site at East Farm, Barnham, Suffolk, 1989–94* (eds N Ashton, S G Lewis and S Parfitt), Brit Mus Occas Pap 125, 245–50, London

Donahue, R E, 1999 The microwear analysis of the flint artefacts from Upper Ninepence, in Gibson, A, *The Walton Basin project: excavation and survey in a prehistoric landscape, 1993–7*, CBA Res Rep 118, 100–12, York

Donahue, R E, Burroni, D B, Coles, G M, Colten, R H, and Hunt, C O, 1992 Petriolo III south: implications for the transition to agriculture in Tuscany, *Current Anthropol* 33(3), 328–31

Drummond-Murray, J, 1994 Wolseley Street, land adjacent to the Fire Station, SE1, London Borough of Southwark: an archaeological evaluation, unpub MoLAS archive rep

Drummond-Murray, J, Saxby, D, and Watson, B, 1995 Recent archaeological work in the Bermondsey district of Southwark, *London Archaeol* 7(10), 251–57

Drummond-Murray, J, and Thompson, P, with Cowan, C, 2002 *Settlement in Roman Southwark: archaeological excavations (1991–8) for the London Underground Limited Jubilee Line Extension Project*, MoLAS Monogr Ser 12, London

Drury, P J, 1978 *Excavations at Little Waltham 1970–1*, CBA Res Rep 26, London

Dumont, J V, 1989 Star Carr: the results of a microwear study, in *The Mesolithic in Europe: papers presented at the 3rd international symposium, Edinburgh 1985* (ed C Bonsall), 231–40, Edinburgh

Editors, 1974–2001 London fieldwork and publication roundup, *London Archaeol* 2–9

Editors, 1980–2000 Archaeology in Surrey, *Surrey Archaeol Collect* 72–87

Elsden, N J, 2001 Excavations at 36–46 Tanner Street and 159–161 Tower Bridge Road, Bermondsey, *London Archaeol* 9(10), 275–82

English Heritage 1991 *The management of archaeological projects*, London

Evans, J G, 1972 *Land snails in archaeology*, London

Evans, J G, 1975 *The environment of early man in the British Isles*, London

Filer, J, 1991 Excavation round-up 1990, part 2: London boroughs, *London Archaeol* 6(11), 301–9

Fischer, A, 1989 Hunting with flint-tipped arrows: results and experiences from practical experiments, in *The Mesolithic in Europe: papers presented at the 3rd international symposium, Edinburgh 1985* (ed C Bonsall), 29–39, Edinburgh

Fischer, A, Hansen, P V, and Rasmussen, P, 1984. Macro and microwear traces on lithic projectile points. *J Danish Archaeol* 3, 19–46

Franks, A W, 1864–7 *Proc Soc Antiq London*, 2 ser, 342–4

Gerloff, S, 1975 The Early Bronze Age daggers in Great Britain, and a reconsideration of the Wessex culture, *Prähistorische Bronzefunde*, 6.2

Gibbard, P L, 1994 *The Pleistocene history of the lower Thames valley*, Cambridge

Gibson, A M, 1995 First impressions: a review of Peterborough ware in Wales, in *Unbaked urns of rudely shape: essays on British and Irish pottery* (eds I Kinnes and G Varndell), Oxbow Monogr 55, 23–39, Oxford

Gibson, A M, 1997 The prehistoric pottery from Hopton Street, London, unpub Pre-Construct Archaeology archive rep

Gibson, A M, and Kinnes, I, 1997 On the urns of a dilemma: radiocarbon and the Peterborough problem, *Oxford J Archaeol* 16, 65–71

Gilman, P J, 1993 Archaeology in Essex 1992, *Essex Archaeol Hist* 24, 195–210

Giorgi, J A, 2001 The plant remains, in Watson, B, Brigham, T, and Dyson, T, *London bridge: 2000 years of a river crossing*, MoLAS Monogr Ser 8, London

Girardon, S, and Heathcote, J, 1988 Excavation round-up 1987, part 2: London boroughs, *London Archaeol* 5(10), 270–8

Girardon, S, and Heathcote, J, 1989 Excavation round-up 1988, part 2: London boroughs, *London Archaeol* 6(2), 72–80

Girling, M A, 1988 The bark beetle *Scolytus scolytus* (Fabricius) and the possible role of elm disease in the Early Neolithic, in *Archaeology and the flora of the British Isles* (ed M Jones), Oxford Univ Comm Archaeol Monogr 14, 34–8, Oxford

Godwin, H, 1956 *The history of the British flora. A factual basis for phytogeography*, Cambridge

Grace, R, 1992 Use wear analysis, in Healy et al 1992, 53–63

Graham, A H, 1978 The geology of north Southwark and its topographical development in the post-Pleistocene period, in Bird et al 1978, 501–17

Green, H S, 1980 *The flint arrowheads of the British Isles*, BAR Brit Ser 75, Oxford

Greenwood, P, 2001 Uphall Camp, Ilford – an update, *London Archaeol* 9(8), 207–16

Greenwood, P, and Thompson, A, 1992 Excavation round-up 1991: Part 2, Greater London, *London Archaeol* 6(15), 415–23

Greenwood, P, and Maloney, C, 1995 London fieldwork and publication round-up 1994, *London Archaeol* 7(13), 333–54

Greenwood, P, and Maloney, C, 1996 London fieldwork and publication round-up 1995, *London Archaeol* 8(1), 1–27

Greenwood, P, Maloney, C, and Gostick, T J, 1997 London fieldwork and publication round-up 1996, *London Archaeol* 8(2), 31–64

Grimes, W F, and Close-Brooks, J, 1993 The excavation of Caesar's Camp, Heathrow, Harmondsworth, Middlesex, 1944, *Proc Prehist Soc* 59, 303–60

Greig, J, 1992 The deforestation of London, *Rev Palaeobotany Palynology* 73, 71–86

Haggart, B A, 1995 A re-examination of some data relating to Holocene sea-level changes in the Thames estuary, in *The Quaternary of the lower Thames* (eds D R Bridgland, P Allen and A Haggart), Quat Res Ass, 329–38, London

Hammer, F, in prep *Industry in north-west Roman Southwark: excavations 1984–8*, MoLAS Monogr Ser, London

Haughey, F, 1999 The archaeology of the Thames: prehistory within a dynamic landscape, *London Archaeol* 9(1), 16–21

Healy, F, Heaton, M, and Lobb, S, 1992 Excavations of a Mesolithic site at Thatcham, Berkshire, *Proc Prehist Soc* 58, 41–76

Heard, K, 1996 The hinterland of Roman Southwark: Part 1, *London Archaeol* 8(3), 76–82

Heard, K, Sheldon, H, and Thompson, P, 1990 Mapping Roman Southwark, *Antiquity* 64, 608–19

Heathcote, J, 1990, Excavation round-up 1989: Part 2, London boroughs, *London Archaeol* 6(7), 188–95

Hedges, R E M, Bronk, C R, and Housley, R A 1989 The Oxford accelerator mass spectrometry facility: technical developments in routine dating, *Archaeometry* 31, 99–113

Hill, J D, 1999 Settlement, landscape and regionality: Norfolk and Suffolk in the pre-Roman Iron Age of Britain and beyond, in *Land of the Iceni: the Iron Age in northern East Anglia* (eds J Davies and T Williamson), Stud East Anglia History 4, 185–207

Hinton, P (ed), 1988 *Excavations in Southwark 1973–6 and 1973–9*, London Middlesex Archaeol Soc and Surrey Archaeol Soc Joint Pub 3, London

Hinton, P, and Thomas, R, 1997 The Greater London publication programme, *Archaeol J* 154, 196–213

Hodges, H W M, 1958 A hunting camp at Cullyhanna Lough near Newtown Hamilton, County Armagh, *Ulster J Archaeol* 3 ser 21, 7–13

Howe, T, Jackson, G, Maloney, C, and Saich, D, 2000 Archaeology in Surrey 1997–9, *Surrey Archaeol Collect* 87, 183–218

Iversen, J, 1941 Landnam i Danmarks Stenalder, *Danmmarks Geologiske Undersøgelse* 2 ser 66, 1–67

Jackson, G, Maloney, C, and Saich, D, 1999 Archaeology in Surrey 1996–7, *Surrey Archaeol Collect* 86, 217–55

Jacobi, R, 1976 The Mesolithic of Sussex, in Drewett, P L, *Archaeology in Sussex to AD 1500*, CBA Res Rep 29, 15–22, London

Juel Jensen, H, 1994 *Flint tools in plant working*, Aarhus

Jones, H, 1991 Excavations at the former Bricklayers Arms Railway Depot site, unpub MoLAS rep (July 1989, updated May 1991)

Jones, P, 1990 Neolithic field monuments and occupation at Staines Road Farm, Shepperton, *Surrey Archaeol Soc Bull* 252

Keeley, L H, 1980 *Experimental determination of stone tool uses: a microwear analysis*, Chicago

Keeley, L H, 1988 Lithic economy, style and use: a comparison of three Late Magdalenian sites, *Lithic Technol* 17(1), 19–25.

Kennard, A S, and Warren, S H, 1903 On a section of the Thames alluvium in Bermondsey, *Geol Mag* 10, 456–60

Kenyon, K M, 1959 *Excavations in Southwark 1945–7*, Surrey Archaeol Soc Res Pap 5

Lacaille, A D, 1966 Mesolithic facies in the transpontine fringes, *Surrey Archaeol Collect* 63, 1–43

Lawrence, G F, 1929 Antiquities from the Middle Thames, *Archaeol J* 86, 69–98

Layard N F, 1922 Prehistoric cooking-places in Norfolk, *Proc Prehist Soc East Anglia* 3, 483–98

Levi Sala, I, 1986a Experimental replication of post-depositional surface modification on flint, in *Technical aspects of microwear studies on stone tools* (eds L Owen and G Unrath), Early Man News 9/10/11, 103–9

Levi Sala, I, 1986b Use wear and post-depositional surface modification: a word of caution, *J Archaeol Sci* 13, 229–44

Lewis, J C S, 1991 A Lateglacial and Early Postglacial site at Three Ways Wharf, Uxbridge, England: interim report, in *Lateglacial settlement in northern Europe: human adaptation and environmental change at the end of the Pleistocene* (eds R N E Barton, A J Roberts and D A Roe), CBA Res Rep 77, 246–55, London

Lewis, J C S, 1994a Appendix 6: the flints, in Drummond-Murray 1994, 20–4

Lewis, J C S, 1994b The flintwork, in Bruce, P, 21–35 *Marlborough Grove, London SE1, London Borough of Southwark: an archaeological excavation*, unpub MoLAS archive rep, 8–21

Lewis, J C S, 2000 The Upper Palaeolithic and Mesolithic periods, in *The archaeology of Greater London* (ed MoLAS), 45–62, London

Lewis, J C S, in prep *Excavations at a Lateglacial/Early Holocene site at Three Ways Wharf, Uxbridge*, MoLAS Monogr Ser, London

Lewis, J S C, Wiltshire, P E J, and Macphail, R I, 1992 A Late Devensian/Early Flandrian site at Three Ways Wharf, Uxbridge: environmental implications, in *Alluvial archaeology in Britain* (eds S Needham and M Macklin), Oxbow Monogr 27, 235–47, Oxford

Long, A J, 1995 Sea-level and crustal movements in the Thames estuary, Essex and East Kent, in *The Quaternary of the lower Thames* (eds D R Bridgland, P Allen and A Haggart), Quat Res Ass, 99–105, London

Long, A J, Scaife, R G , and Edwards, R J, 2000 Stratigraphic architecture, relative sea-level and models of estuary development in southern England: new data from Southampton Water, in *Coastal and estuary environments: sedimentology, geomorphology and geoarchaeology* (eds K Pye and J Allen), Geol Soc Spec Pub 175, 253–80

Longley, D, 1976 The archaeological implications of gravel extraction in north-west Surrey, *Surrey Archaeol Soc Res Vol 3*, 1–35

Longley, D, 1980 Runnymede Bridge 1976: excavations on the site of a Late Bronze Age settlement, *Surrey Archaeol Soc Res Vol 6*

McCormac, F G, 1992 Liquid scintillation counter characterization, optimization, and benzene purity correction, *Radiocarbon 34*, 37–45

McCormac, F G, Kalin, RM, and Long, A, 1993 Radiocarbon dating beyond 50,000 years by liquid scintillation counting, in *Liquid scintillation spectrometry* (eds J E Noakes, F Shonhofer and H A Polach), 125–33, Tucson, Arizona

McKinley, J I, 1997 Bronze Age 'barrows' and funerary rites and rituals of cremation, *Proc Prehist Soc 63*, 129–45

McKinley J I, 1998 Archaeological manifestations of cremation, *The Archaeologist 36*, 18–20

McKinley J I, 1999 Human bone and funerary deposits, in Walker, K F, *M3 Bar End to Compton: archaeological investigations at Twyford Down*, Hampshire Fld Club Monogr 9, 85–119

Macphail, R I, Courty, M A, and Gebhardt, A, 1990 Soil micromorphological evidence of early agriculture in north-west Europe, *World Archaeol 22*, 53–69

Maloney, C, and Gostick, T J, 1998 London fieldwork and publication round-up 1997, *London Archaeol 8(3)*, 75–109

Maloney, C, and Holroyd, I, 2000 London fieldwork and publication round-up 1999, *London Archaeol 9(2)*, 35–65

Maloney, C, and Holroyd, I, 2001 London fieldwork and publication round-up 2000, *London Archaeol 9(3)*, 67–97

Mason, S, 1991 Jubilee Line Extension: report on the archaeological evaluation at Canada Water, Rotherhithe, unpub Museum of London archive rep

May, J, Elsdon, S M, Phillips, P, Guir, H, and Donahue, R, 1996 Earlier Neolithic artefacts from pits and hollows, in *Dragonby: report on excavations at an Iron Age and Romano-British settlement in North Lincolnshire, I* (ed J May), 38–41, Oxford

Meddens, F M, 1996 Sites from the Thames estuary wetlands, England, and their Bronze Age use, *Antiquity 70*, 325–34

Mellars, P, and Dark, P, 1998 *Star Carr in context: new archaeological and palaeoecological investigations at the Early Mesolithic site of Star Carr, North Yorkshire*, McDonald Institute Monographs, Cambridge

Merriman, N, nd a Phoenix Wharf: the flint assemblage, unpub Museum of London archive rep

Merriman, N, nd b Prehistoric flintwork from Bricklayers Arms (BLA87), unpub Museum of London archive rep

Merriman, N, 1987 A prehistory for central London?, *London Archaeol 5(12)*, 318–26

Merriman, N, 1990 *Prehistoric London*, London

Merriman, N, 1992 Predicting the unexpected: prehistoric sites recently discovered under alluvium in central London, in *Alluvial archaeology in Britain* (eds S Needham and M Macklin), Oxbow Monogr 27, 261–7, Oxford

Merriman, N, 2000 Changing approaches to the first millennium BC, in *The archaeology of London* (eds I Haynes, L Hannigan and H Sheldon), Oxbow, 35–51, Oxford

Millett, M, 1990 *The Romanization of Britain: an essay in archaeological interpretation*, Cambridge

Milne, G, Battarbee, R, Straker, V, and Yule, B, 1983 The River Thames in London in the mid 1st century AD, *Trans London Middlesex Archaeol Soc 34*, 19–30

Mook, W G, 1986 Business meeting: recommendations/resolutions adopted by the 12th international radiocarbon conference, *Radiocarbon 28*, 799

Moore, J, and Jennings, D, 1992 *Reading Business Park: a Bronze Age landscape*, Oxford Univ Comm Archaeol, Oxford

Needham, S P, 1987 The Bronze Age, in *The Archaeology of Surrey to 1540* (eds J Bird and D G Bird), 97–137, Dorking

Needham, S P, 1990 *The Petters Late Bronze Age metalwork: an analytical study of Thames valley metalworking in its settlement context*, Brit Mus Occas Pap 70, London

Needham, S P, 1991 *Excavation and salvage at Runnymede Bridge, 1978: the Late Bronze Age waterfront site*, London

Needham, S P, 2000 *The passage of the Thames: Holocene environment and settlement at Runnymede*, Runnymede Bridge Research Excavations Vol 1, London

Needham, S P, and Burgess, C, 1980 The later Bronze Age in the lower Thames valley: the metalwork evidence, in *Settlement and society in the British later Bronze Age* (eds J Barrett and R Bradley), BAR Brit Ser 83, 437–69, Oxford

Needham, S P, and Longley, D, 1980 Runnymede Bridge, Egham: a Late Bronze Age riverside settlement, in *Settlement and society in the British later Bronze Age* (eds J Barrett and R Bradley), BAR Brit Ser 83, 397–435, Oxford

Noakes, J E, Kim, S M, and Stipp, J J, 1965 Chemical and counting advances in liquid scintillation age dating, in *Proceedings of the 6th international conference on radiocarbon and tritium dating* (eds E A Olsson and R M Chatters), 68–92

Noort, R van de, Fletcher, W, Thomas, G, Carstairs, I, and Patrick, D, 2001 *Monuments at risk in England's wetlands*, Engl Heritage Consultation Document, London

O'Drisceoil, D, 1988 Burnt mounds: cooking or bathing?, *Antiquity* 62, 671–80

Odell, G H, and Cowan, F, 1986 Experiments with spears and arrows on animal targets, *J Fld Archaeol* 13, 195–212

Pearson, G W, 1984 The development of high-precision ^{14}C measurement and its application to archaeological time-scale problems, unpub PhD thesis, Queens Univ Belfast

Poole, C, 1984 Clay weights, in Cunliffe, B, *Danebury: an Iron Age hillfort in Hampshire: Vol 2, The excavations 1969–78: the finds*, CBA Res Rep 52, 401–6, London

Prehistoric Ceramics Research Group, 1995 (rev edn 1997) *The study of later prehistoric pottery: general policies and guidelines for analysis and publication*, Occas Pap 1 and 2, np

Proctor, J, 2000 Phased summary and assessment document of an archaeological evaluation at 1–2 Three Oaks Lane, Southwark, unpub Pre-Construct Archaeology archive rep

Pryor, F, 1998 *Farmers in prehistoric Britain*, Chalford

Rackham, D J, 1994 Prehistory in the Lower Thames floodplain, *London Archaeol* 7(7), 191–6

Rackham, D J, and Sidell, E J, 2000 London's landscapes; the changing environment, in *The archaeology of Greater London* (ed MoLAS), 11–27, London

Rankine, W F, and Rankine, W M, 1960 Further excavations at a Mesolithic site at Oakhanger, Selbourne, Hampshire, *Proc Prehist Soc* 12, 246–62

Rayner, L J, in prep, The prehistoric pottery, in Thomas, C, Cowie, R, and Sidell, J, *Excavations at Thorney Island, Westminster: archaeological excavations (1991–8) for the London Underground Limited Jubilee Line Extension Project*, MoLAS Monogr Ser, London

Reynier, M J, 1998 Early Mesolithic settlement in England and Wales: some preliminary observations, in *Stone Age archaeology: essays in honour of John Wymer* (eds N Ashton, F Healy and P Pettitt), Oxbow Monogr 102, 174–84, Oxford

Reynolds, P, 1981 Deadstock and livestock, in Mercer, R, *Farming practice in British prehistory*, 97–122, Edinburgh

Richardson, B, 1977 Excavation round-up 1976, *London Archaeol* 3(2), 36–53

Richardson, B, 1978 Excavation round-up 1977, *London Archaeol* 3(6), 159–63

Richardson, B, 1980 Excavation round-up 1979, *London Archaeol* 3(14), 384–9

Richardson, B, 1984 Excavation round-up 1983, *London Archaeol* 4(14), 384–91

Richardson, B, 1985 Excavation round-up 1984, *London Archaeol* 5(2), 47–52

Richardson, B, 1986 Excavation round-up 1985, *London Archaeol* 5(6), 157–64

Richardson, B, 1987 Excavation round-up 1986, *London Archaeol* 5(10), 270–8

Ridgeway, V, with Butler, J, 1999 Prehistoric finds at Hopton Street in Southwark, *London Archaeol* 9(3), 72–5

Ridgeway, V, and Meddens, F, 2001 Changing prehistoric environments on a Southwark island margin, at Butler's Wharf Estate, *London Archaeol* 9(10), 283–90

Robertson-Mackay, M E, 1987 The causewayed enclosure at Staines, Surrey: excavations 1961–3, *Proc Prehist Soc* 52, 23–128

Rogers, W, 1990 Mesolithic and Neolithic flint tool-manufacturing areas buried beneath Roman Watling Street in Southwark, *London Archaeol* 6(9), 227–31

Rowlands, M J, 1976 *The production and distribution of metalwork in the Middle Bronze Age in southern Britain*, BAR Brit Ser 31, Oxford

Rowley-Conwy, P, 1987 The interpretation of ard marks, *Antiquity* 61, 263–6

Scaife, R G, 1988 The elm decline in the pollen record of south-east England and its relationship to early agriculture, in *Archaeology and the flora of the British Isles* (ed M Jones), Oxford Univ Comm Archaeol Monogr 14, 21–33, Oxford

Schadla-Hall, R T, 1989 The Vale of Pickering in the Early Mesolithic in context, in *The Mesolithic in Europe: papers presented at the 3rd international symposium, Edinburgh 1985* (ed C Bonsall), 218–24, Edinburgh

Sheldon, H, 1974 Excavations at Toppings and Sun Wharves, Southwark 1970–2, *Trans London Middlesex Archaeol Soc* 25, 1–116

Sheldon, H, 1978 The 1972–4 excavations; their contribution to Southwark's history, in Bird et al 1978, 11–49

Shennan, S, 1997 *Quantifying archaeology*, 2 edn, Edinburgh

Sidell, E J, Scaife, R G, Tucker, S, and Wilkinson, K N, 1995 Palaeoenvironmental investigations at Bryan Road, Rotherhithe, *London Archaeol* 7(11), 279–85

Sidell, E J, Wilkinson, K N, Scaife, R G, and Cameron, N, 2000 *The Holocene evolution of the London Thames: archaeological investigations (1991–8) in advance of the London Underground Limited Jubilee Line Extension*, MoLAS Monogr Ser 5, London

Sloane, D, 1998 An archaeological evaluation at the Bankside Pontoon, Southwark, unpub MoLAS archive rep

Smith, A G, and Pilcher, J R, 1973 Radiocarbon dates and the vegetational history of the British Isles, *New Phytologist* 72, 903–14

Smith, C, 1989 British antler mattocks, in *The Mesolithic in Europe: papers presented at the 3rd international symposium, Edinburgh 1985* (ed C Bonsall), 272–83, Edinburgh

Smith, C, 1992 *Late Stone Age hunters of the British Isles*, New York

Smith, C R, 1854 *Catalogue of the Museum of London Antiquities*, privately printed

Smithson, S, 1984 The burnt mounds of Chalfont St Giles: a survey, *Rec Buckinghamshire* 26, 113–16

Spurrell, F C J, 1885 Early sites and embankments on the margins of the Thames estuary, *Archaeol J* 42, 269–302

Spurrell, F C J, 1889 On the estuary of the River Thames and its alluvium, *Proc Geol Ass* 11, 210–30

Steele, A, in prep *Excavations at the monastery of St Saviour, Bermondsey, Southwark*. MoLAS Monogr Ser

Steier, P, and Rom, W, 2000 The use of Bayesian statistics for ^{14}C dates of chronologically ordered samples: a critical analysis, *Radiocarbon* 42, 183–98

Stuiver, M, and Kra, R S, 1986 Editorial comment, *Radiocarbon* 28(2B), ii

Stuiver, M, and Polach, H A, 1977 Discussion: reporting of ^{14}C data, *Radiocarbon* 19, 355–63

Stuiver, M, and Reimer, P J, 1986 A computer program for radiocarbon age calculation, *Radiocarbon* 28, 1022–30

Stuiver, M, and Reimer, P J, 1993 Extended ^{14}C data base and revised CALIB 3.0 ^{14}C age calibration program, *Radiocarbon* 35, 215–30

Stuiver, M, Reimer, P J, Bard, E, Beck, J W, Burr, G S, Hughen, K A, Kromer, B, McCormac, F G, van der Plicht, J, and Spurk, M, 1998 INTCAL98 radiocarbon age calibration, 24,000–0 cal BP, *Radiocarbon* 40, 1041–84

Swain, H, 1992 Prehistoric pottery, in Cowan 1992, 67–70

Swain, H, nd The prehistoric pottery from Coronation Buildings (COR89), unpub Dept of Greater London Archaeol archive rep

Taylor, H, 1996 Time and tide: a study of a site at Erith in the Thames estuary, unpub undergraduate dissertation, Univ Sheffield

Thomas, C, and Rackham, J (eds), 1996 Bramcote Green, Bermondsey: a Bronze Age trackway and palaeoenvironmental sequence, *Proc Prehist Soc* 62, 221–53

Thomas, C, Cowie, R, and Sidell, J, in prep *Excavations at Thorney Island, Westminster: archaeological excavations (1991–8) for the London Underground Limited Jubilee Line Extension Project*, MoLAS Monogr Ser

Thompson, A, Westman, A, and Dyson, T (eds), 1998 *A guide to records of excavations by the Museum of London*, MoL Archaeol Gazetteer Ser 2, London

Thompson, I, 1982 *Grog-tempered 'Belgic' pottery of south-eastern England*, BAR Brit Ser 108, Oxford

Thompson, L (ed), 1998 A post-excavation report on an archaeological evaluation carried out in 1997, at Brockham Street, Southwark, London SE1, unpub Birkbeck College Univ London archive rep 54

Timby J R, 1996 The pottery, in An archaeological excavation on land adjacent to Snowy Fielder Waye, Isleworth (ed C Bell), *Trans London Middlesex Archaeol Soc* 47, 42–50

Turner, J, 1962 The Tilia decline: an anthropogenic interpretation, *New Phytologist* 61, 328–41

Tyers, I, 1988 The prehistoric peat layers (Tilbury IV), in Hinton 1988, 5–12

Tyers, P A, 1996 Late Iron Age and early Roman pottery traditions of the London region, in *Form and fabric: studies in Rome's material past in honour of B R Hartley* (eds J Bird, M Hassall and H Sheldon), Oxbow Monogr 80, 139–45, Oxford

Wait, G, and Cotton, J F, 2000 The Iron Age, in *The archaeology of Greater London* (ed MoLAS), 101–18, London

Waller, M, 1994 Paludification and pollen representation: the influence of wetland size on *Tilia* representation in pollen diagrams, *The Holocene* 4, 430–34

Ward, G K, and Wilson, S R, 1978 Procedures for comparing and combining radiocarbon age determinations: a critique, *Archaeometry* 20, 19–31

Watson, B, Brigham, T, and Dyson, T, 2001 *London bridge: 2000 years of a river crossing*, MoLAS Monogr 8, London

Webber, M, 1999 *The Thames archaeological survey 1996–9*, London

Westman, A, 1997 The topography and prehistory of Southwark and Lambeth: updated project design for research and publication, unpub MoLAS Engl Heritage project design

Wilkinson, K N, 1995 A geoarchaeological assessment of the boreholes from Masthouse Terrace, Isle of Dogs, unpub Cotswold Archaeol Trust archive rep

Wilkinson, K N, Scaife, R G, and Sidell, E J, 2000 Environmental and sea level changes in London from 10,500 BP to the present: a case study from Silvertown, *Proc Geol Ass* 111, 41–54

Wilkinson, K N, Scaife, R G, and Sidell, E J, in prep Mesolithic environment and humans in London; new evidence from Wandsworth, *J Environmental Archaeol*

Wilkinson, K N, and Sidell, E J, in prep *The Neolithic Thames of central London: its evolution and archaeological significance*, Neolithic Stud Group/Oxbow Monograph

Wilkinson, T, 1988 *Archaeology and environment in south Essex*, E Anglian Archaeol 42, Gressenhall

Wilkinson, T J and Murphy, P L, 1995 *The archaeology of the Essex coast: Vol I, The Hullbridge survey*, E Anglian Archaeol 71, Gressenhall

Willcox, G H, 1975 Problems and possible conclusions relating to the history and archaeology of the Thames in the London region, *Trans London Middlesex Archaeol Soc* 26, 185–92

Williams, J, and Brown, N (eds), 1999 *An archaeological research framework for the Greater Thames estuary*, Essex County Council, Kent County Council, The Thames Estuary Partnership and Engl Heritage

Woodbridge, K P, 1998 Holocene sediments from the River Thames foreshore at Bermondsey, London, *Quat Res Ass Newsl* 85, 9–20

Wymer, J J, 1962 Excavations at the Maglemosian sites at Thatcham, Berkshire, England, *Proc Prehist Soc* 28, 329–61

Wymer, J J, 1968 *Lower Palaeolithic archaeology in Britain as represented by the Thames valley*, London

Yates, D T, 1999 Bronze Age field systems in the Thames valley, *Oxford J Archaeol* 18, 157–70

Yates, D T, 2001 Bronze Age agricultural intensification in the Thames valley and estuary, in *Landscape and settlement in Bronze Age Britain* (ed J Brück), Oxbow Monogr, Oxford

Yeaxlee, R, 1998 Prehistoric pottery appendix II, in A post-excavation report on an archaeological evaluation carried out in 1997, at Brockham Street, Southwark, London SE1 (ed L Thompson), unpub Birkbeck College Univ London archive rep 54

Yule, B, 1988 The natural topography of north Southwark, in Hinton 1988, 13–18

INDEX

Compiled by Susanne Atkin

Page numbers in **bold** refer to illustrations
Gaz = gazetteer; for other abbreviations see p 56